WHO OWNS THE BIBLE?

WHO OWNS THE BIBLE?

Toward the Recovery of a Christian Hermeneutic

K ARL P AUL D ONFRIED

A Herder & Herder Book
The Crossroad Publishing Company
New York

The Crossroad Publishing Company
16 Penn Plaza — 481 Eighth Avenue, Suite 1550
New York, NY 10001

This book is set in 10/13 Sabon.

Printed in the United States of America

Library of Congress Cataloging-in-Publication Data

Donfried, Karl P.
    Who owns the Bible? : toward the recovery of a Christian hermeneutic
/ Karl Paul Donfried.
        p. cm. — (Companions to the New Testament)
    "A Herder & Herder book."
    Includes bibliographical references and index.
    ISBN 0-8245-2390-3 (alk. paper)
    1. Bible—Criticism, interpretation, etc. 2. Bible—Hermeneutics.
I. Title. II. Series.
BS511.3.D66 2006
220.6'01—dc22

                                                2006002911

        1   2   3   4   5   6   7   8   9   10   10   09   08   07   06

WITH GRATITUDE

For My Distinguished Colleagues and Friends

Past and Present

Department of Religion and Biblical Literature

Smith College

~

For the Clergy and the Faithful People of God

Past and Present

Christ Church Cathedral

Springfield, Massachusetts

Contents

Preface to the Series

THE COMPANIONS TO THE NEW TESTAMENT SERIES aims to unite New Testament study with theological concerns in a clear and concise manner. Each volume:

- engages the New Testament text directly.
- focuses on the religious (theological/ethical) content of the New Testament.
- is written out of respect for the integrity of the religious tradition being studied. This means that the New Testament is studied in terms of its own time and place. It is allowed to speak in its own terms, out of its own assumptions, espousing its own values.
- involves cutting-edge research, bringing the results of scholarly discussions to the general reader
- provides resources for the reader who wishes to enter more deeply into the scholarly discussion.

The contributors to the series are established scholars who have studied and taught the New Testament for many years and who can now reap a wide-ranging harvest from the fruits of their labors. Multiple theological perspectives and denominational identities are represented. Each author is free to address the issues from his or her own social and religious location, within the parameters set for the series.

It is our hope that these small volumes will make some contribution to the recovery of the vision of the New Testament world for our time.

Charles H. Talbert
Baylor University

Preface

I HAVE BEEN PRIVILEGED with exceptional teachers throughout my academic career, and issues of biblical interpretation have been present throughout. In the process of writing this book I have come to realize my considerable indebtedness especially to Paul Tillich, Krister Stendahl, and G. Ernest Wright at Harvard, John Knox at Union, and Günther Bornkamm and Hans von Campenhausen at the University of Heidelberg. During this same period I was profoundly influenced by Karl Barth's seminar in Basel in 1966 on the Vatican II document *De Divina Revelatione* and his sustained criticism of Ernst Käsemann's exegetical method, especially its consequences for preaching. In the 1970s I was fortunate to be named a member of the national Lutheran–Roman Catholic dialogue's New Testament panel that produced *Peter in the New Testament* and *Mary in the New Testament*. In this ecumenical context significant and neuralgic hermeneutical issues were regularly encountered; how fortunate to be able to discuss these in a company that included Raymond Brown, Joseph Fitzmyer, John Reumann, and Reginald Fuller. Also very significant were my conversations with Brevard Childs about canonical criticism while I was visiting professor at Yale in 1993 as well as my discussions with Shemaryahu Talmon during and subsequent to the time that I served as visiting professor at Hebrew University in Jerusalem in 1997. It is not only the excellence but also the wide-ranging diversity of these scholars that has contributed greatly to both my thinking and wrestling with the complicated issues of biblical interpretation discussed in the following pages.

As deeply influential as all these experiences have been, none was more preeminently so than my participation in what has come to be known as the Ratzinger Conference on the Bible, which took place for three days in New

York City during January 1988 (*Biblical Interpretation in Crisis: The Ratzinger Conference on Bible and Church*, ed. Richard John Neuhaus [Grand Rapids: Eerdmans, 1989]). To encounter the brilliant mind, deep spirituality, and kindly person of Joseph Ratzinger (now Pope Benedict XVI) in the context of a select group of scholars that included George Lindbeck, Raymond Brown, William Lazareth, and Avery Dulles were moments filled with enormously profound and insightful scholarly and theological dialogue. Ratzinger's lead lecture/essay, "Biblical Interpretation in Crisis" (in the volume cited), is without doubt the most perceptive and substantial essay on hermeneutics that I have encountered during my academic career, and his analysis of the strengths and weaknesses of the historical-critical method is as current today as it was in 1988. I stand deeply in Joseph Ratzinger's debt for his outstanding contributions not only in the area of biblical hermeneutics but also in the field of theology and especially for the profound ecumenical insights contained in his *Principles of Catholic Theology: Building Stones for a Fundamental Theology* (San Francisco: Ignatius, 1987). For our continuing conversation and friendship over many years I remain profoundly grateful.

This volume is dedicated to two groups of treasured friends: (1) my colleagues in the Department of Religion and Biblical Literature at Smith College, who since 1968 have provided the gift of reasoned, gracious, and thoughtful dialogue in the midst of substantial diversity, and; (2) the community of Christ Church Cathedral in the Episcopal Diocese of Western Massachusetts, who since 1977, long before the celebration and inauguration of full communion between the Episcopal and Lutheran churches (2001), have given to me as their Ecumenical Canon a welcoming home in which I have been regularly invited to preside over the holy mysteries, preach the Word, and teach the Scriptures of the Church Catholic, all in the context of a loving and theologically centrist community of believers. I am also most appreciative to others close to me who have critically read my manuscript in its various stages of transformation with great acumen and with considerable attention to detail: my daughter, Dr. Karen Donfried; my wife, Kathy Donfried; my respected colleague Dr. Frank Hughes; and my outstanding research assistant, Anne Stewart. I also wish to thank Dr. Annemarie S. Reynolds not only for her continuing generous hospitality in San Nazzaro but also for over forty-six years of friendship, as well as Karen and Alan for their yearly welcoming in Westport; both are very special places that have contributed significantly to the completion of this book. And, finally, let me say that although I have benefited greatly from all those thanked in these paragraphs, I do not wish in any way to imply that the expression of my profound gratitude suggests agreement with my perspectives nor responsibility for those errors of judgment or inaccuracies that still remain.

Karl Paul Donfried
August 26, 2005
Westport Point, Massachusetts

1

The Bible and the Church

The Problem of Alien Hermeneutics

1.1 To Whom Does the Bible Belong?

The early church fathers raise a fundamental and urgent question: To whom does the Bible belong? Who are its rightful owners, and who is entitled to interpret its texts?[1] These early theologians were in combat with opponents known as Gnostics, adherents of a heretical form of Christianity that was distorting the content and meaning of Scripture as transmitted by the earliest apostles; they argued that these freethinkers were applying "alien hermeneutics" in their exposition of the Bible. Hermeneutics is simply a fancy term for "interpretation"; it comes from the Greek word *hermeneia*, and "alien" implies something that is foreign, strange, or unnatural to the matter at hand. Since the early church understood the incarnation, ministry, suffering, death, and resurrection of Jesus to be central to their proclamation and teaching, anyone who rejected these indispensable components of the Christian narrative would be engaged in an *alien hermeneutic*, namely, an interpretation of the Christ event that was in effect opposed to its essential meaning and dependent on extrabiblical conceptualities.

Before we continue our conversation together a brief word about the term "Christ event" will be useful. John Knox, one of several influential teachers, maintained that the reality of Christ is "so infinitely rich" that it must be understood ". . . under no fewer than three aspects: (1) as the *event* or closely knit series of events in and through which God made himself known; (2) as the *person* who was the center of that event or complex of events; and (3) as the *community* which both came into existence with the event and provided the locus of it."[2] Both in the classroom and in my con-

1

versations with him, Knox maintained that the meaning of Jesus Christ can only be apprehended within the *totality* of God's revelation, including the history of Israel, all events surrounding the person of Jesus (i.e., his ministry, suffering, death, resurrection), and the church that arose as a result of this revelation. Thus, to speak of the "Christ event" implies an indissoluble link within and between all three of these dimensions. To eliminate or to lessen any of them from the discussion of the meaning of Christ is to invite distortion and falsification. Thus, for example, in describing the enduring relationship of Christ with his church, Knox continues: "To speak of the Church in its true identity is to speak of the event in which it arose, the event of which Jesus was the decisive center; and to speak of him in his true and only important identity as Christ and Lord is to speak of the Church, where alone he is known as such. A separation between the two, or even a distinction for purposes of argument or discussion, is as I came to see, quite impossible. *Christology and ecclesiology belong indissolubly together.* The Church's doctrine of Christ is its way of stating its understanding of itself."[3] Throughout our dialogue we will urge that all three aspects of God's revelation—the *events*, including the history of Israel and those related to Jesus in the first century, the *person,* and the *community*—belong indissolubly together. When the person of Jesus Christ is severed from any of these, fertile ground is provided for alien hermeneutics to develop.

Tertullian, a prominent theologian of the third century, apprehensive of both the unintended and the deliberate misinterpretation of Scripture,[4] unequivocally asks the conveyors of such alien hermeneutics: "Who are you, when did you arrive and from where? What are you doing on my property without belonging to me? Who gave you the right, Marcion, to cut my timber? Who gives you permission to divert my springs, Valentinus? By what authority are you moving my boundaries, Apelles? . . . This property belongs to me; I have always possessed it, I have possessed it prior to you and have reliable title-deeds from the original owners of the estate. I am the heir of the apostles."[5] Tertullian's obvious point is that for accurate biblical interpretation to take place there must be a direct continuity between the normative apostolic witness to the Christ event and that of its subsequent interpreters. In a remarkably similar vein, the well-known biblical scholar Raymond E. Brown writes: "What the biblical text said to its first readers should be related to what the text says to me, because I am a Christian heir to the people of Israel and the people of the early church, and *not independent of them.*"[6]

Is Tertullian's concern any less relevant for Christians in the twenty-first century? In our society everyone has the right to go to the local bookshop and purchase whatever version of the Bible one chooses. Must we not, however, ask, together with Tertullian, whether everyone therefore also has the right to interpret normatively the meaning of the Bible for the Church Catholic?[7] Or is this not a prerogative only for those who have received their identity through baptism into the Body of Jesus Christ and have also pledged fidelity to the apostolic witness and teachings transmitted by the orthodox expressions of the church? It has been correctly asserted that "the faith of the living church made the book. There is a reciprocity of the church and the Bible. But there is also a real precedence of the life of the church, because only the life and faith of the church created the Bible as a book."[8] Certainly the Bible is and should be used by a wide range of persons and academics, including literary scholars who are keen to illustrate its story lines, narrative functions, and poetic intensity as well as by historians and archaeologists who wish to illumine the vast array of data preserved in these sacred texts.[9] But the critical question remains: Are such fully appropriate lines of approach *by themselves*, unaccompanied by a deeper penetration of the Christ event in all its fullness, adequate to guide and to confirm the Church Catholic in its task of proclamation, theological interpretation, and teaching? A response to this question requires a description of the current crisis in Christian biblical interpretation.

1.2 The Neglect of the Bible by Mainline Churches

There has been a virtual silencing of the Bible in many churches today.[10] Although this neglect has likely not been intentional, it is, nevertheless, very real. Fewer and fewer sermons are biblically based, and a similar situation exists with regard to the educational activities in the life of local congregations and national church bodies. As one whose teaching and research necessitates a fair amount of travel, my sampling of diverse church life allows me to hear sermons and homilies that more often than not are in the form of stories that contain superficial moralisms and pious platitudes (e.g., God loves you); few, however, really strive to proclaim the specificity of the gospel message from biblical texts that are firmly anchored in the liturgical cycle in the church year. Adult education in many parishes is often nothing more than a collective conversation where virtually any topic that will interest and draw people is discussed—frequently well presented but rarely deriving their generative or critical power from the Scriptures of the Church Catholic. The teaching of the Bible in Vacation Bible Schools and Sunday Schools, when still viable options, has often been reduced to the doing of arts and crafts. How many children and adults in mainline Protestant and Roman Catholic churches have any sense of the major narratives contained in Scripture?

The underlying causes for this neglect are manifold and varied, and they will be examined in the course of our conversation together. To a certain extent contemporary Western culture contributes to the current dilemma. As our society becomes more diverse, multicultural, and secular there is significantly less biblical discourse in the public square. Seldom today does one find a parallel to the late Senator Sam Irvin quoting Scripture repeatedly, naturally, and from memory during the Watergate hearings. In such a cultural context mainline Protestant churches become very vulnerable because there is little that protects them from the erosion of their biblical heritage. One needs to remember that Protestantism emerged in a Western Christian culture in which church and state were often closely linked and supported by the political rulers of the day. In many countries, that protective womb continued well into the twentieth century but has now all but eroded given the secular transformation of Western societies into what can be properly called a post-Christian situation. Without a pope or adequate ecclesial structures that guide church teachings and without a protective and empathetic cultural environment, much of mainstream Protestantism especially is being insidiously invaded, often quite unconsciously and for the first time, especially in the North American and European contexts, by the various extreme ideological forces of the day, whether from the right or the left. In the context of such cultural transformations, the fullness of the Christ event is fragmented, and Scripture as classically understood by the Church Catholic is either silenced or misappropriated.

1.3 The Misuse of the Bible by the Religious Right

Given this intimidating state of affairs for many Christian churches, one understandable response, by both conservative Protestants and Roman Catholics, is to withdraw into environments that protect and defend against this endangering of the faith. For some Catholics the movement is toward a fundamentalist and hierarchical pre-Vatican II fortress mentality that seeks to shield itself theologically from the increasing assaults of a non-Christian culture.[11] For some conservative Protestants this state of affairs leads to the creation of a "paper pope," namely, a literal, rigid, and one-dimensional understanding of the Bible, one that understands its words and actions to be infallibly true and inerrant. Every word of the good book serves as a quotable authority for all human situations, whether personal, communal, or political. It is from this quarter of Christianity that one repeatedly hears the uncritical refrain, "the Bible says. . . ." Whereas the deficiencies of this simplistic and superficial approach are manifold, it has the undeniable power of holding its followers together by providing a defense mechanism during times of rapid and dramatic cultural change. And, so, as mainline Protestant churches have seen sharp declines in membership over the last few decades, conservative churches with their unflinchingly fundamentalist grasp of Scripture have grown dramatically, largely through their readiness and willingness to confront courageously the various secular ideologies of the day. Although distorting and deforming the Scriptures of the Church Catholic they have not silenced them; herein lies a strategic evangelistic advantage over mainline Protestantism, which has all but discarded the central message of the Christian Bible.

There are serious problems with this fundamentalism of the religious right. Since the media as well as the religious left have focused considerable attention on these issues, we can be relatively brief in our attention to these challenges. (1) By refusing to give serious heed to the contributions of critical biblical scholarship, such a biblical hermeneutic refuses to understand the original historical and literary contexts of the various individual writings, thus collapsing the distance between the ancient and the contemporary worldviews and imposing the latter upon the former. (2) Such an approach to the Bible refuses to comprehend fully the radically transformative effect that the death and resurrection of Jesus Christ have for the understanding of the whole of Scripture. Christ as the center, fulfillment, and interpretative key for *all* Scripture seems frequently to be ignored. Since according to a conservative fundamentalist perspective all Scripture is inspired by God, the consequence for many is that one can randomly pick and choose biblical texts that one wishes to apply to any given current personal, cultural, religious, or political situation. In such a way the historical settings of the biblical books are disregarded, and their relationship to the Christ event ignored. Almost as if he had the religious right in mind, Tertullian, the straight-talking theologian of the early church, writes: "False exegesis injures truth just as much as a corrupt text."[12]

The distortions resulting from such a hermeneutic alien to the full and essential meaning of Scripture include heavy emphasis on the end-time, the desire to "Christianize" this nation as well as the world, the misappropriation of the biblical texts for political purposes and their misapplication for the purpose of authenticating a soft, comfortable suburban faith for its churchly consumers that renders impotent the hard words of Jesus and, in fact, silences him in a way quite analogous to the silencing current in main-line Protestantism. Whether it is Franklin Graham, the son of Billy Graham, arguing the merits of the Iraq war on the basis of the fact that God himself had been involved in holy wars in the Old Testament,[13] or Tim LaHaye and his *Left Behind* books,[14] or megachurch pastor Joel Osteen's attempt to co-opt God to serve self-centered individuals in his *Your Best Life Now*,[15] all reveal similar defects: a fragmentation of Scripture into self-serving texts that refuse to take seriously the contexts of the original biblical authors as well as their relationship to the fullness of the Christ event as an indissoluble link between the events of Israel, the revelation of God in Christ, and the life of the church.

For the early Christian movement the understanding of the Old Testament was significantly and substantially reshaped by the New. The Scripture of the emerging church was the Jewish Bible, and it is for that reason that the New Testament appears like "a skin on every square inch of which the Old Testament is tattooed."[16] Simultaneously, however, the New radically transforms those skins because for the Christian community of the new covenant the interpretative center of the entire biblical narrative is rooted in and fulfilled by the redemptive death and resurrection of Jesus Christ. Thus, for example, the horrific and violent death of Jesus by means of crucifixion at the hands of the Romans was to be the cessation, from the perspective of God, of all further human violence. The violence perpetrated by Joshua (*yeshua‘*) has been transformed by the violence committed by the Romans against God Incarnate, Jesus (*yeshua‘*); and, as a result, the violent death of Jesus on the cross brings to an end the violence found throughout the Old Testament. The Christian can no longer be the initiator of violence or an advocate of the preemptive use of force. "Through his incarnation and now his death," Jack Miles writes with profound insight, God "has found a way to infuse the closing stanzas of Psalm 22, as well as innumerable other statements in the Old Testament expressing what those stanzas express, with a new meaning that transcends rather than negates the old meaning. It has cost him everything to make this cataclysmic change, but he has made it, and—*na‘aśah*—it is accomplished. He bows his head and breathes out his last breath."[17] The crucifixion and the resurrection compel a new reading of the Old Testament in light of the "transformative expansion"[18] initiated by the Christ event, and this new reading disallows interpretations that simply play "Bible Land,"[19] the precarious game that allows one to pick and choose texts uncritically and at will without attention either to the context or the relationship with the central events of the New Testament.

1.4 The Misuse of the Bible by the Religious Left

Although the Protestant Christian right does not fully grasp the implications of this "transformative expansion" of the Bible by the fullness of the Christ event, it does, despite its fragmented approach, attempt to pay attention to both the Old and the New Testaments, even if its ill-considered methods are problematic and fraught with perilous implications. Liberal Protestantism, however, captive to its trivialized refrain devoid of serious ethical reflection and determined biblical penetration that "God is love, God loves us," has little use for the major themes in the Old Testament. Increasingly "justice causes" occupy a good deal of preaching time, but the full and rich potential of the Old Testament is scarcely queried since the interpretative key for the concept of "justice" is more often secular than biblical. A deeper probing of Scripture would, in fact, substantially revise the more simplistic notions of "justice" that are currently being bandied about.

The ethicist Philip Turner makes a distinction between two contrasting theologies that are at work in much of mainline Protestantism: a theology of acceptance and a theology of redemption. The theology of acceptance has reduced the mystery of God to one who simply wants us to love one another with an emphasis on the affirmation of the other, especially those who have been marginalized by society. This results in a "practical equivalence between the Gospel of the Kingdom of God and particular form of social justice."[20] The problem for Turner is that such a biblically ill-considered approach produces "a quasi-deist theology that posits a benevolent God who favors love and justice as inclusion but acts neither to save us from our sins nor to raise us to new life after the pattern of Christ. . . . In a theology dominated by radical inclusion, terms such as 'faith,' 'justification,' 'repentance,' and 'holiness of life' seem to belong to an antique vocabulary that must be outgrown or reinterpreted."[21]

The religious left has replaced this "theology of redemption" with a "theology of inclusion."[22] The former is biblical, insists on "costly grace,"[23] recognizes the power of sin, acknowledges that evil can only be overcome through the death and resurrection of Jesus Christ, and accentuates the call to discipleship, that is, the "exclusive inclusivity"[24] of Jesus Christ, as a call to holiness. The latter, in contrast, is alien and secular, characterized by "cheap grace,"[25] understands the incarnation as some vague expression of divine love that results in the inclusion of all, and it "produces an ethic of tolerant affirmation that carries with it no call to conversion and radical holiness."[26]

Representative of this fundamentalism of the religious left[27] is John Shelby Spong,[28] who insists that "the beating scenes or the sadism evidenced in the blood from the crown of thorns streaming down the face of Jesus in Mel Gibson's controversial motion picture *The Passion of the Christ* will finally be enough to make us see the violence that Christianity has fostered. . . ."[29] The crucifixion, so the argument proceeds, "portrays the holy God involved in a cruel act of divine child abuse. . . ."[30] With such simplistic argumentation the crucifixion is dismissed as irrelevant for Christianity, and Spong's doctrine of a "new consciousness" that "Jesus did not die for our sins" is substituted.[31] One finds here not only a blatant example of a hermeneutic alien to the New Testament but one that fundamentally and willfully distorts a Trinitarian interpretation of Scripture, namely, that the Bible discloses the Triune God on the basis of an incoherently articulated ideology of "new consciousness" that calls Christianity into a "universal human consciousness."[32] Such an alien hermeneutic is driven by subjectivity, cultural relativism, and the turn to personal experience.[33]

What exactly is meant by the reference to a *Trinitarian hermeneutic of Scripture*? In the first place such an interpretation recognizes, together with the church's earliest theologians, that Jesus is the definitive revelation of God. His life and ministry, his suffering, crucifixion, death, and resurrection are not only a word about God, they are the Word of God incarnate, the Word made flesh, the *humanation* of God.[34] The continued presence of the risen Jesus through the Spirit in the community that worships him leads to the affirmation of a Trinitarian theology of God as Father, Son, and Holy Spirit as the most adequate manner in which to understand the revelation of God in creation, in the history of Israel, in Jesus, and in the church. Because "Jesus Christ is the same yesterday and today and forever" (Heb 13:8), a Trinitarian hermeneutic must of necessity be a hermeneutic of consistency and coherence. We will return to this theme in chapters 5 and 6 where it will be asked, for example, whether a theological position maintained coherently and consistently throughout the canon of Scripture can be contradicted and altered and, if so, by what justification.[35]

Cloaked by their disdain for the Christian tradition as well as their specious argumentation, the crisis created by the religious left for biblical interpretation is considerable. Buoyed by the enormous advances of biblical scholarship in the twentieth century, liberal Protestantism has employed these insights, properly in my judgment, to free itself from rigid dogmatic, pietistic, and fundamentalistic interpretations of Scripture; however, in the process it has created a fundamentalism of its own. By overlooking the forest for the trees, this fundamentalism of the left has so concentrated on the historical settings and prehistories of individual texts that the broader, biblical interpretative landscape is lost. Using a different analogy, Jack Miles articulates this dilemma with great insight: "What attracts viewers, believing or unbelieving, to the great rose window of the Bible is neither what can be seen through it nor how the glass for it was stained and assembled, but what the window looks like in and for itself and what all those jagged fragments of light and color, working together, make happen behind the eye of the beholder."[36] Modern readers often seem no longer able to appreciate the beauty of the cathedral's rose window in its magnificent totality, since often the focus has been exclusively on this or that pane to the exclusion of the entire work of art.[37] Consequently, texts are frequently disconnected from their broader narrational whole, anchored in the death and resurrection of Jesus Christ, and, as a result, they can be co-opted effortlessly by a nonbiblical, alien hermeneutic. Once their canonical location has been relocated into other ideological contexts, the potential for distortion becomes enormous. By displacing texts from their original setting, they can then be read in a manner more congenial to interpreters who find the original canonical and Trinitarian context to be too narrow, uncongenial, or simply discomforting. Following this trajectory, liberal Protestantism becomes increasingly captive to the fundamentalism of the religious left and a results-based interpretation, not dissimilar to the phenomenon of judicial activism, thus replacing a careful listening to biblical texts within their canonical fullness.[38] The hermeneutics driven by both the religious right and the religious left suffer from a common ailment which is stated succinctly by George Lindbeck: ". . . from fundamentalist rigorists to hyperskeptical liberals, the narrative meaning [has] collapsed into the factual and disappeared."[39] Lindbeck maintains that both are "instances of capitulation to an Enlightenment collapse of the rich salvation narrative into very limited notions of fact."[40]

1.5 Transitions in the Academic Study of Religion

Another critical element factoring into the current crisis in biblical interpretation is the role of the academy, not only in terms of institutions of higher learning and biblical societies but also in the changed social location of the individual interpreters. The last few decades have revealed a fundamental shift in the hermeneutical context in which biblical studies are taught at many American interdenominational divinity schools and theological seminaries. When I was a graduate student in the 1960s virtually all of my professors were male, ordained clergy with a deep sense of commitment to the Christian church in its various manifestations. This situation has changed dramatically and with no uncertain gains in terms of the variety and diversity of persons teaching biblical studies today, including far more minorities, women, nonordained persons and non-Christians. In fact, one of my best students, a leading New Testament scholar at a major divinity school, is a Jew.[41] In so many ways this new situation brings with it major benefits in terms of accessing the biblical text from a considerably more expansive interfaith, cultural, and historical perspective. For those who simultaneously participate in this all-inclusive academic arena and who still remain committed to doing biblical interpretation in a Christocentric, Trinitarian manner, the environment for such teaching and research will have changed dramatically; and, for the most part, churches have failed to recognize the impact of this extraordinary transition of social location. The intrinsic linkage between Jesus and community, so important for John Knox,[42] still exists, but the nature of community has shifted from Christian to non-Christian. The fact that most of the church's interpreters of Scripture are trained in non-Christian academic settings and continue to engage their colleagues in such locations is a major factor in the inability of some to advocate a Trinitarian interpretation of Scripture within the church.

George Lindbeck has referred to biblical studies in the academy as "foundationless hermeneutical enterprises,"[43] and by this he means that it can no longer be assumed that any of these scholarly activities will necessarily attempt to interpret a given biblical theme or passage within its canonical situation. More often than not, the texts or topics in question are consciously removed from that context so as to probe their historical, social, and archaeological situations. Now, on the one hand, this is an important advance, and it represents one of the great contributions of the historical-critical method. But, on the other hand, there are risks involved in concentrating on such narrowly delimited historical trajectories, for such diachronic[44] interpretations often overlook the broader synchronic[45] context of Scripture. Lindbeck analyzes the contemporary crisis in this way: "Theologians start with historical reconstructions of the biblical message which are inescapably diverse, tentative, and changing; and then seek to translate these reconstructions into contemporary conceptualities which are also diverse and variable. Not surprisingly, the results are often mutually unintelligible. There is no single overarching universe of biblical discourse with which differences can be discussed."[46]

What has occurred, then, over the last several decades is a shift in the context in which Scripture is interpreted, a shift from the church to the academy; and for many of those in the academy who claim to be its inter-preters, the Bible is no longer seen as standing in the service of the church. Therefore those who are committed to a Christian, Trinitarian hermeneutic must be concerned with reclaiming the Bible for the church with an inten-sity similar to that displayed by Irenaeus,[47] Tertullian, and other leaders in the early church.

1.6 A Trinitarian Hermeneutic of Scripture and the Academy

Working from the perspective of a Trinitarian hermeneutic of Scripture, it can be argued that the observation of "foundationless hermeneutics" as a descriptor for the current situation does not go far enough. Are the con-temporary circumstances, in fact, that benign and disengaged? Is there really ever anything that is "foundationless"? Are not all interpretative enterprises driven by a deeper ultimate concern, viewpoint, or ideology? What makes the current state of affairs so complex and precarious is that this social shift from the church to the academy often finds some members of the academy forging a variety of alliances with ideologies that are in opposition to the classical expressions of the Christian faith. In the name of history, which often is a pretense for an ideological theology, classical and normative expressions of Christian theology are frequently attacked, at times overtly and at times more invidiously and subtly. One need only think of such books as Burton Mack's *The Lost Gospel*,[48] Jan Schaberg's *The Ille-gitimacy of Jesus: A Feminist Theological Interpretation of the Infancy Nar-ratives*,[49] or *The Five Gospels*,[50] produced by the Jesus seminar. All of these works are consciously trying to develop an alternative image of Jesus. With regard to the Jesus Seminar, Richard Hays asks: "Does the passive, politi-cally correct, laconic sage who speaks in the red type of *The Five Gospels* have the capacity to remake our imaginative world and provide a new fic-tion within which millions might find meaning for their lives? Surely not."[51]

While those who share Hays's classical hermeneutical perspective will concur with his conclusion, one must not overlook the fact that this trun-cated, avant-garde version of Jesus, unrelated either to the Old Testament or to the church, has become influential and no doubt stands behind the theology of acceptance infusing much of mainline Protestantism. The quest for the "real" Jesus is as alive and well today as it was in the eighteenth and nineteenth centuries. By simply changing the name of some of the charac-ters, Albert Schweitzer's reproach of the so-called old quest for the histori-cal Jesus is as insightful today as when it was published in 1906.[52] Many in the professional guild of biblical scholarship are satisfied to offer private ideological speculations, yielding with regularity a myriad of conflicting options distant from the canonical witness and alien to its major theological testimonies.

To a large degree the distorting effects of this social shift can be observed in a variety of secular interpretations that are often removed from the faith and practice of those communities who worship Christ as Lord within a Trinitarian theology and ecclesiology. What lies at the core of many of these nontrinitarian hermeneutical enterprises is an assumption that historical knowledge is omniscient and that it determines theological truth.[53] As a result certain biblical texts are disabled and removed from their synchronic, canonical construct; this "disabling" function takes place either through a process of "bracketing" and/or "fixing." Already in the third century Tertullian is troubled by similar tendencies. What heresy "accepts, it perverts with both additions and subtractions to suit its own teachings. . . ."[54]

The phenomenon of "bracketing" can be illustrated by reference to Ephesians 5:21-32:[55]

> [21]*Be subject to one another out of reverence for Christ.* [22]*Wives, be subject to your husbands as you are to the Lord.* [23]*For the husband is the head of the wife just as Christ is the head of the church, the body of which he is the Savior.* [24]*Just as the church is subject to Christ, so also wives ought to be, in everything, to their husbands.* [25]*Husbands, love your wives, just as Christ loved the church and gave himself up for her,* [26]*in order to make her holy by cleansing her with the washing of water by the word,* [27]*so as to present the church to himself in splendor, without a spot or wrinkle or anything of the kind—yes, so that she may be holy and without blemish.* [28]*In the same way, husbands should love their wives as they do their own bodies. He who loves his wife loves himself.* [29]*For no one ever hates his own body, but he nourishes and tenderly cares for it, just as Christ does for the church,* [30]*because we are members of his body.* [31]*"For this reason a man will leave his father and mother and be joined to his wife, and the two will become one flesh."* [32]*This is a great mystery, and I am applying it to Christ and the church.*

In *The Lectionary for the Christian People*, the symbol § is placed before Ephesians 5:21-23.[56] This and other similar texts are described as "essentially sexist in speaking specifically of a subordinate position of women. Such problematic lessons are translated faithful to the original, with the hope that future lectionary revisions will choose other readings as more appropriate for today's church. Such lessons are marked with a §."[57] Why is this text bracketed, that is, rejected, from the public liturgical reading of the Bible without any further examination concerning its coherence and consistency with the remainder of Scripture? Why should the people of God be deprived from hearing biblical texts without editorial filters? Because a results-based feminist hermeneutic has declared that it is in conflict with its ideological premises.

The goal of "fixing" is similar to "bracketing" to the degree that selected texts are made dysfunctional and, thus it is hoped, eliminated from contemporary theological dialogue and discourse. Several prominent New Testament scholars have, for example, attempted to disable Romans 1:26-28, a text to which we will return in chapter 5, in precisely such a way.[58]

> For this reason God gave them up to degrading passions. Their women exchanged natural intercourse for unnatural, and in the same way also the men, giving up natural intercourse with women, were consumed with passion for one another. Men committed shameless acts with men and received in their own persons the due penalty for their error. And since they did not see fit to acknowledge God, God gave them up to a debased mind and to things that should not be done.

The sins of the Gentile world that Paul has itemized no longer speak, it is argued, to current discussions of sexuality because the position expressed belongs to the apostle's Jewish-Hellenistic worldview, which is in conflict with our own. Such a perspective, it is maintained, can be discarded since it has been superseded by the "insights" of the social sciences. What emerges here is an appeal to history, the philosophical presuppositions of which are seldom, if ever, discussed, coupled with an invocation of the social sciences; together they become the epistemological keys that arbitrate the appropriateness of biblical texts for the moral teachings of the contemporary church.

Rather than offering critical discernment in the midst of this assortment of contradictory choices, many seminary faculty embrace these ambiguities with enthusiasm. Thus, Terrence Fretheim, a seminary professor of Old Testament, maintains that an "increasingly diverse church facing complex challenges ought to rejoice in the indeterminacy of meaning; the church will need more readings to speak to the variety of people and situations it will face."[59] Was the missionary success of early Christianity among radically diverse populations based on the "indeterminacy of meaning"? When Vincent of Lerins, a theologian of the fifth century, argued that the center of the

Christian faith is "that which has been believed everywhere, always and by all"[60] he was referring to a theology that was specifically focused on the rule of faith, apostolic authority, and the canon of Scripture; it was not based on the "indeterminacy of meaning."

The Church Catholic must indeed ask: What are the criteria of discernment that can be usefully employed at this moment in Christian history to sort out the multiplicity of polyphonic and polyvalent claims of "responsible biblical scholarship" established on "the fragile vessel of historiography posing as theology"?[61] Then, too, there are the supplications being imposed upon readers everywhere by virtually all religious publishers intent on selling the "newest contributions" and "radical breakthroughs" of biblical scholarship.

1.7 The Continued Relevance of Historical Biblical Criticism

It has become quite fashionable today, in reaction to the problems just outlined, to assume that *the* major obstacle in reclaiming the Bible for the church is the "historical-critical method" of biblical study. To begin with, one needs to be clear that there is no such thing as a single "historical-critical method."[62] Rather, there are a variety of methods and hermeneutics in which various components used in the task of historical biblical criticism —that is, textual criticism, literary criticism, form criticism, redaction criticism, just to cite a few—can be employed, often with strikingly different, if not contradictory, results. It is far more accurate to use the phrase "historical biblical criticism," by which is meant the attempt to understand by the use of all available critical tools what the biblical author wished to convey to the original audience for which he wrote. *Since all Christians, including especially preachers and theologians, must be subject to the control of the written, canonical text and not to spiritual or ideological speculations unrelated to the text, historical biblical criticism, as thus defined, becomes an indispensable tool.* Therefore it is important to acknowledge the enormous advances and contributions that have been made by biblical scholars throughout the world over the last two centuries toward a better understanding of what the biblical authors intended to communicate to their original audiences.[63]

In an earlier book, *The Dynamic Word*, I asserted that it is impossible to effectively preach or to do theology without first attempting to understand the original audience to which the biblical books were addressed, and I continue to maintain the decisive significance of this perspective.[64] It would be naïve to think that a modern person can, without effort, understand the intention of authors writing almost two thousand years ago in other languages, with different worldviews and to destinations unknown to many of us. While the insights resulting from historical biblical criticism have been significant and in many ways indispensable, it must also be admitted that many historical issues remain unresolved or, at least, uncertain. Nevertheless, this critical task remains foundational for the entire theological enterprise since the treasure that is ours in Scripture is contained "in earthen vessels" (2 Cor 4:7, RSV), in texts that are shaped and transmitted by ancient Israel and the first-century church. It is important to remember that faith "relies upon human forms of expression and interpretation, dialogue and communication, all of which are fragile and all too often fragmented embodiments, none of which is completely adequate, of the mystery which has been revealed."[65]

The issue, then, is not with the tools employed by historical biblical critics—otherwise one would have to put into question the very text of Scripture as well as its translations—but *the domain of meaning into which the results of such critical study are placed. Every* hermeneutic represents and presupposes a *domain of meaning*; therefore, the real challenge for biblical interpretation is not only the critical task itself but especially the conceptual world of meaning in which such interpretation takes place. Thus, when a given domain of meaning further influences tentative and variable scholarly results, the consequent interpretation of any biblical text is significantly affected. Many today, presuming that historical critical exegesis is more definitive than it is and imagining that it represents a neutral, impartial hermeneutic, fall captive to an imperialistic perception that such biblical criticism, in effect, exhausts the complete meaning of the biblical text. When this occurs Scripture becomes susceptible to an ideological capture devoid of Christological and Trinitarian context yet often claiming to be fully "Christian," the very technique employed by the heretical Gnostics with whom Tertullian collided and whom he chided.

One way to illustrate the decisive importance of historical biblical criticism is to refer to recent scholarly discussion regarding Paul's letter to the Romans.[66] An important aspect of this dialogue has been to determine the occasion and purpose of Romans. To do so effectively involves specific knowledge about the rich diversity of Judaism in the period know as Second Temple Judaism,[67] the Graeco-Roman world, inscriptions, the sociological structure of the Jewish and Christian communities in Rome, form criticism, rhetorical and epistolary theory, just to mention a few of the necessary components of the critical task. Such historical inquiry has contributed valuable information and shed new light on the situation of Roman Christianity and, further, has advanced a consensus concerning the actual situations that Paul may have been addressing as he wrote this letter. Yet despite the positive contributions of this dialogue, seen as a whole, one can observe some troubling trends: (1) a tendency on the part of some scholars toward atomistic fixations and fanciful reconstructions with little basis in fact and to which no critical controls are applied; (2) a tendency to permit issues external to the text, important as they may be in their own right, such as the contemporary Jewish-Christian dialogue, to determine the evaluation of the theology of Romans; (3) a tendency to get mired in historical issues without returning to the central concerns of the letter itself, including how this new knowledge helps the interpreter to understand Paul's theological message to the believers in Rome. Despite these aberrant tendencies, many encouraging contributions have been made by critical scholars, as is evident in a number of helpful essays in *The Romans Debate*,[68] one of many examples of how historical biblical criticism effectively contributes to a more profound understanding of the central theological themes of the New Testament.

Although historical biblical criticism runs the risk of being involved in historical reconstruction for its own sake and at times thinking that such exercises alone exhaust the meaning of Scripture, it is not unimportant to be aware of the opposite fallacy: to think that one can resolve the excesses of historical reconstruction by reverting to a new form of biblical literalism. To understand the proper historical setting of the canonical texts is essential, while at the same time recognizing the necessary limits of this information. To reject such a historical approach risks the danger not only of succumbing to an uninformed literalist reading of Scripture, but also of catering to one of the major delusions of the modern age: a self-referential reading in which the only meaning of a text is what it says to me: I alone make the final determination of meaning and significance. The Trinitarian church has always rejected such an introverted and distorted hermeneutic represented by an unrestrained individualism, and the church must continue to do so today. The insightful words of Raymond Brown bear repeating again: "What the biblical text said to its first readers, should be related to what the text says to me, because I am a Christian heir to the people of Israel and the people of the early church, and *not independent of them*."[69]

Notes

1. Tertullian, *Prescription against Heretics*, 15. For English translations, see S. L. Greenslade, *Early Latin Theology* (Library of Christian Classics 5; Philadelphia: Westminster, 1956) 14.

2. John Knox, *Jesus: Lord and Christ* (New York: Harper, 1958) 206 (italics mine).

3. John Knox, *Limits of Unbelief* (London: Collins, 1970) 67 (italics mine). Of course, John Knox is not to be held responsible for the different nuances and emphases that I attribute to the term "Christ event." My own work with the Dead Sea Scrolls, for example, has led to a far greater emphasis on the role of Judaism in all dimensions of the Christ event than Knox was able to realize at the time he wrote.

4. Ca. 160–ca. 225.

5. *Prescription against Heretics*, 37.3ff.; modified translation from S. L. Greenslade, *Early Latin Theology*, 58.

6. Raymond E. Brown, "The Contribution of Historical Biblical Criticism to Ecumenical Church Discussion," in Richard John Neuhaus, *Biblical Interpretation in Crisis: The Ratzinger Conference on Bible and Church* (Grand Rapids: Eerdmans, 1989) 46 (italics mine).

7. With the term "Church Catholic" I am attempting to express the universality (i.e., East and West) of the Christian church in its classical and orthodox expression both at the time of Tertullian and in subsequent history, including the present.

8. Joseph Ratzinger, in Neuhaus, *Biblical Interpretation in Crisis*, 171.

9. See my discussion of this point in Neuhaus, *Biblical Interpretation in Crisis*, 141-45.

10. See, for example, Scott W. Gustafson, *Biblical Amnesia: A Forgotten Story of Redemption, Resistance and Renewal* (West Conshohocken, Pa.: Infinity, 2004).

11. See further, Philip Jenkins, *The New Anti-Catholicism: The Last Acceptable Prejudice* (New York: Oxford, 2004).

12. *Prescription against Heretics*, 17, in S. L. Greenslade, *Early Latin Theology*, 42. "Exegesis" comes from the Greek word meaning "interpretation" or "explanation."

13. See www.newsmax.com/archives/articles/2001/11/17/190533.shtml.

14. For example, Tim La Haye and Jerry B. Jenkins, *Glorious Appearing: The End of Days* (Left Behind Series 12; Wheaton, Ill: Tyndale, 2004).

15. Joel Osteen, *Your Best Life Now: 7 Steps to Living at Your Full Potential* (New York: Warner, 2004).

16. Jack Miles, *Christ: A Crisis in the Life of God* (New York: Vintage, 2002) 65.

17. Ibid., 235.

18. Ibid., 47.

19. Krister Stendahl, *The Bible and the Role of Women: A Case Study in Hermeneutics* (Philadelphia: Fortress, 1966) 40.

20. Philip Turner, "An Unworkable Theology," *First Things* 154 (June/July 2005) 10-12, here 11.

21. Ibid., 12.

22. Ibid., 10-12.

23. Dietrich Bonhoeffer, *The Cost of Discipleship* (New York: Collier, 1963) 45-47.

24. Joseph Ratzinger, *Principles of Catholic Theology: Building Stones for a Fundamental Theology* (San Francisco: Ignatius, 1987) 281.

25. Bonhoeffer, *Cost of Discipleship*, 45-47.

26. Turner, "An Unworkable Theology," 11.

27. Characteristic of a fundamentalism of the right or of the left is the tendency of both to impose on the biblical text rigid adherence to unyielding doctrinal or ideological perspectives and to separate the interpretation of the Bible from the tradition of historic Christianity. With regard to such deviant tendencies the Pontifical Biblical Commission in "The Interpretation of the Bible in the Church" (*Origins* 23/29 [January 6, 1994] 497-524) summarizes the matter well: "It fails to realize that the New Testament took form within the Christian church and that it is the Holy Scripture of this church, the existence of which preceded the composition of texts" (510).

28. The retired Episcopal bishop of the Diocese of Newark.

29. John Shelby Spong, *The Sins of Scripture: Exposing the Bible's Texts of Hate to Reveal the God of Love* (San Francisco: HarperSanFrancisco, 2005) 171.

30. Ibid.

31. Ibid., 174.

32. Ibid., 125, 229.

33. See Marcus Borg, *Reading the Bible Again for the First Time* (San Francisco: HarperSanFrancisco, 2001) 1-18.

34. See Leo Steinberg, *The Sexuality of Christ in Renaissance Art and in Modern Oblivion* (Chicago: University of Chicago Press, 1983) 15.

35. The term *canon* refers to those biblical books that the Church Catholic understood as comprising Holy Scripture.

36. Miles, *Christ*, 289.

37. Ibid., 265-89.

38. A primary example of such an orientation is the work of the American *Jesus Seminar*. See Raymond E. Brown for a critical discussion of both the intentions and the fallacies of this approach in *An Introduction to the New Testament* (Anchor Bible Reference Library; New York: Doubleday, 1997) 820-23.

39. George Lindbeck, "Scripture, Consensus, and Community," in Neuhaus, *Biblical Interpretation in Crisis*, 74-101, here 83.

40. Neuhaus, *Biblical Interpretation in Crisis*, 146

41. Professor Amy-Jill Levine at Vanderbilt University.

42. See pages 1-2 in this volume.

43. Neuhaus, *Biblical Interpretation in Crisis*, 97.

44. "Diachronic" derives from Greek, meaning "through time." Here it refers to developments over a significant period of time.

45. "Synchronic," as opposed to "diachronic," does not refer to developments over a period of time but rather at a particular point in time or, as here, the interconnections within a given canonical set of texts.

46. Neuhaus, *Biblical Interpretation in Crisis*, 88.

47. Irenaeus, ca. 130–ca. 200, was the bishop of Lyons.

48. Burton Mack, *The Lost Gospel: The Book of Q and Christian Origins* (San Francisco: Harper, 1993).

49. Jane Schaberg, *The Illegitimacy of Jesus: A Feminist Theological Interpretation of the Infancy Narratives* (San Francisco: Harper, 1987).

50. Robert W. Funk, Roy W. Hoover, and the Jesus Seminar, *The Five Gospels: The Search for the Authentic Words of Jesus* (New York: Macmillan, 1993).

51. Richard B. Hays, "The Corrected Jesus," *First Things* 43 (May 1994) 48.

52. Albert Schweitzer, *The Quest of the Historical Jesus* (Minneapolis, Minn.: Fortress, 2001). The first English edition appeared in 1910, a translation from the first German edition in 1906 entitled *Von Reimarus zu Wrede*. Schweitzer (1875-1965) was a distinguished German New Testament scholar, physician, and organist.

53. See the review essay by Luke Timothy Johnson, "The Crisis in Biblical Scholarship," *Commonweal* (December 3, 1993) 18-21.

54. *Prescription against Heretics*, 17, in S. L. Greenslade, *Early Latin Theology*, 42.

55. All quotations from the Bible are taken from the New Revised Standard Version (NRSV) unless noted otherwise.

56. *The Lectionary for the Christian People*, edited by Gordon W. Lathrop and Gail Ramshaw-Schmidt (Cycle A and B; New York: Pueblo Publishing Company, 1986-87), B 202.

57. *The Lectionary for the Christian People*, A xiv.

58. See, for example, Arland Hultgren, "Being Faithful to the Scriptures: Romans 1:26-27 as a Case in Point," *Word & World* 14 (Winter 1994) 6-11; Krister Stendahl in a lecture given to west coast clergy, Fall, 1993.

59. Terence E. Fretheim and Karlfried Froehlich, *The Bible as Word of God in a Post-modern Age* (Eugene, Or.: Wipf & Stock, 2001) 95.

60. Vincent of Lerins, *Commonitorium*, in Henry Bettenson, *Documents of the Christian Church* (Oxford: Oxford University Press, 1963) 83.

61. Johnson, "The Crisis in Biblical Scholarship," 20.

62. One may wish to consult Edgar Krentz, *The Historical-Critical Method* (Philadelphia: Fortress, 1975). For an excellent discussion of the function and value of historical biblical criticism, see the report of the Pontifical Biblical Commission, "The Interpretation of the Bible in the Church," 500-502.

63. Exemplary among such contributions is Raymond E. Brown, *An Introduction to the New Testament*.

64. Karl Paul Donfried, *The Dynamic Word: New Testament Insights for Contemporary Christians* (San Francisco: Harper, 1981).

65. *A Treasure in Earthen Vessels: An Instrument for an Ecumenical Reflection on Hermeneutics* (Faith and Order Paper No. 182; Geneva: World Council of Churches/Faith and Order, 1998) 7.

66. See Karl P. Donfried, *The Romans Debate* (Peabody, Mass.: Hendrickson, 2001).

67. This time period begins with the call of Haggai and Zechariah (520-15 BCE) for the construction of the Temple that had been destroyed by Nebuchadnezzar in 587/586 BCE and ends with its destruction in 70 CE by the Romans.

68. See, for example, the contribution by Peter Stuhlmacher, "The Theme of Romans," in Donfried, *The Romans Debate*, 333-45.

69. Raymond E. Brown, "The Contribution of Historical Biblical Criticism to Ecumenical Church Discussion," in Neuhaus, *Biblical Interpretation in Crisis*, 24-49, here 46 (italics mine).

2

The Bible and the Church

Christian Presuppositions

2.1 Toward the Praxis of a Trinitarian Hermeneutic

How does the interpretation of the Bible function appropriately within a Trinitarian hermeneutic? How does such a hermeneutic inform us about the Triune God, his relationship to us, and the doing of his will? In a preliminary way it can be said that such a hermeneutic takes seriously the entire canonical context of the Christian Bible as a narrational and theological whole, beginning with Genesis and ending with Revelation, centered in the Trinitarian God who has disclosed himself definitively in the life, death, and resurrection of Jesus Christ and continues to reveal himself to the community of believers through his Holy Spirit. In this way a Trinitarian hermeneutic "redescribes reality within the scriptural framework rather than translating scripture into extrascriptural categories. It is the text so to speak which absorbs the world, rather than the world the text."[1] Only in such a way does the Bible become the Scripture of the Christian church and resist capture by "self-interested misreadings."[2]

Some might wonder whether the church's teaching about the Trinity, brought to clear expression only in the fourth century, is germane to the interpretation of biblical texts written considerably earlier. The Bible that Christianity accepts as Scripture is, however, only given its final and normative canonical form by the universal church meeting in council, under the guidance of the Holy Spirit, considerably after its composition. This canonical process was guided by the same rule of faith, creeds, and councils that gave final expression to the church's understanding of the Triune God. Reginald Fuller reminds us that the critical decisions of early Christianity bring

20

to fruition a set of trajectories actually beginning in the New Testament. Thus the canonical decisions of the church fathers and councils are already found in "embryonic form" in the New Testament even though its "basic shape does not emerge until towards the end of the 2nd century." Similarly, the

> concept of a confession or creed is present, but creeds likewise do not emerge until the end of the 2nd century. The liturgy is beginning to take shape, but it is not until the 2nd century that its pattern is clearly discerned. Finally, the institutional ministry is beginning to emerge in Acts and the Pastorals, replacing the charismatics on the one hand and the purely governmental presbyteries on the other. But this institutional ministry does not achieve its classical form until the second century, with the threefold ministry of bishops, presbyters and deacons.[3]

The church of Jesus Christ that came into existence *prior* to the writing of the New Testament as a result of the resurrection is the *same* church that gives final shape to the New Testament, the Christian canon of Scripture, and the doctrine of the Trinity. Thus, what we emphasized in our discussion of the Christ event[4] bears repetition: Christology cannot be separated from ecclesiology, in the same way that Jesus can never be understood apart from his church.

2.2 Canonical Criticism as a Starting Point for a Trinitarian Hermeneutic

A magnificent contribution toward a renewed understanding of biblical hermeneutics is the magisterial contribution of Brevard S. Childs, *Biblical Theology of the Old and New Testaments: Theological Reflection on the Christian Bible.*[5] Although both the fragmentation of the biblical text and its removal from its canonical context by many biblical scholars are appropriately criticized, Childs recognizes that one cannot and should not attempt to turn the clock back as if the late-nineteenth- and twentieth-century developments in historical biblical criticism had never occurred. While fully cognizant of the misuses to which these advances have been put, he rightly applauds some of their significant contributions. Childs is especially to be commended for his attempt to recognize that *both* the trajectory leading to the final redaction (i.e., editing) of texts *and* their canonical placement are critical if the community of faith is to engage in a conversation with Scripture. To eliminate the first opens the door to a naïve fundamentalism or a dogmatic misuse of the coherent, consistent gospel articulated in contingent, specific contexts;[6] to ignore the second creates a biblical scholarship based on a fragmented hermeneutic likely to distort the canonical context of the biblical witness to the reality of the Triune God in the pages of Scripture. When such a fractionalized, alien hermeneutic infuses various levels of ecclesial structures, then Christianity can easily be seduced by well-intentioned ideologies, often set forth as an ethic of love, yet, often unsuspectingly, deceptive in their consequences.[7]

An adequate biblical hermeneutic requires the ability to hold a wide variety of factors together in creative tension and thoughtful balance. To properly interpret the various redactional levels in concert with the final, canonical form of Scripture requires not only a profound knowledge of the primary text of Scripture but also academic learning and theological insight; Childs displays both splendidly. Further, his contribution is to be lauded for seeing the necessity of both biblical and theological reflection based on the discreet witness of both the New *and* the Old Testament, as well as the necessity for dialogue between biblical and dogmatic theology. One of the significant contributions of this volume is to point us toward a more balanced interpretation of Scripture as well as to begin a long-overdue conversation between biblical interpreters and their systematic counterparts in the theological enterprise.

2.3 The Unity of Old and New Testaments

A Trinitarian interpretation of Scripture presupposes the canonical unity of both testaments, and the common terminology used by Christians, Old and New Testaments, is a reflection of this oneness. In most academic settings the Bible is taught over two semesters, and therefore the academic year necessitates a division, for pedagogical reasons, between the Old and New Testaments. In virtually all secular colleges and universities, and not a few divinity schools, the current language used to describe the two parts of the Christian Bible is "Hebrew Bible" and "Christian Scriptures." The intent is quite correct, since what Christians refer to as "Old Testament" belongs to Judaism as well as Christianity, and it is imperative to make such a distinction in an academic environment. Yet the choice of these descriptors, especially the reference to "Christian Scriptures" in preference to the New Testament, is far from ideal for several reasons. The phrase "Hebrew Bible," the somewhat less problematic of the two, is a construct of American scholarship and, among other things, it does not immediately make evident to the student that some small parts of this literature were written in Aramaic and that the whole was also circulating in Greek translation in the centuries prior to Philo of Alexandria[8] and Jesus of Nazareth. The designation "Christian Scriptures" in reference to the New Testament is particularly misleading because for Christianity its Scriptures are not merely the twenty-seven books of the New Testament but include also the thirty-nine of the Jewish Bible, that is, that which becomes the Christian Old Testament.[9] It is imperative for the proper interpretation of the Christian Bible to recognize that it begins with Genesis, not Matthew.

This terminological problem involved in describing the two parts of the Christian Bible in non-Christian settings is indeed difficult. Other alternative designations for the two testaments that have been suggested, especially in broad academic settings, include "Bible I/II," and "First/Second Covenant." Both such references take seriously the distinction between the Jewish and the Christian sacred texts, and the former allows for the use of the term Bible as distinct canonical entities for each, but in ways that reflect their uniqueness within their respective traditions. In non-Christian contexts the Old Testament might also appropriately be referred to as either the Jewish Bible or by the acronym Tanakh.[10]

2.3.1 Luke 24:44-48: The Fulfillment of the Old Testament

A Christian interpretation of Scripture must, however, refer to the Bible as Old and New Testaments. To announce a reading during a liturgical service as taken from the Hebrew Scriptures misses the point that the Hebrew Scriptures are part of the Christian canon. Further, theologically the first testament must be referred to as the Old Testament to denote its completion and transformation—*not* its supercession or rejection—as a result of the Christ event; the second is called the New Testament by way of the inauguration of a "new" or "renewed" covenant or testament through this same Christ event.[11] The conceptual categories of promise/fulfillment and old/new (renewed) covenant are among the basic presuppositions of the earliest Jesus movement. A text that will prove helpful for our consideration is found in the gospel of Luke 24:44-48:

> Then he [Jesus] said to them, "These are my words that I spoke to you while I was still with you—that everything written about me in the law of Moses, the prophets, and the psalms must be fulfilled." Then he

opened their minds to understand the scriptures, and he said to them, "Thus it is written, that the Messiah is to suffer and to rise from the dead on the third day, and that repentance and forgiveness of sins is to be proclaimed in his name to all nations, beginning from Jerusalem. You are witnesses of these things. And see, I am sending upon you what my Father promised so stay here in the city until you have been clothed with power from on high."

Several aspects found in this text are significant for an understanding of the interconnectedness of the Old and New Testaments:

a. *The theme of promise and fulfillment: what has been promised by God in the Torah, the prophets, and the psalms has been fulfilled in Jesus.* This is precisely the point that Luke accentuates as well in the beginning of his gospel. After Jesus reads from the Isaiah scroll on the Sabbath in the synagogue in Nazareth, he proclaims: "Today this scripture has been fulfilled in your hearing" (4:21). For Jesus and his followers, there is an unbreakable bond between the promises made to Israel and the Christ event. Under the guidance of the Spirit, they claimed these promises of old were now being fulfilled. Thus, without a thoroughgoing knowledge of the content of the promises made to the Israelites in the Old Testament it becomes difficult, if not impossible, to know what is being fulfilled during the ministry, death, and resurrection of Christ.

b. *Jesus, as the one who suffered, died, and been resurrected, is able to open the minds of his disciples so that they can understand the Scriptures in a renewed way.* It is precisely this Jesus, understood as part of the broader Christ event, who not only holds the old covenant and new covenant together but who also reveals how the new covenant in Christ makes the first covenant comprehensible in a new and more profound way. The followers of Jesus are given new "eyeglasses" by which they are able to read their Scriptures, which at this point was solely the Old Testament.

This second observation, namely, that Jesus "opened their minds," is anticipated earlier in this same chapter in Luke. Following the appearance of the risen Lord in their midst they said to each other, "Were not our hearts burning within us while he was talking to us on the road, while he was opening the scriptures to us?" (24:32). To have the Risen One open the minds of his followers is just as essential today for a genuinely Christian and canonical interpretation of Scripture. When Christ himself is present through his Holy Spirit, then all of Scripture is opened and illumined in a new way: it refers all who truly seek to understand his word to himself and to his self-giving life in the context of God's salvation history. The goal of any preacher, theologian, or interpreter of Christian Scripture is to penetrate the mystery of Christ, and that can take place only when his Spirit opens it as a word from God,[12] illumines the mind of the believer, and allows for an understanding more profound than that available simply through critical biblical study, as indispensable as such study is.

2.3.2 The Jesus Movement and the Dead Sea Scrolls

The Jewish group from which many of the Dead Sea Scrolls originate, most likely the Essenes[13] or a group closely related to them, provides us with interesting insights and similarities with the Jesus movement, especially given their relatively unique interpretation of the Tanakh in the context of such shared themes as community, fulfillment, and covenant. When a Bedouin shepherd threw a stone into a cave at Khirbet Qumran in 1947, our understanding of "Judaism" and "Christianity" in the first century CE changed dramatically. The vast majority of the 900 texts found in these caves have since been published. On the basis of these texts scholarship in the twenty-first century will need to rewrite the complex phenomenon known as Second Temple Judaism,[14] the history of the early Jesus movement, and the interaction of the two. No longer can we speak about Judaism and Christianity in the first century as distinct religions in sharp conflict with one another; rather we must recognize the enormous diversity and breadth of Judaism, an inclusivity so extensive that it included the earliest followers of Jesus. The texts of the Dead Sea Scrolls illustrate that the interaction of these distinct forms of Judaisms was far greater than scholars had previously recognized.

The movement revealed in the scrolls referred to itself as the community of the renewed covenant or simply, the *yahad*.[15] Part of this group relocated from Jerusalem to Qumran in the late second century BCE and remained there until 68 CE when the Romans destroyed it as they marched toward Masada fresh from having conquered and burned Jerusalem. Josephus, the first-century Jewish historian, calls attention to the fact that there were Essenes resident in an area located in the southwest corner of Jerusalem.[16] From the Damascus Document (CD), one of the major texts found in Cave 4, researchers are aware that the Essene movement was also spread throughout the land that we now know as Israel.[17]And with a membership of four thousand it was not a small movement when compared to the Pharisees, who numbered six thousand.[18]

These texts from the Dead Sea have dramatically altered our perception of this period. As a result of their discovery, we now have many original texts describing this community, thus shedding enormous light, sometimes directly and sometimes indirectly, on the entire shape of the Judaisms[19] of this period, including the Sadducees, the Pharisees, the Essenes, and the early Jesus movement. The Dead Sea Scrolls have not only made available a large quantity of hitherto unknown texts but they have also provided a new context for comprehending (1) the complexity of Second Temple Judaism, (2) the intention of Jesus of Nazareth and his movement, and (3), especially, the great missionary of this movement, the apostle Paul.

2.3.2a Fulfillment and Covenant

The term "new covenant" is used only once in the Old Testament. In Jeremiah 31:31-34 we hear these words:

> The days are surely coming, says the Lord, when I will make a new covenant with the house of Israel and the house of Judah. It will not be like the covenant that I made with their ancestors when I took them by the hand to bring them out of the land of Egypt—a covenant that they broke, though I was their husband, says the Lord. But this is the covenant that I will make with the house of Israel after those days, says the Lord: I will put my law within them, and I will write it on their hearts; and I will be their God, and they shall be my people. No longer shall they teach one another, or say to each other, "Know the Lord," for they shall all know me, from the least of them to the greatest, says the Lord; for I will forgive their iniquity, and remember their sin no more.

This phrase is taken up in several places in the New Testament and among the best known are Luke 22:20 ("And he did the same with the cup after supper, saying, 'This cup that is poured out for you is the *new covenant* in my blood . . .'") and 2 Corinthians 3:5-6 ("Not that we are competent of ourselves to claim anything as coming from us; our competence is from God, who has made us competent to be ministers of a *new covenant*, not of letter but of spirit; for the letter kills, but the Spirit gives life"). Not of little interest is the fact that in late Second Temple Judaism it was not the Jesus movement that first used the term "new covenant," but rather it was the Essenes, the community represented in this text found among the Dead Sea Scrolls: "And so it is with all the men who enter the *New Covenant* in the land of Damascus" (CD 8:21).

Since in the New Testament there is considerable tension between Jesus, his followers, and the Pharisees, it is not insignificant that the New Testament's understanding of new covenant is considerably closer to that of the Essenes than of the Pharisees. The Qumran community's understanding of covenant was virtually absent from the pharisaic movement. Shemaryahu Talmon suggests that the Rabbis "did not develop the notion that in their days, and with their community, God had renewed his covenant of old with the people of Israel."[20] In contrast to the specific *communal* thrust of the Essene concept of covenant, it is the act of circumcision with the focus on the individual that is pivotal in the rabbinic considerations of covenant. In light of this strikingly different usage between these two Torah schools, it is of considerable interest to note the New Testament's, and especially Paul's, affinity for the Essene use of "covenant," particularly in the context of an ecclesial, communal comparison of the new covenant with the old in 2 Corinthians 3:6 and 3:14. Given the fact that we have no texts over a period of 500 to 600 years since Jeremiah that refer to a "new covenant," it is quite remarkable that the only two Jewish communities that accentuate and interpret the new covenant are the Essenes and the early Jesus movement, both active in the first century.

Anticipating our subsequent discussion of Pauline theology, the reader should be alerted to the fact that Talmon has consciously translated the Hebrew for "new covenant" as "renewed covenant."[21] He urges that the "thread of Israel's historical past, which had snapped when Jerusalem and the temple were destroyed, is retied with the establishment of the *yahad*'s 'renewed covenant.'"[22] What "snapped," it is argued, is not an irrevocable rupture; rather, there is an indissoluble bond, a strong linkage, with the earlier and the current covenant. Does Talmon's hesitation in translating the Hebrew as "old covenant" have possible relevance for Christian usage of the terminology "old" and "new" covenants? Given that both Jesus and Paul were Jews who never renounced this profoundly determinative religious context, did they advocate a sustained severance between old and new covenant? If not, Talmon's language may be relevant for the relationship of the two testaments as well. The phrase "old covenant" is used only once (2 Cor 3:14) in the entire New Testament. When Paul uses the term *palaios* for "old," does he necessarily mean "antiquated" or "obsolete," or is he able to retain the other sense of this adjective, namely, "venerable," "being in existence for a long time"? In antiquity both senses are possible,[23] and for Matthew's Jesus the latter is emphasized in Matthew 13:52: "And he said to them, 'Therefore every scribe who has been trained for the kingdom of heaven is like the master of a household who brings out of his treasure what is new and what is old.'" Even the author of Hebrews with his sharp, negative use of "obsolete" in 8:13 speaks on more than one occasion, in very nuanced language, both in terms of a "better covenant" (7:22) as well as a "first covenant" (8:7). Talmon's observations should give Christian scholars great pause in the all-too-frequent radical separation of the two covenants, a separation that has had profoundly negative theological and interfaith consequences.

2.3.2b Interpreting the Bible: Qumran, Jesus, and Paul

Having learned from the similarities between the Essenes and the early Jesus movement in the way they use the term "covenant," one will better understand the manner in which the Essenes and the Jesus movement, both reflective of the Judaisms of the Second Temple period, interpret their Jewish Bible. The *yahad* used a *"pesher"*[24] method of biblical interpretation, a contemporizing form of interpretation in which prophetic texts are understood as referring to present events in the life of their community. More specifically, in its use of biblical texts it divided the law into distinct categories, that is, the revealed (*nigleh*) and the hidden (*nistar*). The revealed law was known to all of Israel, but the hidden was known only to the *yahad*. The use of the category "revealed" can be found in the *Community Rule* (1QS 8:15-16), one of the community's foundational documents: "This (path) is the study of the Law which He commanded by the hand of Moses, that they may do according to all that has been revealed (*nigleh*) from age to age, and as the Prophets have revealed by His Holy Spirit."[25] Most of Israel, however, was rebellious: "For they are not reckoned in His Covenant. They have neither inquired nor sought after Him concerning His laws that they might know the hidden things[26] in which they have sinfully erred; and matters revealed[27] they have treated with insolence" (1QS 5:11-12). As a result, the "hidden laws" were progressively revealed only to the Qumran Community, that is, the Community of the Renewed Covenant.[28] This entire approach has remarkable resemblance to the texts in Luke 4 and 24, which were discussed earlier. In each set of these Lukan verses, the Old Testament texts are understood as referring to a contemporary moment in the life of Jesus or his followers, and the newness of the interpretation is only fully comprehended as a result of the Spirit's activity.

Krister Stendahl[29] has shown with great clarity that the dozen or so formula quotations in Matthew's gospel, for example in Matthew 1:22, "All this took place to fulfill what had been spoken by the Lord through the prophet . . . ," share a remarkable resemblance to the *pesher* type of biblical interpretation of some of the scrolls found at Qumran. The assumption is that the prophets had written with a veiled, eschatological meaning and that their correct interpretation could only be made by the community living in the end-time to whom special knowledge had been revealed, in the one case through the Teacher of Righteousness,[30] and, in the other, Jesus of Nazareth. And so for Matthew's community the Isaiah 7:14 text, "Look, the virgin shall conceive and bear a son, and they shall call him Emmanuel," is intended to point to the birth and incarnation of Jesus (Matt 1:21-23). Similarly, the Commentary on Habakkuk (1QpHab) found among the Dead Sea Scrolls understands the process of interpretation in a very similar way. Commenting on Hab 2:4b, "But the righteous shall live by his faith," the writer continues: "Interpreted, this concerns all those who observe the Law in the House of Judah, whom God will deliver from the House of Judgement because of their suffering and because of their faith in the Teacher of Righteousness."[31] It is quite apparent that the words of the prophet Habakkuk are being directly applied to the life of the *yahad* living close to the final period of Second Temple Judaism, just as Isaiah was directly related to the Christ event by his followers.

The apostle Paul not only cites this identical Habakkuk text in Romans and interprets it according to the same pesher technique, but quite interestingly comes to a very different conclusion with regard to the meaning of the text. Paul writes to the Romans: "For I am not ashamed of the gospel; it is the power of God for salvation to everyone who has faith, to the Jew first and also to the Greek. For in it the righteousness of God is revealed through faith for faith; as it is written, 'The one who is righteous will live by faith'" (Rom 1:16-17). Here the application is not to having faith in the Teacher of Righteousness, but in Jesus Christ. Paul's conviction that Jesus is the Messiah, the Christ, becomes determinative for his understanding of Habakkuk and, of course, all the other prophets that he cites with great frequency in his letters. Although the center of Paul's hermeneutic, the death and resurrection of Jesus the Messiah, is radically different from that of Qumran, he uses virtually identical introductory formulas, for example, "it is written in the law," "for it has been written," as those found in the literature of the Dead Sea Scrolls. These commonalities between the *yahad* and the Jesus movement allow us to better understand the connections between the two and the way in which the Tanakh functions within their theology.

The tensions that were previously observed between the Pharisees and the Essenes, two of the several Jewish groups within the broader framework of Second Temple Judaism, are also evident in their differing perspectives of biblical interpretation. Shemaryahu Talmon maintains that in the texts of the Dead Sea Scrolls there is in evidence a confrontation between a prophet-ically inspired movement inclined toward apocalypticism (i.e., a revelation of otherworldly secrets that disclose the future overthrow of the present age and the establishment of God's rule at the End of Days) and a rationalist stream that will ultimately develop into Rabbinic Judaism.[32] He observes, further, that "Rabbinic Judaism shelved prophetic inspiration and progres-sively developed a rationalist stance. . . . By contrast, the *yahad* embraces unreservedly the Bible's high appreciation of prophetic teaching and con-tinues to subject the life of the individual and the community to the guid-ance of personalities who were possessed of the divine spirit. . . . In this respect, the Covenanters and nascent Christianity are on the same wave length. The acceptance of inspiration as the paramount principle of indi-vidual and communal life informs also the followers of Jesus."[33] The words of Paul to the Corinthians reflect such a perspective: "And we speak of these things in words not taught by human wisdom but taught by the Spirit, inter-preting spiritual things to those who are spiritual" (1 Cor 2:13). It is for like reasons that a Christian hermeneutic of Scripture, understood as the Old and New Testaments integrally interwoven into a single canon, cannot be satisfied that historical biblical criticism *alone* exhausts the meaning of Scripture or that interpretations of the sacred texts from those outside the community are *necessarily* adequate to the life and ministry of the church. For only when Scripture is placed before the Triune God will the crucified and risen Lord become present as a definitive word.

Notes

1. George Lindbeck, *The Nature of Doctrine: Religion and Theology in a Postliberal Age* (Philadelphia: Westminster, 1984) 118.

2. George Lindbeck, "Scripture, Consensus, and Community," in Richard John Neuhaus, *Biblical Interpretation in Crisis: The Ratzinger Conference on Bible and Church* (Grand Rapids: Eerdmans, 1989), 74-101, here 79.

3. Reginald Fuller, "The Development of the Ministry," in *Lutheran-Episcopal Dialogue: A Progress Report* (Cincinnati: Forward Movement Publications, 1973) 88.

4. See pages 1-2 in this volume.

5. Minneapolis: Fortress, 1993.

6. In using the terms "coherent" and "contingent" I am indebted to the work of J. Chris-tian Beker, *Paul the Apostle* (Philadelphia: Fortress, 1980), especially 11-16, although he is not to be held responsible for the particular way in which I interpret and apply this terminology.

7. See Philip Turner, "An Unworkable Theology," *First Things* 154 (June/July 2005) 10-12.

8. Ca. 20 BCE–ca. 50 CE.

9. In addition the Roman Catholic Bible contains the Apocrypha, books that are included in the Greek Old Testament (Septuagint) but not contained in the Tanakh.

10. The word Tanakh (also Tanach) is an acronym based on the initial Hebrew letters of each of the Hebrew Bible's three parts: Torah, the Law; Nevi'im, the Prophets; and Ketuvim, the Writings.

11. See pages 26-27 in this volume.

12. For a discussion of the Bible as Word of God, see section 3.2, "Scripture and the Word of God."

13. See Joseph A. Fitzmyer, *The Dead Sea Scrolls and Christian Origins* (Grand Rapids: Eerdmans, 2000) 249-60.

14. See note 67 (p. 19) above.

15. See Shemaryahu Talmon, "The Community of the Renewed Covenant," in *The Community of the Renewed Covenant: The Notre Dame Symposium on the Dead Sea Scrolls,* ed. Eugene Ulrich and James VanderKam (Christianity and Judaism in Antiquity Series 10; Notre Dame, Ind.: University of Notre Dame, 1994) 3-24, here 8.

16. Josephus, *Jewish War* 5.145.

17. For example, *Damascus Document* 7:6-9.

18. Josephus, *Jewish Antiquities* 18.18-22. For a more complete discussion of the Judaisms of the period, see Shaye J. D. Cohen, *From the Maccabees to the Mishnah* (Library of Early Christianity; Philadelphia: Westminster, 1987).

19. The term Judaisms is used intentionally in order to indicate the diversity and non-monolithic character of Second Temple Judaism.

20. Talmon, "The Community," 14-15.

21. ברית חדשׁה

22. Talmon, "The Community," 13.

23. See further Henry George Liddell and Robert Scott, *A Greek-English Lexicon* (Oxford: Clarendon, 1996); and Frederick William Danker, *A Greek-English Lexicon of the New Testament and Other Early Christian Literature* (Chicago: University of Chicago, 2000).

24. *Pesher* derives from the Hebrew word "to explain" and is the method of interpretation found in some of the Dead Sea Scrolls in which prophecy is applied to events current in the life of the Qumran community.

25. Translation by Geza Vermes, *The Complete Dead Sea Scrolls in English* (New York: Penguin, 1997).

26. נסתרות

27. נגלות

28. See further Lawrence H. Schiffman, *Reclaiming the Dead Sea Scrolls: The History of Judaism, the Background of Christianity, the Lost Library of Qumran* (Philadelphia and Jerusalem: Jewish Publication Society, 1994) 248.

29. Krister Stendahl, *The School of St. Matthew and Its Use of the Old Testament* (Philadelphia: Fortress, 1969).

30. The Teacher of Righteousness was an influential leader of the *yahad* soon after its founding.

31. Vermes, *The Complete Dead Sea Scrolls in English,* 482.

32. Talmon, "The Community," 22.

33. Ibid., 20-21.

3

The Bible and the Church

Scripture as School of the Word

3.1 Scripture as School of the Word

Since the Old Testament finds its fulfillment in the new/renewed covenant brought into being through the death and resurrection of Jesus, it is this Christ event in its rich fullness that shapes the understanding of Scripture, and it is the Risen Christ, present through the Holy Spirit, who gives insight in apprehending the deeper levels of meaning inherent in the biblical texts. Such a recognition brings with it important consequences, perhaps the most significant is that all biblical texts are not equal and, specifically, that Old Testament texts must be interpreted through the lens of Christological fulfillment. Thus, to randomly select texts to support one's cause contributes to the disintegration of Scripture and leads to its distortion. This point is nicely illustrated in the gospel of John. Jesus, in dialogue with his fellow Jews, remarks:

> You search the scriptures because you think that in them you have eternal life; and it is they that testify on my behalf. Yet you refuse to come to me to have life. I do not accept glory from human beings. But I know that you do not have the love of God in you. I have come in my Father's name, and you do not accept me; if another comes in his own name, you will accept him. How can you believe when you accept glory from one another and do not seek the glory that comes from the one who alone is God? Do not think that I will accuse you before the Father; your accuser is Moses, on whom you have set your hope. If you believed Moses, you would believe me, for he wrote about me.

> But if you do not believe what he wrote, how will you believe what I say? (John 5:39-47)

Not only does this passage presuppose that the first covenant points forward in a convincing way to the new/renewed covenant (vv. 45-46), but it also makes clear that all of Scripture is to "testify on my behalf." It is to Christ, his life, suffering, death, and resurrection that all biblical writings point, and it is from him that they receive their significance. Picking and choosing texts in an isolated and noncontextual manner without reference to the Christ event is precluded by a Trinitarian hermeneutic because it is the life, suffering, death, and resurrection of Jesus that give meaning to the whole. The significance of the Christ event for the correct interpretation of Scripture may be compared to the punch line of a joke: without it one simply doesn't get the point of the joke, and without Jesus as the crucified and risen Lord at the center of Scripture one is unable to understand its full intention.

3.1.1 Scripture as the Presence of God in Jesus Christ

If Scripture has its fulfillment in the death and resurrection of Jesus, then it is this event that becomes foundational and pivotal for the interpretation of the entire Bible, and any Christian *lectio divina* must have this event as its alpha and omega, its beginning and end. *Lectio divina* is a "reading, on an individual or communal level, of a more or less lengthy passage of Scripture, received as the word of God and leading, at the prompting of the Spirit, to meditation, prayer and contemplation."[1] The eminent biblical scholar Carlo Maria Martini has suggested that there are *four major presuppositions* at work in such a reading of Scripture:[2]

a. *The unity of Scripture.* For the Christian reader, Scripture is a unified whole from Genesis through Revelation with its interpretative center found in the Christ event. Every page refers to God's great plan of salvation, and the reference to the cross allows all texts, "even those that at first glance have little to do with this message" to be related to this "unifying mystery. . . ."[3] Jesus, his earliest followers, and the writers of the New Testament understood such an intimate relationship to the Old Testament story to be self-evident, whether the references were to Moses, Jonah, David, Isaiah, Melchizedek, or to the Psalms. In the New Testament, God's revelation to his people Israel remains foundational and is now actualized anew through his self-giving in the incarnation of Jesus of Nazareth.

b. *The existential relevance of Scripture.* Not only do the Scriptures "speak to human beings; they give expression to the deepest treasures of the human heart, to the restlessness, sufferings, aspirations, desires, and fears that all human beings share." As a result the Bible allows humanity to understand itself "as individuals and as a community, without which they cannot grasp their own unity or their true relationship to others."[4] One of the most powerful examples of this existential application is that of the towering theologian of Christianity Saint Augustine. In both his *Confessions* and in the *City of God* he repeatedly refers to the Bible as illustrating and illuminating the dramatic issues of his life and his society. As contemporary Western society struggles with such complex issues as human rights and justice, the question needs to be repeatedly raised whether such concepts can be given their fullest meaning in a context other than transcendence? If our norms for proper action to the neighbor near and far are left only to human values, the result, as Scripture repeatedly indicates, will be continued rivalry and jealousy resulting in a continuous pattern of violence and destruction among both individuals and nations.

c. *The dynamic character of values.* Since Christians are people on a journey, Scripture "interacts with human life in a constant movement from life to the word of God and from the word of God back to life,"[5] and therefore gives us insights and values that allow us to move beyond ourselves. The God of Abraham, Isaac, Jacob, and Jesus constantly calls his people to otherness, toward the holiness of God, away from idolatry, so that his will might be carried out and his people may live in the fullness of life that he has promised. This is exactly the point that Paul wishes to make as he writes to the Romans: "Do not be conformed to this world, but be transformed by the renewing of your minds, so that you may discern what is the will of God—what is good and acceptable and perfect" (Rom 12:2).

d. *The Scriptures are a real presence of Jesus.* In a most helpful way Martini emphasizes what has been characteristic for much of the Christian tradition, namely, that Christ is present to his people in Word and Sacrament. Thus when those "in Christ"[6] read Scripture "they can enter into a real communion with Jesus. The expression 'real communion' may startle because it echoes the language applied to eucharistic presence, but Vatican II does not hesitate to assert that the risen Christ is present in the Scriptures and that when we read them or listen to them we can experience this presence."[7] When the apostle Paul reminds the Corinthian believers that they actually "stand" (1 Cor 15:1) in the gospel or when he encourages the church at Thessalonica to remember that they accepted the word of God, the gospel, "not as a human word but as what it really is, God's word, which is also at work in you believers" (1 Thess 2:13), he is expressing exactly what the disciples experienced in their encounter with their risen

Lord in Luke 24:32, "They said to each other, 'Were not our hearts burning within us while he was talking to us on the road, while he was opening the scriptures to us?'"

3.1.2 Scripture as Communion with Jesus Christ

To actualize the Word in the life of the believer, at least *four focal points* are necessary to establish genuine communion with Jesus in the reading and reflection of biblical texts. They are: reading, meditation, prayer, and contemplation. Before considering these approaches more fully, it will be helpful to select a specific text for purposes of illustration. Luke 15:11-32 contains a parable that is often referred to as the "Parable of the Prodigal and His Brother,"[8] although it might more appropriately be described as the "Parable of the Merciful Father."

> Then Jesus said, "There was a man who had two sons. The younger of them said to his father, 'Father, give me the share of the property that will belong to me.' So he divided his property between them. A few days later the younger son gathered all he had and traveled to a distant country, and there he squandered his property in dissolute living. When he had spent everything, a severe famine took place throughout that country, and he began to be in need. So he went and hired himself out to one of the citizens of that country, who sent him to his fields to feed the pigs. He would gladly have filled himself with the pods that the pigs were eating; and no one gave him anything. But when he came to himself he said, 'How many of my father's hired hands have bread enough and to spare, but here I am dying of hunger! I will get up and go to my father, and I will say to him, "Father, I have sinned against heaven and before you; I am no longer worthy to be called your son; treat me like one of your hired hands."' So he set off and went to his father. But while he was still far off, his father saw him and was filled with compassion; he ran and put his arms around him and kissed him. Then the son said to him, 'Father, I have sinned against heaven and before you; I am no longer worthy to be called your son.' But the father said to his slaves, 'Quickly, bring out a robe—the best one—and put it on him; put a ring on his finger and sandals on his feet. And get the fatted calf and kill it, and let us eat and celebrate; for this son of mine was dead and is alive again; he was lost and is found!' And they began to celebrate.
>
> "Now his elder son was in the field; and when he came and

approached the house, he heard music and dancing. He called one of the slaves and asked what was going on. He replied, 'Your brother has come, and your father has killed the fatted calf, because he has got him back safe and sound.' Then he became angry and refused to go in. His father came out and began to plead with him. But he answered his father, 'Listen! For all these years I have been working like a slave for you, and I have never disobeyed your command; yet you have never given me even a young goat so that I might celebrate with my friends. But when this son of yours came back, who has devoured your property with prostitutes, you killed the fatted calf for him!' Then the father said to him, 'Son, you are always with me, and all that is mine is yours. But we had to celebrate and rejoice, because this brother of yours was dead and has come to life; he was lost and has been found.'" (Luke 15:11-32)

Let us now consider these four focal points with this parable in mind.

1. *Reading*. An essential first step is a careful reading and study of the text in its original context.[9] Important here is the discovery of the central elements of the text, which might include, by way of example, "actions, verbs, acting subjects, attitudes and thoughts, settings, motives for acting."[10] A careful reading of the parable must examine the text in light of these possible questions, adapting them as might be relevant to the particular text under consideration. So in response to the question about acting subjects, one will note that there is a father, a younger son, an older son, and a variety of other participants. The attitudes include the rejection of the father as well as a rethinking of that position by the younger son, the anger and jealousy of the older son, and the compassion toward both sons by the father. The actions, movements, and the use of verbs is revealing: the movement away from and then toward the father by the younger son; the older son remaining distant from the house in anger; the somewhat surprisingly active movement of the father toward each son. The father rushed toward the younger son "while he was still far off" (v. 20), and, despite the anger of the older son, the father moved toward him and began to entreat him. Once a sense of the story line has been obtained and some attention has been given to the internal dynamics of the text, one is in a better position to meditate upon this powerful parable, awaiting with surprise the disclosure of its deep and profound levels of meaning.

2. *Meditation*. Having considered the specific context and message of this parable, it will then be necessary to meditate on the abiding value of the text in an effort to hear an authentic word of God in a continuing attempt

to discover our "authentic selves."[11] Meditation on the parable can take many forms, especially if one seeks a word of God that will help to discover our inner being, both in terms of weakness and renewed possibility. What human frailties do both sons reveal? What is the point of the theological confession, "Father, I have sinned against heaven and before you; I am no longer worthy to be called your son; treat me like one of your hired hands," and what is the father's response to it? Why does the return of the younger, often called the "prodigal son," occasion a time of festivity and celebration? In what manner does the father respond to each son? The older son asserts before his father, "I have never disobeyed your command; yet you have never given me even a young goat so that I might celebrate with my friends. But when this son of yours came back, who has devoured your property with prostitutes, you killed the fatted calf for him!" Are there ways in which this attitude helps to reveal aspects of our attitudes? And, finally, one should ask what might well be the most penetrating question of all: What is the father attempting to communicate to his older son and to us with the closing words of the parable: "Son, you are always with me, and all that is mine is yours. But we had to celebrate and rejoice, because this brother of yours was dead and has come to life; he was lost and has been found"? What, in fact, is "the mine" that is "yours"? In what way has the younger brother, whom the older son refuses to name as "brother" in the parable, "come to life" by entering into a new communion with his estranged father?

3. *Prayer.* The significant themes emerging as a result of meditation become motives "for praise, thanksgiving, intercession, petition, forgiveness,"[12] and the seeking of guidance, sustenance, and strength for the ongoing Christian pilgrimage. In asking many questions of the text and meditating on them, one inevitably is moved to prayer, to conversation with the Father himself; and surely the first utterances will be those of praise and thanksgiving for a father who rejects neither the waywardness or callousness of his sons but who takes the initiative to approach each with compassion and who does not rebuke the younger son but who, rather, inaugurates a time of passionate celebration and rejoicing. Prayer also becomes a time of intercession and petition for all those times we as well as others have strayed from the loving father as if he did not really matter in our lives. Then, too, there are those moments when we pitted our arrogant and selfish perspectives against his compassion, thus alienating ourselves from God the loving father and the many others with whom we interact both within our families but also well beyond. Intercession, then, surrenders the self to the very heart of prayer, forgiveness!

4. *Contemplation.* Praying with, through, and under a biblical text

allows for a deeper penetration into the holy mysteries of God. "At some point," urges Cardinal Martini, "the multiplicity of sentiments, reflections, and prayers are reduced to unity in contemplation of the mystery of Jesus, the Son of God, a mystery that is contained in every page. This is especially true of the gospels but it is also true in varying degrees of every passage in the Bible."[13] Now comes the moment for the careful reader of the Parable of the Merciful Father in Luke 15 to inquire how the mystery of Jesus becomes manifest as a result of studying, meditating upon, and praying with this biblical text. Surely the mystery of Jesus emerges at several possible points, but, perhaps, most compellingly in the father's response to the older son: "Son, you are always with me, and all that is mine is yours" (v. 31). Is not this the offer of intimacy and life abundant with the Father that the younger son had accepted earlier as a gift in the context of joy and celebration? And is it not now this very same gift that is being offered to the elder son as well? Does not, perhaps, the parable end without indication of response because this is an offer made to every hearer of the parable, including you and me? To accept the offer of the Father signifies the end of our own artificially constructed world and entrance into the banquet of intimacy, love, and joy—what Jesus refers to as the kingdom of God. Günther Bornkamm, the influential German New Testament scholar of the twentieth century, has rightly observed that to "make the reality of God present: this is the essential mystery of Jesus."[14]

3.1.3 Scripture as the Enabler of Spirit-Guided Discernment, Decision, and Action

Penetrating toward the central mysteries of Scripture and making use of the approaches just discussed, the Christian reader is faced with an urgent question: "In what way are my life, my activity, my apostolate becoming a word of God in the light of the definitive Word that is Jesus Christ, present in the Scriptures?"[15] Real communion with Christ will now help to shape three interrelated activities as the reader of Scripture encounters the real presence of the Word in discernment, decision, and action.

a. *Discernment.* Following a process of reading, meditating, praying, and contemplating with Scripture, Christians develop the ability "with the grace of the Holy Spirit, to see in their lives what is or is not in conformity with the gospel. It is a discernment of what is best, at a given moment in history, for themselves, for others, for the church."[16] The pattern here would not be dissimilar to the recognition by the younger son in the Parable of the Merciful Father that his life was moving in the wrong direction. "But when he came to himself . . ." is the way Luke describes his moment of discernment (Luke 15:17).

b. *Decision.* Discernment leads to conscious assessment and decisions concerning what actions in the believer's life are in agreement with the gospel. Similarly the younger son, as a result of his discernment, makes a momentous decision: "I will get up and go to my father . . ." (Luke 15:18).

c. *Action.* Action is a consequence of discernment and decision. Martini puts the matter in this way: "Only the kind of Christian acting, doing, and thinking that is guided by the Holy Spirit can truly be called spiritual activity 'according to God.'"[17] Luke describes the action of the younger son, an action based on his discernment and decision, in simple terms: "So he set off and went to his father." And, as we know, this results in a moment of profound grace: "But while he was still far off, his father saw him and was filled with compassion; he ran and put his arms around him and kissed him . . ." and then declares, "let us eat and celebrate; for this son of mine was dead and is alive again; he was lost and is found! And they began to celebrate" (Luke 15:19-24).

It is hoped that these reflections on the reading and use of Scripture will not only provide for a fuller understanding of what is meant by a Trinitarian hermeneutic but will also allow Scripture to become increasingly a Trinitarian reality, namely, the presence of *God* as real communion with *Jesus Christ* who enables *Spirit*-guided acting, doing, and thinking.

3.2 Scripture and the Word of God

Before moving on to the next section dealing with faith and the moral life, it will be important to clarify the relationship of the terms "word of God" and "gospel" that have been used interchangeably, both in the discussion concerning the "School of the Word" as well as elsewhere in our conversation about the interpretation of Scripture.

What is meant by "word," and how does it relate to such common terms as "word of God," "gospel," and "Christ event"? What is this "word" that is being dynamically actualized in the Bible? "Word" as it is used in these pages means "word of God" in the sense of gospel, the proclamation of good news of what God has done in Christ. These two terms are set side by side and used interchangeably by the apostle Paul in his letter to the church at Philippi.

I want you to know, brethren, that what has happened to me has really served to advance the gospel, so that it has become known through-

out the whole praetorian guard and to all the rest that my imprisonment is for Christ; and most of the brethren have been made confident
in the Lord because of my imprisonment, and are much more bold to
speak the word of God without fear. (1:12-14)

The gospel in early Christianity is the oral proclamation of what God has
done in Jesus Christ, the good news of God's salvation.[18] Although the specific actualization of the gospel varies with the audience, it does have definite features. Paul gives a summary of the essential contents of the gospel as
he proclaimed it to the Corinthian church:

For I delivered to you as of first importance what I also received, that
Christ died for our sins in accordance with the scriptures, that he was
buried, that he was raised on the third day in accordance with the
scriptures, and that he appeared to Cephas, then to the twelve. Then
he appeared to more than five hundred brethren at one time, most of
whom are still alive, though some have fallen asleep. (1 Cor 15:3-6)

Although the content of the gospel is articulated in a variety of ways,
Paul expresses its normative character as he concludes this section in verse
11: "Whether then it was I or they, so we preach and so you believed." Precisely in this Corinthian church that had known not only Paul as preacher,
but others as well, *all* proclaim the *same* gospel. It is a gospel of good news
and joy because it declares God's gracious offer of redemption and new life
to a lost world. To proclaim this gospel of God's mercy lies at the center of
the entire New Testament.

To return for a moment to the Philippian text just cited, one will have
noticed that Paul uses the term "word of God" interchangeably with
"gospel." It is a word about what God has done in the salvific event of Jesus
Christ, a word that changes the lives of those who receive and believe it, a
word that creates new meaning and community. This is exactly what Paul
is expressing to the Christians at Thessalonica:

And we also thank God constantly for this, that when you received the
word of God which you heard from us, you accepted it not as the
word of men but as what it really is, the word of God, which is at
work in you believers. (1 Thess 2:13)

Surely part of the task of the biblical interpreter is to demonstrate how this
word of God, this gospel, was proclaimed and expressed by different

authors in diverse communities. To witness the actualization of the gospel in the literature of the New Testament is both energizing and challenging.

Although understanding the term "word of God" as the gospel is the dominant usage of the phrase in this volume, it is important to recognize that there are two other common ways in which the phrase "word" or "word of God" is understood. The first of these is explicitly biblical: in the opening of John's gospel and at the closing of the book of Revelation, Jesus is identified as the Word. In the latter reference Jesus is described as "clad in a robe dipped in blood, and the name by which he is called is The Word of God" (Rev 19:13). Without question, this usage of the term "word of God" is the primary one in the New Testament: Jesus is the expression, the revelation, of the reality of God. Therefore, the reference to the word of God as gospel, as dynamic and energizing word, is subsidiary to this primary meaning, because it is always a word about what God has accomplished in the Christ event.

A final way in which the term "word of God" can be used relates to Scripture itself. Because the Old and New Testaments, as Christian Scripture, are themselves witnesses to Christ, the Bible itself can also be referred to as word of God. While such an affirmation can be made with integrity, one must guard against a misguided impulse to view paper and ink as identical to the word of God in its primary sense, that is, the incarnation of God. Only as the word is proclaimed and uttered in the urgency of each new situation does it become a dynamic word. Scripture contains the word of God, witnesses to the word of God, and proclaims the word of God only as the risen Lord inspires his servants to proclaim the Christ event anew for each generation. Particularly helpful in this regard is to recall the discussion between Jesus and nonbelievers in John 5, a text that has already been noted. In the midst of an exasperating dialogue in which they refuse to understand and accept who Jesus is, he responds to them: "You search the scriptures, because you think that in them you have eternal life; and it is they that bear witness to me; yet you refuse to come to me that you may have life" (John 5:39-40). Eternal life cannot be found in the texts of Scripture, but these texts reveal the deep mysteries of the one to whom they bear witness; only in this sense can one speak properly of Scripture as the word of God. Scripture always has the potential to become revelatory, yet such revelation is never the guaranteed possession of the reader.

In summary: the concept "word of God" in the New Testament refers in its primary sense to Jesus Christ, the center of God's revelation. The good news about this Christ event, which is always proclaimed anew, is also referred to in the New Testament as the word of God; it is a dynamic word spoken concretely amid a wide diversity of situations to which the New Testament bears witness. And, finally, all Scripture, Old and New Testaments, can be referred to as the word of God, since it bears powerful witness to *the* Word, Jesus, and to the continued and repeated proclamation of the Christ event as a dynamic word.

Notes

1. Pontifical Biblical Commission, "The Interpretation of the Bible in the Church," *Origins* 23/29 (January 6, 1994) 497-524, here 522.

2. Here and in the comments that follow I am indebted to the work of Carlo Maria Cardinal Martini, "The School of the Word," *Worship* 61 (1987) 194-98.

3. Ibid., 196.

4. Ibid.

5. Ibid.

6. A term frequently use by Paul in his letters to indicate that believers in Christ as a result of their baptism are participants in his risen life and are incorporated into his body, the church.

7. Martini, "The School of the Word," 196.

8. *The HarperCollins Study Bible: New Revised Standard Edition*, ed. Wayne Meeks et al. (San Francisco: HarperSanFrancisco, 1993) 1990.

9. See further, Karl Paul Donfried, *The Dynamic Word: New Testament Insights for Contemporary Christians* (San Francisco: Harper, 1981).

10. Martini, "The School of the Word," 197.

11. Ibid.

12. Ibid.

13. Ibid.

14. Günther Bornkamm, *Jesus of Nazareth* (New York: Harper, 1960) 62.

15. Martini, "The School of the Word," 197.

16. Ibid., 198.

17. Ibid.

18. For a discussion of the pagan background of the term "gospel" in early Christianity, see Karl P. Donfried, "The Cults of Thessalonica and the Thessalonian Correspondence," in *Paul, Thessalonica and Early Christianity* (Grand Rapids: Eerdmans, 2002) 21-48.

4

The Bible and the Church

Faith and the Moral Life

4.1 Jesus and the Moral Life

Scripture testifies that God has become human in Jesus of Nazareth and that as a result of his life, teaching, suffering, death, and resurrection, forgiveness and reconciliation are available to those who respond to his offer of unmerited grace in and through the act of faith. This would certainly be the *sensus fidelium*[1] throughout the Church Catholic. But today opinions differ sharply regarding the relationship of faith and morals, that is, the ethical formation and structure of the Christian life. It is this relationship that the apostle Paul has in mind when he tells the Christian communities in Galatia that faith must work through love, that faith must be active in love (Gal 5:6). Similarly the apostle can speak of "progress and joy in faith" (Phil 1:25) and urges his Philippian brothers and sisters to "work out your own salvation with fear and trembling; for it is God who is at work in you, enabling you both to will and to work for his good pleasure" (Phil 2:12-13). Faith involves a new orientation of one's entire life, and its consequences need to be articulated and actualized in concrete circumstances. Thus, it is little wonder that most of the New Testament literature deals with teaching, instruction, and moral exhortation precisely in order to allow progress in faith and to enable faith to be active in love. Without such ethical guidance, the continued transformation of the new life of discipleship ever more into the image of Christ would be an impossibility. For this reason Paul writes to the Corinthian Christians that "all of us, with unveiled faces, seeing the glory of the Lord as though reflected in a mirror, are being transformed into the same image from one degree of glory to another; for this comes from the Lord, the Spirit" (2 Cor 3:18).

43

Earlier in our discussion we made a distinction between two contrasting theologies: a theology of acceptance and a theology of redemption. A theology of acceptance reduces the mystery of God to one who simply wants us to love one another with an emphasis on the affirmation of the other. Such "a quasi-deist theology," writes Turner, "that posits a benevolent god who favors love and justice as inclusion but acts neither to save us from our sins nor to raise us to new life after the pattern of Christ . . . in a theology dominated by radical inclusion, terms such as 'faith,' 'justification,' 'repentance,' and 'holiness of life' seem to belong to an antique vocabulary that must be outgrown or reinterpreted."[2] Much like the Gnostics who misinterpreted Paul in the early church, modern-day "inclusivists" reduce the Pauline language of justification by faith, as well as Jesus' call to discipleship, to a rhetoric of acceptance. Essential components in a theology of redemption grounded in the redeeming death of Jesus are diminished and urgent ethical consequences of the new life in Christ, whether personal, communal, or global, are often diluted or disregarded. In contrast the biblical call to discipleship is not one of tolerant and casual acceptance of any given culture, but is always a summons to the "exclusive inclusivity" of Jesus Christ.[3]

This theology of acceptance creates a further dilemma by cheapening the biblical sense of justice. Justice becomes first and foremost a social justice of inclusion and affirmation, thus not only marginalizing the call to discipleship and redemption, but also trivializing the great prophetic call to global judgment before the God of creation and the Lord of history. While those adhering to a theology of acceptance often make imprecise and pretentious political judgments, these declarations, whether uttered by the religious left or right, are frequently not rooted in a proper biblical understanding of sin and are, as a result, not only largely irrelevant but they also further complicate and exacerbate the issues they had intended to address. One thinks here of the right's accusations of certain nations as belonging to an "axis of evil" and the left's unrelenting criticism of Mel Gibson's film *The Passion of the Christ*. The former never seems to consider the fact that the United States itself may be involved in substantial forms of evil, and the latter fails to recognize that the ambiguity of artistic portrayals may also embrace fundamental truths with reference to the suffering and death of Jesus Christ.

The influential Protestant ethicist and moral theologian Reinhold Niebuhr worried a great deal about the "triviality and irrelevance" of the churches because "the terrors of the day have tempted the church to flee into the cellars of irrelevance"[4] precisely by neglecting and relinquishing their extensive moral and ethical responsibilities. Reflecting on the post–World War II era with its horrors both of mass annihilation and nuclear catastrophe, Niebuhr "continued to be appalled by the superficiality and self-contented pride of America's churches . . . ," and he even went so far as to say that in the seminary he served so long and so faithfully "piety has been reduced to triviality here, and indeed in the whole church."[5] One of the perennial temptations of Christianity is to divorce faith from morals and to disconnect faith from the political realities of the day. But this temptation is not unique to Christianity, for the prophets of Israel uttered similar concerns and warnings. The recurrent message of Scripture is that faith and the moral life, involving the life of discipleship in the context of global responsibility, are intrinsically interwoven, and when these intimate bonds are loosened one needs to join with the apostle Paul as he writes to the Christians in Thessalonica that "we pray that we may . . . restore whatever is lacking in your faith" (1 Thess 3:10). Biblically understood, there can be no individual holiness that is not cognizant of its global responsibilities, and there can be no social justice that is not rooted in the life of holiness to which Christ calls.

4.1.1 The Life of Discipleship:
The Perspective of Matthew's Gospel[6]

Rather than present an abstract picture of Jesus, it may be more helpful to present his teachings about the life of discipleship through the eyes of one gospel writer, Matthew, whose gospel is particularly concerned with this theme. Matthew's concern with "making disciples" dominates the final verses of the gospel: "Go therefore and make disciples of all nations, baptizing them in the name of the Father and of the Son and of the Holy Spirit" (Matt 28:19). Of the many rich insights scholars offer with regard to Matthew's gospel, Krister Stendahl's suggestion that it was intended, at least partially, to be a catechetical handbook is especially useful.[7] The word "catechetical," which comes from the Greek term *catechesis*, refers to instruction. In this sense, one of the primary functions of Matthew's gospel is to instruct its community in the fundamentals of living the life of Christian discipleship.

Because of this teaching purpose, Matthew's gospel is organized in a way that makes it easy to master. The central organizing principle appears to be five major teaching narratives. The evangelist has taken *Jesus material* and *church tradition* and fashioned them into theologically coherent units. The hand of Matthew is visible not only in his theological emphasis, but also in the phrase "when Jesus had finished . . . ," a framing device that concludes each of the five teaching narratives. The five major sections are the following:

1. Matthew 5–7, the Sermon on the Mount, concludes in Matthew 7:28-29, "*Now when Jesus had finished* saying these things, the crowds were astounded at his teaching, for he taught them as one having authority, and not as their scribes."
2. Matthew 10, instructions to the disciples, concludes in Matthew 11:1, "*Now when Jesus had finished* instructing his twelve disciples, he went on from there to teach and proclaim his message in their cities."
3. Matthew 13, eschatological parables, concludes in Matthew 13:53, "*When Jesus had finished* these parables, he left that place. . . ."
4. Matthew 18, teachings on mercy, discipline, and forgiveness, concludes in Matthew 19:1, "*When Jesus had finished* saying these things, he left Galilee. . . ."
5. Matthew 23–25, instructions and warnings concerning the last day, the day of judgment, concludes in Matthew 26:1, "*When Jesus had finished* saying all these things, he said to his disciples. . . ."

These five teaching narratives are followed frequently by miracle stories, emphasizing that Jesus is the messiah of word *and* deed. The five sections in their entirety are preceded by Jesus' birth and temptation, found in Matthew 1–4 and followed by the narratives giving an account of his death and resurrection in Matthew 25–28.

As with every document in the New Testament one must inquire about the audience—for whom and to whom was this gospel addressed? The eminent New Testament scholar W. D. Davies proposes that the formation of Matthew's gospel must be placed in the context of post–70 CE Judaism, following the destruction of the temple and Jerusalem in 70 CE by the Romans, a horror that left Judaism shaken to its foundations.[8] In fact, so fierce was this destructive blow that only one of the several first-century Jewish groups survived, the Pharisees. This post-destruction period, which coincides with the last quarter of the first-century CE, is a period of reconstruction and codification, a phenomenon that eventually develops into what is referred to as Rabbinic Judaism. This post–70 CE Judaism is defensive and sees emergent Christianity as a competitor, and, as a result, both Judaism and Matthew's community interact and influence each other in negative ways. One will not adequately understand Matthew's setting unless the relationship with the synagogue "across the street" as well as the stance of that synagogue toward Matthew's congregation is taken into account.

4.1.1a Ethical Perspectives: The Sermon on the Mount

The congregation to which the gospel of Matthew is addressed was Jewish in origin, but also included a goodly number of Gentiles who had come to believe that Jesus the Jew was the Messiah. For the most part Matthew's gospel is quite intelligible when viewed as an attempt to assist former Jews in understanding the newness of their commitment to Jesus. There is perhaps a tendency within this group to view this responsibility as requiring a less rigorous understanding and application of the religious life than they had previously experienced. Matthew rejects such a perspective and urges that "unless your righteousness exceeds that of the scribes and Pharisees, you will never enter the kingdom of heaven" (5:20). This verse is key to understanding the entire gospel.

The thesis of Matthew 5:20 is applied to the structure of the gospel by means of an emphasis on ethics and eschatology.[9] Ethics refers to the new lifestyle that is now possible to the disciple because of God's entry into history through Jesus Christ; eschatology represents the complex of events dealing with the end-time: the last judgment, death, resurrection, and the consummation of history. Not only are these categories prominent throughout the gospel, they actually shape its composition. The first teaching narrative, the Sermon on the Mount found in Matthew 5–7, stresses the theme of ethics, and the final teaching section in Matthew 23–25 emphasizes the theme of eschatology with symbolic portrayals of God's judgment on the last day. While each of these opening and closing discourses has a specific concentration, they always incorporate both themes. Matthew 5–7 stresses ethics, but never abstractly; ethics are understood in light of eschatology, which is a major accent at the end of the Sermon on the Mount. Similarly, while Matthew 23–25 is concerned primarily with eschatology, God's judgment on the last day is clearly dependent on obedience to his will as described earlier in the gospel. Further, not only are the themes of ethics and eschatology intertwined in the first and last discourses, but throughout the gospel as well. All of these interrelationships flow, as we have observed, from the key verse of Matthew 5:20: "For I tell you, unless your righteousness exceeds that of the scribes and Pharisees, you will never enter the kingdom of heaven." Righteousness is specifically related to final entrance into the kingdom, or put another way, the ethical character of discipleship lived as a result of grace becomes the basis for the eschatological judgment. This point can be seen in Matthew 7:13-23:

Enter through the narrow gate; for the gate is wide and the road is easy that leads to destruction, and there are many who take it. For the gate is narrow and the road is hard that leads to life, and there are few who find it. Beware of false prophets, who come to you in sheep's clothing but inwardly are ravenous wolves. You will know them by their fruits. Are grapes gathered from thorns, or figs from thistles? In the same way, every good tree bears good fruit, but the bad tree bears bad fruit. A good tree cannot bear bad fruit, nor can a bad tree bear good fruit. Every tree that does not bear good fruit is cut down and thrown into the fire. Thus you will know them by their fruits. Not everyone who says to me, "Lord, Lord," will enter the kingdom of heaven, but only the one who does the will of my Father in heaven. On that day many will say to me, "Lord, Lord, did we not prophesy in your name, and cast out demons in your name, and do many deeds of power in your name?" Then I will declare to them, "I never knew you; go away from me, you evildoers."

The opening words (vv. 13-14) are a summary of the previous ethical instructions that began in chapter 5. The life of discipleship is difficult and entrance into the kingdom is via a narrow gate. The phrase "the gate is narrow and the road is hard" is characteristic of Matthew's portrayal of discipleship throughout his gospel. The middle verses (vv. 15-20) warn that there will be false prophets who come in the name of Jesus, a theme found elsewhere in the New Testament. The criterion laid down for testing whether prophets are true or false is their fruits, that is, their works. Even this criterion is seen in light of eschatology: "Every tree that does not bear good fruit is cut down and thrown into the fire. Thus you will know them by their fruits" (vv. 19-20). Since a Trinitarian hermeneutic must discern the continuity between the original and the contemporary meaning of a text, it is not unimportant for the present-day church to be mindful of this correlation between ethics and eschatology. Contemporary reflection on these themes prompts several questions. Are there false prophets in the Church Catholic today? Is the theology of acceptance previously referred to an example of false teaching? What are the criteria used in making such discernments? What makes them false? In what ways do false teachers generate irreparable harm to the communion of saints? Although these may seem unusual questions to many who have been influenced by a laissez-faire culture in which everything goes—"I'm ok, you're ok"—yet, any serious reading of Scripture compels the contemporary consideration of concerns that were real to Jesus and his followers. For, according to many of these biblical texts, Jesus as Lord will ask some uncompromising questions of both the communities of disciples as well as the individual follower of Jesus—past, present, and future—at the consummation of history, a theme especially emphasized in Matthew 25.

One of the clearest examples of the close interconnection between the themes of ethics and eschatology in sections one and five is to be seen in Matthew 7:21-23. Here again the concern is with entering the kingdom, the final eschatological goal of the Christian. It is not simply lip service, "Lord, Lord," but it is, rather, doing "the will of my Father in heaven" that will be the decisive factor. As the next verse makes clear, it is finally not frenetic activity in the name of Jesus but doing the will of the Father that is the significant criterion. To underline the seriousness of this, verse 23 represents a categorical rejection of those who have confused misguided activity for fidelity to the will of the Father: "Then I will declare to them, 'I never knew you; go away from me, you evildoers.'" The interconnections between this theme and Matthew 25 are striking. At the end of the allegory of the ten virgins in Matthew 25:11-12 one reads: "'Lord, Lord, open to us.' But he replied, 'Truly, I tell you, I do not know you.'" Two phrases just encountered in Matthew 7 recur: "Lord, Lord" and "I do not know you." Matthew is consciously linking the first and last teaching narratives. They are both concerned with ethics and eschatology, the essential difference being that Matthew 25 puts the major stress on eschatology, viewing ethics in light of the impending end-time.

The Sermon on the Mount in its present form is a composition of Matthew.[10] As is characteristic of Matthew's gospel throughout, Matthew collects Jesus material and church interpretation and places them in the context of his own theological perspective. In the Sermon on the Mount, Matthew assembles words of Jesus found in different parts of the received tradition and places them into a unified whole. In comparison with the gospel of Luke, one will find that much of the material in Matthew 5–7 is found also in Luke, but in the third gospel it is scattered throughout. As a result of redaction criticism, emphasizing the final editorial/authorial work of the gospel writer, scholars have learned that it is Matthew's technique to bring unified expression to materials originally found in different locations. But even without this knowledge it seems more likely that an author would bring together that which is scattered rather than to scatter throughout one's gospel that which has been already unified.

At the beginning of the Sermon on the Mount we hear these words: "When Jesus saw the crowds, he went up the mountain; and after he sat down, his disciples came to him." The setting places Jesus on a mountain to give ethical instruction to his disciples. Other than the frequent Old Testament reference to the mountain as a place of revelation, it is also the place where Moses goes to receive ethical instruction. There are indeed striking analogies, if not conscious typologies, between the structure and content of Matthew's gospel and the Old Testament. One need only remember that Matthew has five teaching narratives and that the Torah is comprised of five books. Is this purely coincidental? Hardly. With regard to this opening verse two additional points should be noted: (1) Jesus sits down, in good rabbinic fashion, to give instruction; and (2) instruction is given to the disciples. This is not an ethic intended for everyone to follow, but for those who have responded to the call of discipleship, an unambiguous illustration of "exclusive inclusivity." Further, if one views the kingdom of God as a phrase implying political rhetoric, one recognizes that the kingdom has a king, the Father; a constitution, the will of the Father; and that it is comprised of a people, the disciples. What follows is the "constitution" for the constituency of the kingdom: the will of God revealed through Jesus for those who respond to the call of faith.

The Sermon on the Mount opens with a section frequently referred to as "the beatitudes," a term taken from the opening word of the central verses, *makarioi*, from which the English word "makarism" is derived. The translation of *makarios* as "blessed" is not especially helpful, however, since for most Americans it is not an everyday expression. More effective is the suggested translation by W. F. Albright, "fortunate are those. . . ."[11] "Fortunate" captures the sense of the eschatological, which is central to these beatitudes. Those who participate in the lifestyle outlined in the beatitudes are fortunate for they shall "enter," they shall receive the joys of the kingdom on the last day. The practice that leads to entrance in the kingdom is here detailed in general terms that will be made even more concrete in the remainder of this first teaching section. One should note that according to verses 3 and 10, there is already *now* a participation, however preliminary, in the kingdom, and this is one of several reasons for the repeated call to holiness of life in the New Testament. The second half of these verses is not situated in the future but in the present. "Blessed are the poor in spirit, for theirs *is* the kingdom of heaven." Those who are humble already now participate in that kingdom which has been inaugurated in the coming of Jesus of Nazareth. Likewise, verse 10: "Fortunate are those who are persecuted for righteousness' sake, for theirs is the kingdom of heaven." An important sign of participation in the kingdom is that one runs the high risk of persecution. Although this is a reality for the disciple now, it will with certainty bring its reward in the consummation of the kingdom on the last day (vv. 11-12).

The beatitudes provide a fascinating example of how Matthew actualizes the gospel tradition for the needs of his congregation as well as how they are considerably amplified beyond what we find in Luke and, hence, in their common source, Q.[12] Leaving aside the obvious parallel to Matthew 5:11 (the persecution makarism) in Luke 6:22, the beatitudes as found in Luke 6:20-21 are unusually brief and read as follows:

> Blessed are you who are poor,
>   for yours is the kingdom of God.
> Blessed are you who are hungry now,
>   for you will be filled.
> Blessed are you who weep now,
>   for you will laugh.

Not only has Matthew expanded these verses by adding additional beatitudes, but he has also altered and expanded the Lucan parallel. Throughout, Matthew shifts from the second person "you" to a generalized third person. More significantly one should note that Matthew alters "Blessed are you poor" into "Blessed are the poor in spirit." As can be seen from the remainder of Matthew's gospel, he certainly is not unconcerned about the poor. Rather, at this point in his gospel Matthew is concerned with the necessity of humility as an essential criterion of the disciple's life. Thus he changes what he received from the Q source by adding "in spirit" since this was a major concern for his congregation. One should also observe that Matthew's alteration of "kingdom of God" to "kingdom of heaven," a change he frequently, but not always, makes in his gospel, undoubtedly reflects his Jewish background and his reluctance to use the divine name.

Before we proceed, it may be useful to say a further word about alterations and additions to the gospel traditions by the authors of the gospels. First, what motivates their changes to the received traditions? For Matthew and the primitive church, Jesus is the risen Lord present in their midst, compelling them always to make his word a dynamic word. Second, as certain changes in the beatitudes are reviewed, it will be made clear that Matthew is not fabricating this material *de novo*. It is not a creation *ex nihilo*, out of nothing. Matthew, as well as the other evangelists, is formulating, shaping, and interpreting certain elements he received from the early church's oral and written traditions and guided by the risen Christ in order to emphasize and to actualize them for the needs of his congregation. We see here the inseparable correlation between Christology and ecclesiology characteristic of the Christ event; it is this that gives impetus to the process of dynamic actualization, a process for which a Trinitarian hermeneutic and the School of the Word can offer contemporary Christianity guidance.

In Matthew 5:6, the words of the first evangelist once again differ from the Lucan version in 6:21: "Blessed are those who hunger and thirst for righteousness, for they will be filled." Matthew adds a term of central theological importance to him, "righteousness." Matthew 5:6 reads: "Blessed are those who hunger and thirst for *righteousness,* for they shall be filled." In making this change it must once again be stressed that Matthew is not in any way playing down the need for concern with those who are hungry, as he makes abundantly clear in Matthew 25. Rather, he is stressing to his congregation that righteousness, that is, doing the will of the Father, is not optional, but an essential ingredient for entrance into the kingdom on the last day. Concern for poverty and hunger is the appropriate concern of righteousness, but they are not its substitute as a theology of acceptance.

Matthew's ethical rigor is accentuated at another point in the Sermon on the Mount, the Lord's Prayer. This prayer is found only in Matthew and Luke, suggesting that it comes from the Q source, which both had in common. At the point in Matthew 6:10/Luke 11:2 where the original prayer reads, "Your kingdom come," the first evangelist adds, "Your will be done, on earth as it is in heaven." Once again, through these very significant alterations one can recognize concerns of great magnitude that Matthew believes are essential to emphasize for his congregation. To be a follower of Jesus is not simply to talk about the Lord, to advocate some sort of policy of social justice but to participate fully in the ethical and moral responsibility demanded by the redemptive death of Jesus and his unconditional call to discipleship.

At the beginning of this first teaching section Matthew asserts that the disciples of Jesus have been enabled to participate in a lifestyle characterized by humility, righteousness, and peacemaking. Disciples who faithfully participate in such a manner of life will fully inherit the kingdom on the last day. The purpose of the Sermon on the Mount is to outline with clarity the lifestyle of discipleship as well as its rigor. At the outset, in 5:13-16, the distinctive life of discipleship is underscored. Disciples are to be "salt" and "light" in a world that is both "weary" and "dark." Not only do they add a new ingredient to the human situation, the follower of Jesus does so in an actively visible way: "You are the light of the world. A city built on a hill cannot be hid. No one after lighting a lamp puts it under the bushel basket, but on the lampstand, and it gives light to all in the house. In the same way, let your light shine before others, so that they may see your good works and give glory to your Father in heaven" (5:14-16). Disciples are to bear fruit and to do good works not as acts of self-glory but as acts of glory to the Father in heaven in a quite public way.

It is fully possible that some in Matthew's congregation had come to believe that the life of discipleship was easier and less rigorous than their previous religious involvement. This is evident not only from the next few verses to be examined but also from the conclusion to the Sermon on the Mount. Just prior to Matthew 7:15, the verse concerning false prophets, one reads: "Enter through the narrow gate; for the gate is wide and the road is easy that leads to destruction, and there are many who take it. For the gate is narrow and the road is hard that leads to life, and there are few who find it" (7:13-14). This theme echoes throughout Matthew, especially in the familiar words "many are called but few are chosen" (22:14), and stands in striking contrast with the easy inclusion represented by a theology of acceptance.

To call attention to the fact that those who have accepted the message of Jesus are involved in costly rather than cheap grace,[13] Matthew speaks sharply against those in his congregation who would think that the Christian church is involved in a blanket dismissal of the Torah (law) or of the Old Testament itself. This point is made in a brief introduction to a section commonly referred to as the antitheses (5:21-48). The title for this section derives from the formulaic expression, "You have heard that it was said to those of ancient times. . . . But I say to you. . . ." It is in the introduction to these antitheses that one reads: "Do not think that I have come to abolish the law or the prophets; I have come not to abolish but to fulfill" (5:17). This verse underscores the importance of keeping the commandments, and it is followed by the key verse of the gospel: "For I tell you, unless your righteousness exceeds that of the scribes and Pharisees, you will never enter the kingdom of heaven" (5:20).

The immediate questions that come to mind relate to the meaning of the word "fulfill" and the meaning of a righteousness that must "exceed" that of the scribes and Pharisees. That the term "fulfill" in all likelihood means "to bring something to its essential or root meaning" is suggested by the antitheses that follow. The first antithesis summarizes this point concisely:

> You have heard that it was said to those of ancient times, "You shall not murder"; and "whoever murders shall be liable to judgment." But *I* say to you that if you are angry with a brother or sister, you will be liable to judgment; and if you insult a brother or sister, you will be

liable to the council; and if you say, "You fool," you will be liable to the hell of fire. (5:21-22)

Jesus, according to Matthew, does not in any way abolish the commandment "You shall not murder." Rather, he extends it to its root meaning—anger. What is it finally that leads to the external act of murder? Anger! Therefore this antithesis radicalizes the commandment by including anger as well. Jesus goes beyond any possible formal, external, or legal understanding of this commandment so that its root cause might be exposed.

This same pattern can be seen in the second antithesis: "*You* have heard that it was said, 'You shall not commit adultery.' But *I* say to you that everyone who looks at a woman with lust has already committed adultery with her in his heart" (5:27-29). It is not only the external act of adultery that is condemned but the cause of it as well, lust. It is, to give an analogy, not only going to bed with someone else's spouse that is rejected but also lusting over magazine centerfolds. It is by means of such intensification of the Old Testament commandments that the righteousness of the disciple is to exceed that of the scribes and Pharisees. Once again one observes Matthew's unrelenting concern that the connection between faith and ethics, between call and response, are inseparable. To do so brings one into the realm of hypocrisy, a temptation that he roundly condemns in Matthew 23. Given the dramatic lack of concentration on the nature of the moral life in much of contemporary Christianity, Matthew's warning to his congregation is as relevant today as it was in the first century.

Matthew 6 initiates a series of concerns dealing with the practice of the religious life and begins with this warning: "Beware of practicing your piety before others in order to be seen by them; for then you have no reward from your Father in heaven." Hypocrisy, an act of pretending by the use of certain external actions that do not coincide with one's inner attitude, represents a credibility gap that is offensive to Matthew whether it appears among members of the Jesus movement or among the Pharisees (cf. Matthew 23), and he repeatedly warns his congregation about this temptation. The disciple receives his approval from God on the last day, not from human judges in the present. All religious practice has as its authentic motivation the praise of God and not one's own exaltation. Consequently, Matthew stresses in these opening verses that acts of charity and prayer are things that are carried out secretly, "and your Father who sees in secret will reward you" (vv. 4 and 6). Such acts of almsgiving are to be carried out so naturally and unaffectedly that the left hand does not know what the right hand is doing. The point is that a gift or an action on behalf of others should not be accompanied by a plaque designating in bold letters the name of the donor. One of the most vivid illustrations of this theme in contemporary life that immediately comes to mind is the story of a marvelous retired physician who, upon becoming chronically ill, was rejected by his family and placed in what was called, at the time, New York's Welfare Island. In that somewhat depressing institution he was placed in a six-man ward. Whenever the others in his ward had needs, they would be taken care of "miraculously" by means of gifts from this gentleman through a volunteer. His ward-mates never knew the source of their gifts, a classic example of the right hand not knowing what the left hand is doing.

The remainder of the Sermon on the Mount continues to give advice and instruction concerning the life of discipleship. We shall consider one final example from this first teaching narrative in Matthew's gospel, the Lord's Prayer. Insofar as it follows directly upon the sections dealing with praying and giving alms in secret, it continues to give practical advice on the subject of prayer. Here the issue is not that of praying in secret but about the brevity of prayer. "When you are praying, do not heap up empty phrases as the Gentiles do; for they think that they will be heard because of their many words" (6:7). The Lord's Prayer, which follows, is a model of brevity and succinctness, while simultaneously serving as a summary of the teaching of Jesus.

The use of "Father" as a direct address to God was not frequent during the lifetime of Jesus.[14] For many Jews, the political situation from the time of the exile had so deteriorated that God appeared enormously distant, and life was filled with despair. Given this situation, it is in fact rather far-reaching for Jesus to address God as Father. This degree of intimacy and trust is characteristic of Jesus' attitude to God, and it is exactly this dimension of the divine that is being revealed through the ministry of Jesus. This God who is loving, caring, and embracing has already been illustrated in the Parable of the Merciful Father in Luke. The phrase "hallowed be your name" is characteristic of the daily Jewish prayer and would, therefore, unsurprisingly be used by Jesus the Jew. God and his name are most holy and sacred. It may be for this reason, as has already been suggested, that Matthew so often uses the more Jewish phrase "kingdom of heaven" in place of "kingdom of God"; it is a sign of awe and reverence for the divine name. Yet such awe never veils the intimacy that is offered the believer; it does, however, prevent intimacy from dissolving into irreverent sentimentality.

The category "kingdom of God" is absolutely central to the teaching of Jesus, and many of his parables express more fully the content and ethic of this kingdom of God. As shall become evident, it is in and through his ministry that God's kingdom breaks into the human situation in a new way. While this kingdom is already coming to fruition, it is not yet completely fulfilled. Because of this "not yet" dimension, because of this "eschatological reservation," the disciples are taught to pray "your kingdom come." Into this strictly eschatological context, Matthew adds, "Your will be done, on earth as it is in heaven," a phrase that clearly breaks the original connection between verses 9 and 11. Matthew adds verse 10 because of its importance in delineating the gospel for his congregation. They need to be reminded of the necessity of ethical intensity.

Verse 11 is translated by the New Revised Standard Version in this way: "Give us this day our daily bread." An alternative translation appears in a footnote: "Give us our bread for the morrow." Without a doubt this is one of the most difficult verses in the New Testament to translate owing to the unintelligibility of the Greek. Joachim Jeremias advised that the cryptic Greek may be because someone translated an Aramaic (the primary language of Jesus) phrase literally, rather than idiomatically, into the Greek. As many are aware, translation of any foreign language is only successful if one expresses the original thought in the idiom, rather than in some literal, word-for-word rendition. Thus, Jeremias also suggested that a reverse translation from the Greek sentence as it now stands back into Aramaic might be instructive. As a result of this process Jeremias proposes that Jesus originally prayed, "Give us tomorrow's bread today."[15] The request would then be that the bread, the heavenly manna that comes from the kingdom beyond, from that kingdom that has arrived but is not yet fulfilled, be given to his disciples as they live in the midst of this frail, sinful, and broken world. The prayer would be that God's work, God's food, which is a transcendent gift, be made available today and everyday to those disciples who ask for it. That such divine generosity must be shared resonates throughout the gospel: "And forgive us our debts, as we also have forgiven our debtors" (Matt 6:12), a subject that is amplified and illustrated in the Parable of the Unforgiving Servant in Matthew 18:23-25. As God freely forgives, so must the forgiven disciples forgive their brothers and sisters. The final verse of the Lord's Prayer is verse 13, which Jeremias translates as "protect us from the Evil One."[16] While the reality of demonic forces is recognized, so is the assurance of the Father's protecting hand against such forces.

The Sermon on the Mount and especially the Lord's Prayer, set within the context of Matthew's entire gospel, make evident that the life of discipleship is possible only as a result of the death and resurrection of Jesus and that his call to holiness of life is always carried out in anticipation of the final meeting with the Lord. When a contemporary theology of acceptance[17] neglects both holiness and the last judgment it is little wonder that its ethical content is vapid and insipid. This in itself is worrisome; even more regrettable is how such a false theology misleads those who adhere to it, bringing to mind the words of Jesus according to Matthew 15:14: "And if one blind person guides another, both will fall into a pit."

4.1.1b Ethical Perspectives: The Last Judgment

Throughout the Sermon on the Mount, one observes Matthew's overriding concern to illustrate the ethic of the kingdom in light of the last judgment that awaits all, both disciples and nondisciples. In other words, ethics are discussed in light of eschatology. In the fifth and last teaching narrative the emphasis is reversed, and eschatology is discussed in light of ethics. This final narrative section opens in Matthew 23, and this chapter, especially, can only be properly understood as reflecting the current situation in Matthew's congregation in conflict with embryonic Rabbinic Judaism that began to develop following the destruction of the Temple in 70 CE. It begins on a strongly ethical note that dominates all of Matthew 23: "Then said Jesus to the crowds and to his disciples, 'The scribes and the Pharisees sit on Moses' seat; therefore, do whatever they teach you and follow it; but do not do as they do, for they do not practice what they teach.'" The teaching of the Pharisees is not the problem; it is their failure to act on their teaching. It is this lack of credibility, this hypocrisy, that is refuted in an almost liturgically repetitive way in verses 13, 16, 23, 25, 27, and 29. Typical of these "woes" is the passage found in verses 23-24:

> Woe to you, scribes and Pharisees, hypocrites! For you tithe mint, dill, and cumin, and have neglected the weightier matters of the law: justice and mercy and faith. It is these you ought to have practiced without neglecting the others. You blind guides! You strain out a gnat but swallow a camel! (23:23-24)

Not only must one affirm an ethical position, one must act upon it. One cannot simply say "Lord, Lord"; one must bring to fruition the will of the Father. This initial chapter of Matthew's final teaching discourse undoubtedly serves not only as a criticism of the stage of Judaism contemporary with Matthew's congregation but also as a warning to his own congregation that it not fall into this same type of hypocrisy.

Having essentially stressed ethics in chapter 23, Matthew now shifts to a strongly eschatological perspective in chapters 24 and 25. Typical of the flavor of these chapters is 24:44: "Therefore you also must be ready; for the Son of man is coming at an unexpected hour." The stress on eschatology, especially that of meeting the Lord on the last day, is intentional in this first gospel. One of the problems that confronted the Christian communities at the end of the first century is referred to by scholars as "the delay of the parousia." *Parousia* in the Greek New Testament is used frequently to mean "coming" or "advent," especially in the sense of the final messianic advent. The earliest disciples were understandably enthusiastic and excited in the period following the resurrection of Jesus. This together with lines of influence from apocalyptic Judaism led many of these followers to believe that the messianic age that Jesus had inaugurated would be fulfilled at any moment, and certainly within their lifetimes. When this expectation remained unfulfilled after several decades, an understandable disappointment set in. Often this disillusionment led to a decrease in the gravity of the ethical dimension of discipleship, and one effect was that "the love of many will grow cold" (24:12). Therefore Matthew quickly adds in the next verse, "But the one who endures to the end will be saved."

The "delay of the parousia" theme moves center stage at the end of Matthew 24 and occupies much of chapter 25. The concern is well expressed in 24:45-51:

> Who then is the faithful and wise slave, whom his master has put in charge of his household, to give the other slaves their allowance of food at the proper time? Blessed is that slave whom his master will find at work when he arrives. Truly I tell you, he will put that one in charge of all his possessions. But if that wicked slave says to himself, "My master is delayed," and he begins to beat his fellow slaves, and eats and drinks with drunkards, the master of that slave will come on a day when he does not expect him and at an hour that he does not know. He will cut him in pieces and put him with the hypocrites, where there will be weeping and gnashing of teeth.

Note how centrally the concern is expressed: "My master is delayed." If this delay leads a disciple to be unfaithful to the will of the Father, then that servant will be punished on the last day and God will "put him with the hypocrites." Why with the hypocrites? Presumably because she said, "Lord, Lord," but did not practice faithfully her confession with regard to her fellow servants. Matthew is most concerned to point out to his audience that one must be ready; one must be prepared and faithful, "for the Son of Man is coming at an unexpected hour" (24:44). The so-called delay of the parousia dare not become an excuse for ill-defined discipleship.

The delay-of-the-parousia motif also plays a prominent part in the allegory of the ten virgins in 25:1-13. As Matthew deals with this issue he skillfully summarizes major aspects of his theology, and therefore it is a most important passage for our examination.

> Then the kingdom of heaven will be like this. Ten bridesmaids took their lamps and went to meet the bridegroom. Five of them were foolish, and five were wise. When the foolish took their lamps, they took no oil with them; but the wise took flasks of oil with their lamps. As the bridegroom was delayed, all of them became drowsy and slept. But at midnight there was a shout, "Look! Here is the bridegroom! Come out to meet him." Then all those bridesmaids got up and trimmed their lamps. The foolish said to the wise, "Give us some of your oil, for our lamps are going out." But the wise replied, "No! there will not be enough for you and for us; you had better go to the dealers and buy some for yourselves." And while they went to buy it, the bridegroom came, and those who were ready went with him into the wedding banquet; and the door was shut. Later the other bridesmaids came also, saying, "Lord, lord, open to us." But he replied, "Truly I tell you, I do not know you." Keep awake therefore, for you know neither the day nor the hour.

This story illustrates what the kingdom of heaven *shall* be like: it shall be like ten virgins who took their lamps as they were going to meet the bridegroom. It is on the basis of sufficient or insufficient oil that some are and some are not admitted to the marriage feast with the bridegroom; possession of sufficient oil is the basic criterion for admission to the marriage feast. This comparison of the kingdom of heaven with the virgins achieves meaning only if the term "oil" is intelligible to Matthew's congregation; but the immediate context indicates simply that the oil is used as fuel for lamps.

Furthermore, the text does not describe normal Jewish nuptial practice, nor is any description given of the "virgins," of the "bridegroom," of the "marriage feast," or even of the more minor details in the story.[18] These problems push us beyond these thirteen verses for some more intelligible understanding, since it is not reasonable to assume that Matthew would have devoted more than half the story to the lamp/oil motif unless it had some coherent significance for himself and his audience. Since the story does not allow us to discover its meaning or intention within itself, due primarily to the ambiguity of the symbolic language employed, it is more likely an allegory. Various elements in 25:1-13 cohere not with one another but with a theological framework outside the story itself.

John Dominic Crossan distinguishes between two general categories of metaphors: "There are metaphors in which information precedes participation so that the function of metaphor is to illustrate information about the metaphor's referent; but there are also metaphors in which participation precedes information so that the function of metaphor is to create participation in the metaphor's referent."[19] The first type of metaphor is represented in the allegory; the second, in the parable. In addition to this useful distinction, Dan Via suggests that "the structure, shape, and interconnections of an allegory are determined by something outside itself—by its meaning or referent. . . . An allegory, then, communicates to a person what he already knows, though it communicates it in symbolic and altered fashion."[20] What is it that readers of the allegory of the ten virgins know that is here being communicated to them in symbolic and altered fashion?

In attempting to shed light on 25:1-13 in view of the context in Matthew 23–25, it is important to observe that this entire discourse is concerned with practicing and keeping that which has been commanded by Jesus. Both beginning (23:3-4) and conclusion (25:4-46) stress the motif that only by doing the deeds inherent in the life of discipleship will one be found acceptable at the final judgment, and the allegory of the ten virgins is related to this same overall emphasis of the fifth discourse.

A number of themes found in the allegory of the ten virgins are paralleled in Matthew's fifth discourse. The division motif is found not only in 25:2 (five and five) but also in 24:40-41 (one and one). Also, in the Parable of the Talents (25:14-30) Matthew amends the Q source and heightens the separation between those who have multiplied their talents and the one who has buried it. In the virgin allegory the separation is between those who are foolish and those who are wise, whereas in the story of the talents the separation is between the "good and trustworthy slave" (25:21) and the "wicked and lazy slave" (25:26). In 24:45 it is between the "faithful and wise slave" and the one who is not faithful and wise. Throughout the fifth discourse the wise and faithful are the ones who are active in doing good deeds. It is thus likely that the separation between the five foolish virgins and the five wise virgins is related to this overall theme of practicing, observing, and doing (23:3; 24:46; 25:40, 45). It is also probable that the allegory of the virgins is related to the warning not to be like the hypocrites who are condemned in 23:27-28.

The themes of the coming of the master and of eschatological judgment are found throughout (24:30-31, 36-37, 50-51; 25:19-21, 31-33). The coming of the end had been delayed (24:34, 48; 25:5), so Matthew urged those in his congregation not to lessen their performance of good deeds and to remember that "he who endures to the end [in the performance of love] will be saved" (24:13). Matthew deals with the delay of the parousia from at least two different perspectives: the warning to *watchfulness* and the warning about *preparedness*. The allegory of the ten virgins may be intended to deal with the second area of concern. Those who go to sleep (die) prepared will be like the five wise virgins who had enough oil for their lamps, and not like those foolish virgins who had lamps but an insufficient supply of oil. Oil has a critical significance for the story, and given our understanding of the intentions of the fifth discourse, it probably serves as a symbol for the good deeds mentioned throughout, highlighted, and brought to culmination in 25:31-46.

Because of the close connection between Matthew's first and fifth discourses, we return to the Sermon on the Mount, particularly 7:13-27, where parallels to this passage abound. Although 7:24-27 is taken from Q, Matthean redaction is easy to detect. First, Matthew adds the distinction between the "wise" and the "foolish." Second, he modifies and expands Q's account of the second house so that it is now built on a foundation of sand. The foolish man is thus similar to a tree that does not bear fruit (7:17-19) or to a person who says "Lord, Lord" (7:21; 25:11) but does not do the will of the Father; he is, in fact, much like the foolish virgins who do not have sufficient oil.

In addition, the Sermon on the Mount shares an almost identical phrase with the allegory of the virgins. In 7:23 we read, "I never knew you," and in 25:12, "Truly, I tell you, I do not know you." The wording in 25:12 is identical with Luke 13:26-27. It may well be that this Q logion served as a basic element in Matthew's construction of the allegory of the ten virgins and that in 7:23, owing to its probable polemic against a formative and threatening post–70 CE Judaism, Matthew is purposely giving a literal translation of a Jewish *Bannformel,* "formula of exclusion."

In Matthew 25, "I do not know you" serves as a formula of rejection for those who are not properly and adequately prepared; in Matthew 7, for those who hear the words but do not obey them. Those rejected in both places come with certain credentials; they are not rejected because these actions are wrong, but because they are inadequate. If there is any relationship between Matthew 25 and 7, then the likelihood is increased that the oil is another of several symbolic expressions employed by Matthew for the concept "doing the will of the Father." The "door" theme is vital for Matthew. On the eschatological day, Jesus will stand at the door (24:33) and will admit those properly prepared (25:10; 7:21). That entrance through the door is not easy is vividly stressed in 7:13: "Enter through the narrow gate. . . ."

The lamp/oil symbol is also of critical significance in Matthew 25. There are several noteworthy references to lamps and light that are compatible with our suggestion that the oil in Matthew 25 refers explicitly to good deeds. Central among these references is 5:14-16: "You are the light of the world. . . . No one after lighting a lamp puts it under the bushel basket, but on the lampstand, and it gives light to all in the house. In the same way, let your light shine before others, so that they may see your good works and give glory to your Father in heaven." Why does one light a lamp? So that one's good works will give glory to the Father. Similarly the ten virgins lit their lamps before the bridegroom, but in the case of the five foolish virgins, their oil, their good deeds, was not sufficient. When the real test of their oil arrived, the result was similar to the house built on a sandy foundation: it was found to be inadequate.

Now we are in a position to discuss the terms "bridegroom" and "marriage feast" in Matthew. In 9:15 we have not only a connection between the bridegroom and the wedding guests but the explicit identification of Jesus as the bridegroom. The theme of the wedding feast is elaborately presented in 22:1-14, a Q passage editorially enhanced by Matthew, particularly verses 11-14. One guest had no "wedding garment," so was cast into the outer darkness. The wedding garment in Matthew "symbolizes the ethical quality expected in the church."[21]

The delay in the parousia is a nuanced yet characteristic Matthean concern (cf. 24:48; 25:19). And in all those places where Matthew uses the verb *egeirō* independently of his sources he is referring to a real rising from physical death (9:25; 10:8; 16:21; and 17:9). It is likely he intends it to be so understood in 25:7, but then *katheudō* in 13:25 and 25:5 can only mean "death." The symbolic language of 25:5-7, then, refers to the death and resurrection of the virgins. Even if some will die before the delayed parousia comes, they had better not let that factor lead them to believe that the final entrance criteria into the kingdom had become less rigorous.

In the wider New Testament witness, "oil" is used in a variety of ways, but nowhere else with the suggestion of good deeds, as above. But the term "virgins" is illuminated through its use elsewhere in the New Testament. As Jesus is the bridegroom for Matthew, so the church is the virgin who meets her bridegroom at the wedding banquet. The primary support for this comes from Paul in 2 Corinthians 11:2: "I promised you in marriage to one husband, to present you as a chaste virgin to Christ." So "virgin" in Matthew 25 probably refers to all disciples in the interval before the marriage that will occur when Christ returns at the parousia.

There is an exact correlation of "oil" with "good deeds" in the *Midrash Rabbah* to Numbers (Num R. xiii 15, 16). Referring to the phrase "mingled with oil" in Numbers 7:19, the midrash comments that this alludes "to the Torah, the study of which must be mingled with *good deeds*, in accordance with that which we have learned." This usage of oil is identical to what has been suggested the symbol "oil" means in Matthew 25:3, 4, and 8. As there can be no transfer of "oil," "good deeds," or "obedience" from one person to the other, so equally it is absurd to attempt to purchase good deeds from the dealers (25:9).

The fact that 25:1-13 cannot easily be understood on its own terms supports those scholars who have viewed it as an allegory. This factor, coupled with such later concerns as the delay of the parousia, suggests that it does not stem from Jesus in its present form but was created by Matthew on the basis of certain traditions he had received. By focusing primarily on the smaller and larger Matthean contexts, we have discovered not only Matthew's intention in creating the allegory of the ten virgins but also that this allegory summarizes much that is central to the theology of Matthew, especially that the life of discipleship involves both "Gabe *und* Aufgabe,"[22] gift *and* responsibility, a theme that will be explored more fully in our discussion of justification and the ethical life in the Pauline letters.

We now move to the final part of this section, which deals with Matthew's portrayal of the life of discipleship from the perspective, primarily, of the last judgment, and we will take up again the theme of the delay of the parousia, already noted as a major concern of the first evangelist in 24:24 and in 25:5. It is also primary to 25:14-30, the Parable of the Talents. "For it [the kingdom of heaven] is as if a man, going on a journey, summoned his slaves and entrusted his property to them. . . . *After a long time* the master of those slaves came and settled accounts with them" (25:14, 19). The entire action of the parable is concerned with an interval that will continue for a "long time," and it recounts the lives of these persons, each of whom had received different amounts of money.

The servants who had received the five and the two talents, or let us say $5,000 and $2,000, put these gifts immediately to active use. On the last day after the return of the master, the servant who received five talents responds: "'Master, you delivered to me five talents; here I have made five talents more.' Well done, good and trustworthy slave; you have been trustworthy in a few things, I will put you in charge of many things; enter into the joy of your master'" (vv. 20-21). The scene at the last judgment with the servant who received two talents is identical. The major concern in this story is with the servant who received one talent, and it is evident that Matthew is primarily concerned with him as an example of what the disciple ought not to do. Upon receiving his one talent, or in our currency about $1,000, he went and "dug a hole in the ground and hid his master's money" (v. 18). Contrary to the active use to which the other two put their gifts, this servant's performance is striking for its inactivity. This sloth leads to a quite different scenario on the last day, and one should note that about one-half of the entire parable is consumed with this dialogue. The setting is the same: "After a long time the master of those servants came and settled accounts with them" (v. 19). This final servant responds: "Master, I knew that you were a harsh man, reaping where you did not sow, and gathering where you did not scatter seed; so I was afraid, and I went and hid your talent in the ground. Here you have what is yours" (vv. 24-25). Striking is the inconsistency between the servant's declaration about God and his performance. He recognizes that God is both demanding and unusually creative in bringing about results out of nothing. Instead of trusting in this God whom he has just confessed, he is afraid and takes God's talent and puts it in the ground. By placing it in the ground it escapes both God's discipline as well as his creative intention. The master's answer is stinging: "You wicked and lazy slave! You knew, did you, that I reap where I did not sow, and gather where I did not scatter? Then you ought to have invested my money with the bankers, and on my return I would have received what was my own with interest. . . . As for this worthless slave, throw him into the outer darkness, where there will be weeping and gnashing of teeth" (vv. 26-30). Rather than receiving the commendation "Well done, good and faithful servant," the servant with one talent is greeted with a rejection, "You wicked and slothful servant." The negative attribute "wicked and slothful" is important. Not only has this servant done wrong, he had not done what he ought to have done, that is, use the talent in a creative way commensurate with his theological confession. It is also evident from this scene that the final encounter of the disciple with God is not automatically positive but may well contain rejection. One is instantly reminded of such Matthean themes as "Not everyone who says to me, 'Lord, Lord,' will enter the kingdom of heaven, but only the one who does the will of my Father in heaven" (7:21), or "Many are called, but few are chosen" (22:14), as well as Paul's exhortation that "those who do such things will not inherit the kingdom of God" (Gal 5:21). Neither for

Matthew nor for Paul is it possible to confess Jesus authentically unless there is active participation in the new moral life to which he calls; likewise, uttering "Lord, Lord" provides no magical key that opens the door to the kingdom of God.

What is Matthew's point in recounting this particular story in his final eschatological teaching narrative? He is making an analogy between the talents and the life of the disciple, which is to be a life actively using God's gifts in accordance with his will and for his glory. This dimension of actively bearing fruit in the marketplace is what leads to the commendation of the five- and two-talent servants and the rejection of the one-talent servant. Why, one might ask, is the one-talent servant singled out? Perhaps because the majority of disciples are people with one talent rather than five talents and because it is the ordinary person who might feel that his abilities are not significant in God's eyes. To this, Matthew responds that it is God who is the giver and that it is he who is the creative force behind the gift. Therefore precisely the servants with one talent should risk their lives in the hands of the faithful and creative God who both gave the gift and who on the last day will ask for an account of how that gift was used. Matthew's image of God as both firm and munificent, which so dominates Matthew 25, is remarkably similar to Paul's statement in Romans 11:22 that God is a God of severity and kindness.

The consummation of Matthew's eschatological perspective is found in the last part of Matthew 25, verses 31-46. It is an encouragement to ethical seriousness from the viewpoint of the enthroned Son of man on the last day. While many elements in this passage are debated among scholars, it is clear that Matthew wishes to stress that "bearing fruit" and "doing the will of the Father" involve concrete actions to "the least of these my brethren" (RSV) and, further, that Jesus identifies himself precisely with these. To worship Jesus is not an involvement in abstract spirituality but service to those who are hungry, thirsty, strangers, naked, sick, or in prison. On the last day of judgment the exalted Son of Man will exercise his role as judge and will separate the sheep from the goats, the faithful from the unfaithful, not on the basis of whether they have simply confessed "Lord, Lord," but whether they also have done the will of the Father in serving the needs of those who have been marginalized by a competitive and self-serving society.

An examination of the first and last of Matthew's five teaching narratives has made clear that the themes of ethics in the context of eschatology are important themes in Matthew's actualization of the gospel for the needs of his congregation. The analysis of the close interconnections between

Matthew 5–7 and 23–25 has suggested not only the overall structure of Matthew's gospel but also some of his major theological concerns. In light of this background it will now be appropriate to make brief reference to two of the remaining three teaching narratives in order to learn more about Matthew's presentation of Jesus in relationship to the life of discipleship.

4.1.1c Ethical Perspectives: The Church as Corpus Mixtum

The third Matthean teaching section, found in chapter 13, is appropriately referred to as a collection of "eschatological parables." These are a series of parables that reflect on the present nature of the kingdom in light of the final consummation; characteristic is Matthew 13:47-50.

> Again, the kingdom of heaven is like a net that was thrown into the sea and caught fish of every kind; when it was full, they drew it ashore, sat down, and put the good into baskets but threw out the bad. So it will be at the end of the age. The angels will come out and separate the evil from the righteous and throw them into the furnace of fire, where there will be weeping and gnashing of teeth.

The church is presented, to use a phrase of Augustine, as a *corpus mixtum*. Matthew applies these words of Jesus to the community of disciples, which consists of both good and bad here; at the last day, however, there will be a separation and a judgment. That which is more fully expressed in Matthew 25 is already anticipated earlier in this chapter. From the verses just cited it is evident that the first evangelist is attempting to communicate to his audience that in the present age the church is not perfect: it is not fully pure. Further, as will be noted, it is not up to the disciples to "clean house" in order to reach a perfect level of spirituality. Such would be an impossible goal for the earthly manifestation of the kingdom. This perspective is confirmed in the Parable of the Weeds in the Wheat (vv. 24-30) and its allegorical interpretation in verses 36-43, to which we now turn.

> He put before them another parable: "The kingdom of heaven may be compared to someone who sowed good seed in his field; but while everybody was asleep, an enemy came and sowed weeds among the wheat, and then went away. So when the plants came up and bore grain, then the weeds appeared as well. And the slaves of the householder came and said to him, 'Master, did you not sow good seed in your field? Where, then, did these weeds come from?' He answered,

'An enemy has done this.' The slaves said to him, 'Then do you want us to go and gather them?' But he replied, 'No; for in gathering the weeds you would uproot the wheat along with them. Let both of them grow together until the harvest; and at harvest time I will tell the reapers, "Collect the weeds first and bind them in bundles to be burned, but gather the wheat into my barn."'" . . .Then he left the crowds and went into the house. And his disciples approached him, saying, "Explain to us the parable of the weeds of the field." He answered, "The one who sows the good seed is the Son of Man; the field is the world, and the good seed are the children of the kingdom; the weeds are the children of the evil one, and the enemy who sowed them is the devil; the harvest is the end of the age, and the reapers are angels. Just as the weeds are collected and burned up with fire, so will it be at the end of the age. The Son of Man will send his angels, and they will collect out of his kingdom all causes of sin and all evildoers, and they will throw them into the furnace of fire, where there will be weeping and gnashing of teeth. Then the righteous will shine like the sun in the kingdom of their Father. Let anyone with ears listen!"

The focus of the parable, and certainly that of the interpretative allegory, is on a church situation in which it is apparent that there are "false prophets," namely, those who make a confession of faith but do not carry it out in obedience to their heavenly Father. In short, the problem is one of hypocrisy. Is the solution a crusade in the congregation to rid itself of all the undesirable types? Should a new sect be established in order to purify the corrupt church? The response is firmly negative: "No; for in gathering the weeds you would uproot the wheat along with them. Let both of them grow together until the harvest . . ." (vv. 29-30a). This verse is amplified in the interpretation: "Just as the weeds are collected and burned up with fire, so will it be at the end of the age. The Son of Man will send his angels, and they will collect out of his kingdom all causes of sin and all evildoers, and they will throw them into the furnace of fire, where there will be weeping and gnashing of teeth. Then the righteous will shine like the sun in the kingdom of their Father. Let anyone with ears listen!" (vv. 40-43). One notes here several characteristic Matthean emphases: (1) the sharp eschatological stress of what is to happen "at the end of the age"; (2) the motif of separation on the last day that is present in Matthew 24–25 but also in 22:11-14 ("But when the king came in to see the guests, he noticed a man there who was not wearing a wedding robe, and he said to him, 'Friend, how did you get in here without a wedding robe?' And he was speechless. Then the king said to the attendants, 'Bind him hand and foot, and throw him into the outer darkness, where there will be weeping and gnashing of teeth.' For many are called, but few are chosen"); and, (3) the theme that "the righteous will shine like the sun in the kingdom of their Father," which is remarkably similar to the burning lamps in the allegory of the ten virgins.[23]

Matthew 13 is positioned at the mid-point of the gospel and also of the five teaching narratives. It serves to reinforce the teaching previously given and to stress the seriousness of the judgment to come. It functions as a major link between the beginning and the end of the first gospel in Matthew's effort to lift firmly before the eyes of his congregation the critical linkage between ethics and eschatology.

4.1.1d Ethical Perspectives: The Church as a Community of Discipline

In moving toward Matthew 18, the fourth teaching discourse, one must ask whether there is a contradiction between Matthew's warning against premature judgment (Matthew 13) and the firm exhortations about the necessity of discipline (Matthew 18). Before engaging in that discussion, a few introductory remarks about Matthew 18 will be useful. Matthew's primary concern is to communicate that a disciple of Jesus must be humble and forgiving. Such a lifestyle must be expressed especially toward "these little ones who believe in me" (v. 6; see also v. 10). It is in this context of making certain that none "of these little ones should be lost" (v. 14) that one finds the passage dealing with discipline (18:15-20), a text found only in Matthew's gospel. Directly preceding it is the remarkable story of the sheep, with its emphasis on mercy; immediately thereafter one encounters the theme of unlimited forgiveness. Peter comes up to Jesus and asks him, "Lord, if another member of the church sins against me, how often should I forgive? As many as seven times?" (v. 21). Peter undoubtedly thought that he was being quite generous, yet there is a limit beyond which he would not go. To this Jesus responds, "Not seven times, but, I tell you, seventy-seven times" (v. 22). Jesus emphasizes that the ethic of the kingdom is not a calculating one, but one characterized by unlimited mercy and forgiveness. Between these two texts Matthew inserts a section on discipline and ecclesiastical authority (18:15-20):

> If another member of the church sins against you, go and point out the
> fault when the two of you are alone. If the member listens to you, you
> have regained that one. But if you are not listened to, take one or two
> others along with you, so that every word may be confirmed by the
> evidence of two or three witnesses. If the member refuses to listen to

them, tell it to the church; and if the offender refuses to listen even to the church, let such a one be to you as a Gentile and a tax collector. Truly I tell you, whatever you bind on earth will be bound in heaven, and whatever you loose on earth will be loosed in heaven. Again, truly I tell you, if two of you agree on earth about anything you ask, it will be done for you by my Father in heaven. For where two or three are gathered in my name, I am there among them.

The major concern of this passage is how one deals with the fellow disciple who "sins against you." This may strike us strange in an age of permissiveness, where one is expected to tolerate all kinds of action and seldom to criticize or discipline. In verse 15 the advice is explicit: if a member of the community sins against you, such a situation cannot be left to solve itself; concrete action must be taken, and three specific steps are outlined with increasing degrees of severity. The first step is to go to the brother or sister alone, tell the person the fault, and if he or she listens, "you have regained that one" (v. 15). If this initiative fails, then the second course of action is to take one or two others along and to try again. If this second step is not successful, then the final positive step is to "tell it to the church . . ." (v. 17). If there is still at this point a refusal of that one to change attitude and behavior and "and if the offender refuses to listen even to the church, let such a one be to you as a Gentile and a tax collector" (v. 17). Such offenders, then, by their own action have removed themselves from the community; they have technically excommunicated themselves by their refusal to listen. The phrase "exclusive inclusivism" holds these two dimensions in dynamic and creative tension.[24]

Such a process of discipline does not contradict but rather complements Matthew 13, where one finds warnings about premature judgments. The fact that God knows the secrets of the heart and will make the appropriate decision at the eschatological consummation surely does not suggest that any kind of behavior will be tolerated in the church. Quite the contrary; there must be discipline in the present so that none might perish on the last day. When there are flagrant, publicly visible denials of the ethic of Jesus, then those involved must be confronted both for their own sake as well as for that of the community. The foci in Matthew 13 and 18 are quite different, and both need to be held together for the healthy functioning of the community. If, on the one hand, Matthew 13 is pressed to its limits, then a laissez-faire attitude develops in which virtually no correction or discipline takes place; if, on the other hand, Matthew 18 is pushed to an extreme, then a legalistic rigorism sets in that is self-destructive.

How is it that Matthew can attribute such authority to the church? Before one can answer this question one must recognize that Matthew's is the only gospel that uses the term "church," and that it is used only here and in Matthew 16:18. Why? The use of the term "church" *(ekklēsia)* marks a certain developmental point in the history of early Christianity. In Greek there are two virtually synonymous terms used to speak of an assembly of people, usually in the sense of political gathering, *synagōgē* (synagogue) and *ekklēsia* (church). Jews of the diaspora had selected the first term, and the early Jesus movement also used it with little difficulty. This is especially attested in the gospel of John. Only as the break with Judaism develops to the point of rupture is it no longer possible for them to use the term *synagōgē*, and they then select the alternate term *ekklēsia*. Matthew is the only gospel to testify to this state of affairs that is so frequent elsewhere in the New Testament.

From Matthew's perspective at the end of the first century, his church stands in need of renewed instruction about ethical teaching and ecclesiastical structure. Both are commanded by Jesus. In the context of our present discussion, 18:18 is of fundamental importance: "Truly I tell you, whatever you bind on earth will be bound in heaven, and whatever you loose on earth will be loosed in heaven." When this verse is carefully examined, the church is indeed given a staggering responsibility; in the final analysis, however, it is the risen Lord who enables it. It is his authority that makes the church's teachings and structures authoritative; for "all authority in heaven and on earth has been given to me" (28:18). Specifically, in 18:18 the church is given the authority to bind and loose. This is a Jewish idiom that can either mean the communication of authoritative teaching or the exercise of discipline. The former meaning, as will be noted, is apposite to the usage of this phrase in Matthew 16, and the latter meaning is appropriate to our present context. The church, therefore, has a responsibility both to instruct converts and to dismiss flagrant sinners who are unrepentant.

Our passage on ecclesiastical discipline concludes in this way: "Truly I tell you, whatever you bind on earth will be bound in heaven, and whatever you loose on earth will be loosed in heaven. Again, truly I tell you, if two of you agree on earth about anything you ask, it will be done for you by my Father in heaven" (18:18-19). What should be stressed here is that the reference to two or three is not in the first instance where two or three are gathered together for prayer or for worship. Instead, Matthew speaks of two or three gathered together for the process of disciplining a member of the community. It is in the midst of such an action that the Father is present.

There is one other aspect of Matthew's gospel to which attention must be given: the commission to Peter in Matthew 16. Two themes that were found in Matthew 18, "church" and "loosing/binding," also occur in Matthew 16. The critical section of Matthew 16 involves verses 13-20:

> Now when Jesus came into the district of Caesarea Philippi, he asked his disciples, "Who do people say that the Son of Man is?" And they said, "Some say John the Baptist, but others Elijah, and still others Jeremiah or one of the prophets." He said to them, "But who do you say that I am?" Simon Peter answered, "You are the Messiah, the Son of the living God." And Jesus answered him, "Blessed are you, Simon son of Jonah! For flesh and blood has not revealed this to you, but my Father in heaven. And I tell you, you are Peter, and on this rock I will build my church, and the gates of Hades will not prevail against it. I will give you the keys of the kingdom of heaven, and whatever you bind on earth will be bound in heaven, and whatever you loose on earth will be loosed in heaven." Then he sternly ordered the disciples not to tell anyone that he was the Messiah.

One of the reasons this text has invited such lively discussion is that there are no parallels to verses 16b-19 in any of the other gospels. Why? This question becomes even more acute when one realizes the importance that verse 18 especially has had in the development of the papacy: "And I tell you, you are Peter, and on this rock I will build my church, and the gates of Hades will not prevail against it." Because of its strategic importance in the history of the papacy, many Protestants have been inclined to question the authenticity of the text or to argue that the term "rock" could not possibly refer to Peter himself but rather to his confession of faith. Recent New Testament scholarship has moved us beyond these limited options and has opened for us an entirely new perspective.[25]

The starting point for this new perspective is verse 16: "Simon Peter replied, 'You are the Messiah, the Son of the living God.'" Matthew goes beyond the text of Mark by adding the phrase "the Son of the living God." One notes that elsewhere in the New Testament such a confession is usually made about the risen Christ rather than the earthly Jesus. Thus there is an indication that this text represents a postresurrectional setting. This is further suggested by the phrase "flesh and blood." In Galatians 1:15-16 Paul writes these words to the churches of Galatia: "But when God, who had set me apart before I was born and called me through his grace, was pleased to reveal his Son to me, so that I might proclaim him among the Gentiles, I did not confer with any human being [Greek: flesh and blood]." Paul makes clear to the churches of Galatia that the gospel he proclaims was communicated to him by the risen Lord and not through the agency of persons.

In order to understand the Jesus movement it is essential to grasp this phenomenon of postresurrection appearances. The early Christians believed not only in the suffering, death, and resurrection of Jesus, but also that this risen Jesus appeared to certain of his disciples after his resurrection. There are many references to this in the New Testament, perhaps the clearest of which is 1 Corinthians 15. Here Paul is recounting the gospel he had preached to the Corinthians. He begins with this summary: "For I handed on to you as of first importance what I in turn had received: that Christ died for our sins in accordance with the scripture . . ." (v. 3). To stop reading at this point would be to misread Paul, and it would also diminish a perspective of critical significance for the followers of Jesus. Paul's description of the gospel continues as follows: ". . . and that he appeared to Cephas, then to the twelve. Then he appeared to more than five hundred brothers and sisters at one time, most of whom are still alive, though some have died. Then he appeared to James, then to all the apostles" (vv. 5-7). The entire objective of verses 5-7 is to narrate the appearances of the risen one, and here as elsewhere the first of these appearances is to Peter.

Without attempting to be flippant, one must ask whether anything more transpired between the risen Lord and Peter than a swift, passing, "Hi, Pete!" In other words, was there some purpose, some content to the appearance of the risen one to Peter? In *Peter in the New Testament* it is suggested that there was both content and intentionality in this appearance, and it is referred to as a "church-founding" appearance.[26] It was at this moment, through the agency of Peter, that the church as a community of Jesus was actualized, and, in all likelihood, the remembrance of that tradition is contained in Matthew 16:18-19 with a variation of this tradition in John 21:15-17.

In view of this discussion it will be important to view verse 18 more closely: "And I tell you, you are Peter, and on this rock I will build my church, and the gates of Hades shall not prevail against it." Unfortunately, the English translation blurs the fascinating play on words that takes place in the Greek text and in the underlying Aramaic, the language Jesus spoke. If we reconstruct the Aramaic text it reads like this: "And I tell you, you are *Kephā³* and on this *kephā³* I will build my church. . . ." Simon, son of Jonah, is receiving a new name, presumably to describe a new function. Simon receives the additional appellation of "rock." You are "rock" (or in colloquial English, would the rough equivalent be "Rocky"?) and on this "rock" (that is, on you, Simon) I will build my church. This identity of "Peter" and "rock" in Aramaic is without question, and this same relationship is maintained in the Greek text: "You are *Petros* and on this *petra* I will build my church." Here, too, the identity between "Peter" and "rock" is maintained, with the exception that in Greek the word *Kephāʾ* has to be changed into the masculine form *Petros*, since rock in Greek, *petra,* is a feminine form.

Through the human agency of Peter, frail and whimsical as he is, the church has its beginning. This dimension of "beginning" is confirmed by verse 18b and its use of the future tense, *"I will* build my church." The church is possible only because of Christ's resurrection and the church-founding appearance of the risen Lord. In addition to these dramatic divine events, one should not overlook the "miraculous" nature of the selection of Peter, a man who at various times was fickle, weak, and denied his Lord. The miracle, if you will, is that God works through the most ordinary individuals and circumstances. In a very observable way this is what the incarnation (God becoming flesh) is all about: using the most ordinary means of God's creation for his glory.

There are a few additional items that should be examined in this critical section of Matthew's gospel. In verse 18 one finds the only other use of *ekklēsia* (church) in this gospel. The promise is given that this church that is being built and will continue to be built in the future shall be protected from all assaults of the demonic forces operative in the world. The church, and not the "gates of Hades," shall prevail. Verse 19, with its reference to "the keys of the kingdom," strongly influenced by Isaiah 22:15-25, originally referred to permitting persons to enter and to leave the church. John 20:23 provides a helpful parallel to this initial stage in the tradition: "If you forgive the sins of any, they are forgiven them; if you retain the sins of any, they are retained." The earlier formulation "keys of the kingdom" is expanded in Matthew's congregations by the addition of the rabbinic formula of "binding and loosing." In the first place, this addition in Matthew's gospel is addressed in the singular to Peter alone. This is different from its context in Matthew 18, where the "you" is a plural form addressed to the wider group of the disciples.

One will remember that in Matthew 18 the concept of binding and loosing was used in a disciplinary sense. While it may be used in this sense in Matthew 16, it is more likely that here in Matthew 18, in the context of teaching authority, the meaning is that of "permitting" or "forbidding" certain actions. This later interpretation gathers support from the verses just preceding the text under discussion. In 16:11b-12 one reads: "'Beware of the yeast of the Pharisees and Sadducees!' Then they understood that he had not told them to beware of the yeast of bread, but of the teaching of the Pharisees and Sadducees." In this situation of post–70 CE Judaism there is tension between Christianity and Judaism at a number of points, not least of which is the area of authoritative teaching. In such a situation Matthew must reinforce Peter's position as authoritative teacher in the church. This understanding is strengthened at several points in Matthew's gospel where it is Peter who is uniquely the spokesman for the twelve and the communicator of authoritative teaching and interpretation. We have already noticed that it is only in Matthew's gospel that the name "Peter" is inserted as the person who raises the question about forgiveness (18:21). Another clear example of this tendency to elevate Peter as an authoritative interpreter is 17:24-27. The passage begins in this way: "When they reached Capernaum, the collectors of the temple tax came to Peter and said, 'Does your teacher not pay the temple tax?'" After a small dialogue between Peter and Jesus, Matthew has Jesus give this response: "Then the children are free. However, so that we do not give offense to them, go to the sea and cast a hook; take the first fish that comes up; and when you open its mouth, you will find a coin; take that and give it to them for you and me." It is Peter who questions, facilitates, and interprets matters pressing in the life of this church, and Matthew reinforces this position in 16:19. Clearly Peter serves as a model of discipleship and receives a prominence unequaled in the other gospels. Why does Matthew do this? Is he faithful to the gospel tradition?

The simplest way to explain what Matthew is doing is to go back to our previous observations about the postresurrectional character of certain elements in 16:17-19. Matthew takes a postresurrectional church-founding appearance and situates it within the historical ministry of Jesus. In other words, the change of name, or the addition of the name Cephas to Simon, as well as the makarism to Peter, is something that takes place at the moment of the appearance of the risen Lord to Peter. For the purposes of actualizing his gospel message in the midst of a conflict situation with post–70 Judaism, Matthew places it at a much earlier point in his gospel in order to give Peter a prominence that was important for the existential and theological situation of his congregation.

Finally, before leaving this passage in Matthew 16 one should observe its multidimensionality. It is one of the striking examples of the dynamic, creative impulse of early Christianity. In this passage we find words and scenes from the historical Jesus (e.g., the question to Peter about his identity), traditions from the early church (e.g., "binding" and "loosing"), and elements revealing Matthew's own theological perspective (e.g., the editorial and compositional work as a whole as well as the addition of specific items themselves, such as the addition of the name "Jeremiah" in v. 14). While an uninformed reader might categorize postresurrectional appearances as a merely peripheral element in early Christianity, they are quite central for that first generation of followers. Specifically the postresurrectional appearance to Peter is foundational for the entire passage. Once again we have seen how neatly Matthew weaves and molds together many originally disparate elements for the sake of actualizing the teaching of Jesus for the needs of his congregation. Under the guidance of the risen Lord, Matthew takes the gospel tradition and creatively allows it to speak to the uniqueness of his situation. It is to this type of dynamic rather than static theological process, in the context of a Trinitarian hermeneutic, that the entire New Testament invites the contemporary church.

4.2 Paul and the Moral Life[27]

4.2.1 Justification

Resulting largely from the influence of the Protestant Reformation, the term "justification" has appeared frequently in the Christian tradition. But what really is meant by this term? If it refers to sinful human beings who have accepted God's gracious and merciful gift of reconciliation, how does this new reality realize itself in terms of a renewed moral life? Further, one needs to ask in what ways this new life, resulting from God's justifying action to the sinner through Christ, is able to discern and to do the will of God?

The Lutheran-Roman Catholic *Joint Declaration on the Doctrine of Justification (JDDJ)*, agreed to and signed by these churches in Augsburg, Germany, on October 31, 1999, stands among the clearest articulations of the meaning and consequences of "justification":

> In faith we together hold the conviction that justification is the work of the triune God. The Father sent his Son into the world to save sinners. The foundation and presupposition of justification is the incarnation, death and resurrection of Christ. Justification thus means that Christ himself is our righteousness, in which we share through the Holy Spirit in accord with the will of the Father. Together we confess: *By grace alone, in faith in Christ's saving work and not because of any merit on our part, we are accepted by God and receive the Holy Spirit, who renews our hearts while equipping and calling us to good works.*[28]

As a working definition one might say that justification brings to health the diseased, broken relationship between God and humanity, between the Creator and his creation. This healing, this bringing to wholeness, is a completely unmerited gift on the part of God through the blood of Jesus Christ (see Rom 5:9). But what is the intention of this healing power that takes place in the act of justification and reconciliation? What is the relationship of God's gift to his "equipping and calling us to good works"? And, finally, one must ask: if there is a gift, an indicative, is there also a responsibility, an imperative?

The conclusion of the paragraph cited from the *JDDJ* speaks about an irrevocable interrelationship between grace and good works, specifically, that the reception of God's reconciling grace leads to a renewal of the heart and calls us to good works. Particularly in light of polemics at the time of the Reformation, many in the Protestant tradition have become allergic to the term "good works" as if it were some Roman Catholic invention. In fact, the term goes back to Jesus and to the New Testament. "You are the light of the world," says Jesus. "A city built on a hill cannot be hid. No one after lighting a lamp puts it under the bushel basket, but on the lampstand, and it gives light to all in the house. In the same way, let your light shine before others, so that they may see your *good works* and give glory to your Father in heaven" (Matt 5:14-16).[29] Paul rephrases this thought as "faith working through love" (Gal 5:6), and to further help his congregations understand more fully their new life in Christ he uses three terms in overlapping yet distinct ways: justification, sanctification, and salvation.

Although analogies are always imperfect, they may provide, at least to some extent, helpful clarifications. The relationship of grace and good works, so encumbered by the Protestant/Roman Catholic hostilities since the sixteenth-century Reformation and the subsequent Council of Trent, might be viewed in terms of a medical analogy. Following a medical checkup one may be told that a serious disease has set in, perhaps breast or prostate cancer, and that only some form of radical intervention, such as chemotherapy or surgery, will resolve the problem. One can select this solution or one can deny the need for such radical intervention and opt instead for a self-improvement program that might include swimming, a significantly altered diet as well as megadoses of vitamins and herbal formulations. As important as these good efforts, these "good works," may be, they will not resolve the fundamental health problem; only a radical medical intervention from outside oneself contains the potential for healing. This radical entry into the human condition from beyond ourselves can, by analogy, be referred to as "grace," as "free gift."

However, such a radical intervention of grace does not instantaneously complete the process of healing/reconciliation/salvation. When a surgeon, for example, shares the good news following surgery that she was able to remove all the cancerous cells, the patient is certainly not at that moment fully healed. Similarly, one might say that evil, the power of sin and illness have been overcome, but only with the further aid of medication, rest, prayer, and exercise is one able to be what one was meant to be, namely, a healthy human being. Two important points need to be emphasized: (1) that surgery as radical intervention does not lead *immediately* to a state of full recovery, although it does allow for that possibility; (2) recovering from illness results not only in being freed from disease and pain, that is, from self-absorption, but also to be free to serve others.

Justification by faith is a little like this process. The presupposition is that human beings are in a state of ill health, sin, in their relationship with God. This is a theme that is emphasized both by the Pauline letters[30] as well as by some of the texts found in the Dead Sea Scrolls.[31] As a result of God's radical entry into human history through the death and resurrection of Jesus Christ, the diseased state between the human and God can be healed, reconciled, justified. God's radically gracious act of healing and reconciliation cannot be brought into being as a result of human capacity and can only be accepted as an entirely free gift; it has not been achieved through individual efforts, human actions, or through the accumulation of good works. Now, however, that reconciliation, justification, has become a reality, the disciple who has received this healing power for new life in Christ must continue to mature in Christ. This is what Paul has in mind when he speaks of "progress" (Phil 1:25) and "transformation" in 2 Corinthians 3:18: "And all of us, with unveiled faces, seeing the glory of the Lord as though reflected in a mirror, are being transformed into the same image from one degree of glory to another; for this comes from the Lord, the Spirit." Paul stresses that the new life moves toward completeness in Jesus Christ and that this persistent process of transformation is a gift that comes from "the Lord, the Spirit." But this growth in new life is not a private set of activities that takes place only between the believer and Jesus. Quite the contrary, this becoming more like Christ allows the disciple to actualize faith as an activity of love (Gal 5:6) toward the other, toward the neighbor. Supported and nurtured by the Body of Christ, the church, all activities, all such good works, all such acts of love are intended to build up and encourage and console the

entire community of faith (1 Cor 14:3). Because Christ loved us, one is
enabled to be freed from addiction to oneself and so to be liberated in order
to serve the other, which in reality is serving Christ himself, a theme so
evocatively discussed in Matthew 25:34-40:

> Then the king will say to those at his right hand, "Come, you that are
> blessed by my Father, inherit the kingdom prepared for you from the
> foundation of the world; for I was hungry and you gave me food, I
> was thirsty and you gave me something to drink, I was a stranger and
> you welcomed me, I was naked and you gave me clothing, I was sick
> and you took care of me, I was in prison and you visited me." Then
> the righteous will answer him, "Lord, when was it that we saw you
> hungry and gave you food, or thirsty and gave you something to
> drink? And when was it that we saw you a stranger and welcomed
> you, or naked and gave you clothing? And when was it that we saw
> you sick or in prison and visited you?" And the king will answer them,
> "Truly I tell you, just as you did it to one of the least of these who are
> members of my family, you did it to me."

So Luther had it quite right: "Good works do not make a good person,
but a good person does good works."[32] Good works do not bring about
healing, but once healing has taken place one is now free to love the other
with the same sacrificial love that characterized God's self-donation
through the suffering and death of Jesus. As God was wounded for us, so
must we in turn become wounded healers[33] to those who need to be
embraced by the intimacy of Christ's love.

Given the rethinking of Pauline theology among many New Testament
scholars, stimulated by both the availability of the new texts from the Dead
Sea Scrolls and the joint statement on justification issued by Lutherans and
Roman Catholics in 1999,[34] this is a particularly propitious moment to
explore selected aspects of the Pauline meaning of justification more fully,
especially since one's understanding of justification will influence one's biblical hermeneutic as well as the relationship of faith to the moral life.

Ernst Käsemann has compellingly reignited the current discussions
related to this topic.[35] Käsemann argues that justification, together with the
corollary term, "righteousness of God" (Rom 1:17; 3:21),[36] is much more
than simply God's gift to humanity. When understood in this limited way,[37]
not only does the gift character become isolated, resulting in an unbalanced
individualism, but also the eschatological tensions in Pauline theology, particularly between beginning and end, are either reduced to insignificance or

entirely ignored. For Käsemann, justification, as well as the closely related term "righteousness of God," certainly includes the gift character, but he views these themes as part of a much broader historical and eschatological context: the righteousness of God "is seen as God's sovereignty over the world revealing itself eschatologically in Jesus."[38] God's gift in Jesus Christ is a manifestation of the God who has been faithful to his people and who reveals himself in sovereignty and power. When this broader context of the sovereign God revealing himself is ignored, "the inevitable result is that the Pauline anthropology is sucked under the pull of an individualistic outlook."[39] The value of Käsemann's approach to justification is that it avoids this danger of absolutizing the meaning of the term as "gift" in individualistic categories. Faithfully reflecting Paul's intention, justification is regarded as "*Gabe* und *Aufgabe*" ["gift *and* responsibility"]; and it contains not only a present but also a future dimension—it is "a matter of promise *and* expectation."[40]

The gift given in justification does not have *automatic* consequences, that is, some kind of lifetime immunization or guarantee. Rather, it remains a gift only as long as the gift is received with daily fidelity and obedience to Christ. Because this understanding is foundational for the apostle, he is able to integrate present and future judgment as an essential part of his theology, in a manner quite parallel to the teaching of Jesus. The righteousness of God revealed in Christ reclaims the individual created in the image of God for the sovereignty of God; this sovereign God acts not only in mercy but also in judgment[41] to those who reject him, to those who no longer remain obedient, and who consequently fail to actualize his promise. The believer *participates in* but does not possess the righteousness of God.[42]

Fundamental to recent scholarly dialogue[43] is the observation that when Paul speaks of the "gift of righteousness" in Romans 5:17, he is referring to a gift which is both present and future, already received and still expected. God's righteousness is a gift in the present, but a gift that at the same time recognizes God's sovereign authority and the fact that the redeemed person is placed under that power in obedient service.[44] This grace and power of God as "promise" presupposes an eschatological framework of "already"—"not yet." For the justified person salvation is not yet completed in the present; it has yet to be consummated and fulfilled on the last day. Only as the believer waits and hopes in Christ will that person receive the full benefits of salvation (Rom 8:23-25; Gal 5:5).

What is the crucial connection between the already realized dimension of salvation experienced in justification and that future, consummated dimension of salvation if not "obedience"? For Paul faith always means obedience to the will of God, and therefore it contains an active element as a person responds to the claim of God. This interpretation is demonstrated by a careful interpretation of Romans 6, particularly verses 12-23. Sanctification (literally, "holiness" or "holy habits"[45] [6:19]), the development and maturation of the Christian life in Christ, is an integral part of justification and can only be accomplished in obedience to the will of Christ (Rom 6:16). Sanctification serves both to elucidate and to preserve what has taken place in justification. Only when this is carried out in obedience will God fulfill what he has begun.

For Paul, justification both initiates and enables the life in Christ from beginning to end. As human beings participate in the revelation of the sovereign creator in Jesus Christ by faith, or as the apostle alternatively describes such participation as "standing in the gospel" (1 Cor 15:1 [RSV]), their broken relationship with God becomes whole and is restored. God now offers the one in Christ, through the gift of his Spirit, the possibility of leading a new life that is both obedient to him and responsive to the needs of the neighbor. The Spirit permits such a person to live "in holiness," frequently translated from the Greek as "sanctification." The life of sanctification and transformation (2 Cor 3:18), a gift granted by God, will lead to the final fulfillment of that which God began in justification, namely, the gift of salvation to be consummated on the last day.[46]

The fact that sanctification is the process of living out the Christian life between justification and the last day is made clear at several points; specifically Romans 6:19 and 22: "For just as you once presented your members as slaves to impurity and to greater and greater iniquity, so now present your members as slaves to righteousness for *sanctification*. . . . But now that you have been freed from sin and enslaved to God, the advantage you get is sanctification. The end is eternal life." Sanctification, based upon justification and initiated by it, leads to the fulfilled gift of salvation, eternal life.[47] Or, to use slightly different language, holiness (holy habits), based on the gift of reconciliation with God in Christ, will culminate with the final gift of resurrection. That the life of the Christian is in fact a process of transformation that has a beginning and an end-point is also made abundantly clear in 1 Corinthians and Philippians. In language very similar to the synoptic logion that "many are called, but few are chosen" (Matt 22:14), Paul warns the Corinthians that there is nothing automatic about life in Christ. He reminds them that not every athlete receives a prize (1 Cor 9:24-27) and that, in fact, God was not pleased with the behavior of Israel (1 Cor 10:1-13).[48] It is only the believer who both competes in the race and who is pleasing to God (10:5) who will receive the prize. This is exactly Paul's point in

Philippians 2:12 where he urges the Philippians to work out their "own salvation with fear and trembling." The seriousness with which Paul asserts that the already inaugurated gift of salvation is not yet a fully possessed gift is affirmed in Philippians 3:12-14: "Not that I have already obtained this or have already reached the goal; but I press on to make it my own, because Christ Jesus has made me his own. Beloved, I do not consider that I have made it my own; but this one thing I do: forgetting what lies behind and straining forward to what lies ahead, I press on toward the goal for the prize of the heavenly call of God in Christ Jesus." In short, the Christian life, the gift of salvation, is initiated in a continuing, foundational way through justification/reconciliation, is actualized in sanctification/holiness, and is consummated with the ultimate gift of salvation, resurrection from the dead. Critical for this fulfillment of salvation is the believer's continued obedience and continued reception of God's freely offered gift of the Spirit which is at work in the believer as a part of the Body of Christ.[49]

This brief discussion should assist our understanding of a Pauline text that is of fundamental importance, Romans 5:9-10: "Much more surely then, now that we have been justified by his blood, will we be saved through him from the wrath of God. For if while we were enemies, we were reconciled to God through the death of his Son, much more surely, having been reconciled, will we be saved by his life." In this text Paul is speaking to the Roman believers, and he refers to justification as a past and continuing event in which they have already participated and continue to participate, and salvation as a future (and only then consummated) event, the "first fruits" (Rom 8:23) of which they already now experience. In this particular text Paul expresses a strong confidence that the one who is justified will also be saved, that is, receive life eternal. But what is of interest is that despite Paul's strong confidence, he does not simply conflate the final gift of God's salvation with justification, the initiated but not yet fulfilled gift of salvation. They remain two distinct nuances along the trajectory of the Christian life. Nor should one think that Romans 5:9-12 is a unique text. The regular pattern in the Pauline letters is that "to justify" refers to the newly inaugurated life in Christ, and that "to save," together with its cognates, refers to an event already initiated but yet to be consummated. A few examples must suffice. In his discussion of baptism in Romans 6, Paul writes in v. 7: "For whoever has died is freed [perfect tense in Greek] from sin." The event of dying with Christ, as well as justification, are past yet continuing events, and it is exactly in this context that Paul also is very careful to make known that resurrection is a future possibility, *not* a present reality.[50] We died with Christ so that "we too might walk (subjunctive mood in the Greek) in newness of life" (v. 4). Also important as a summary expression of Paul's intent in using the verb "to justify" is the formula, perhaps pre-Pauline,[51] in 1 Corinthians 6:11: "And this is what some of you used to be. But you were washed, you were sanctified, you were justified in the name of the Lord Jesus Christ and in the Spirit of our God." Perhaps even more important than observing the obvious, namely, that justification refers to a past and continuing occurrence for the Christian, is the less frequently noted fact that for Paul "to save" and "salvation" have an unambiguous future reference.

Two texts in particular support Paul's use of the future passive of the verb "to save" (i.e., "will be saved") in Romans 5:9-10 to indicate the futurity of the consummated gift of salvation: 1 Thessalonians 5:8, where he refers to the "hope of salvation," which is immediately followed by the thought that God has destined us to obtain salvation, and Romans 13:11, where the Romans are reminded that "salvation is nearer to us now than when we became believers." This clearly indicates that salvation, in its ultimate sense, is a future event toward which the Christian moves; although already begun, it is not yet completely enjoyed in the present since we still live in a world that is both broken and decaying (Rom 8:18-25). It is unimaginable for Paul[52] that a believer could properly confess "I have been saved," because that would imply complete possession of the resurrection now, the very point for which he rebukes the Christians at Corinth (1 Cor 4:8-13). What those in Christ can assert is that they are in the process of being saved (1 Cor 1:18, "to us who are being saved"), that because of God's radical intervention they are now in the process of being healed. Believers in Christ can give thanks not because they are already saved, that is, restored to full health, but "because God chose you as the first fruits for salvation through sanctification by the Spirit . . ." (2 Thess 2:13), that is, they are still being nursed back to health.

The Pauline configuration of nuances attempting to describe the redeemed life in Christ in all of its aspects, both present and future, might be summarized in this way:

> *justification*—an event that for the believer has already happened and one that has present and continuing power through its actualization in a sanctified, holy life;
>
> *sanctification*—a present event, dependent on a past and continuing event, justification, which anticipates the completed gift of salvation, the resurrection from the dead;
>
> *salvation*—an event already inaugurated through justification and baptism, already partially experienced through justification/reconciliation

with God and sanctification/holiness of life, and whose final fulfillment in the resurrection of the body is already now anticipated with eager longing: "I consider that the sufferings of this present time are not worth comparing with the glory about to be revealed to us. For the creation waits with eager longing for the revealing of the children of God; for the creation was subjected to futility, not of its own will but by the will of the one who subjected it, in hope that the creation itself will be set free from its bondage to decay and will obtain the freedom of the glory of the children of God." (Rom 8:18-21)

Even in those occasional texts where Paul uses the verb "to save" in a present tense, there is no ground for any confusion that would suggest that salvation is now fully possessed or that the process leading to it is automatic. This can be seen in 1 Corinthians 15:1-2: "Now I would remind you, brothers and sisters, of the good news that I proclaimed to you, which you in turn received, in which also you stand, through which also you are being saved, *if* you hold firmly to the message that I proclaimed to you—unless you have come to believe in vain." Yes, the gospel is the means of salvation—but only if one holds fast to its power, only if one is obedient to its claim (Rom 6:16-17). When one does not hold fast, when one is not obedient, then that person has believed in vain (1 Cor 15:2). It is a little like the person who has received the radical therapy of surgery but then undermines the very healing process that is to lead to full recovery. In other words, the gospel is both *Gabe and Aufgabe* ("gift" *and* "responsibility").

In light of these observations, the following preliminary thesis will be proposed concerning the relationship of justification to last judgment, a thesis which of necessity will have to be amplified and clarified as we proceed: Paul is confident that the person who has received the gospel of God's gracious mercy by faith and who has been justified through it will receive the final gift of salvation at the last judgment. This is purely an act of God's grace that believers will receive if they remain obedient to the gift of God and his Spirit. But for those who have been justified and who then make a mockery of God's gift by their gross abuse and disobedience, such will not receive the gift of salvation at the last judgment; rather they will suffer the wrath of God (Rom 5:9-10). Thus the final criterion for Paul at the last judgment is not how many good works one has performed, this is gratuitous since it is the Spirit which enables one to do these deeds of love, but, rather, whether one has held fast and remained obedient to his new life in Christ.[53] It is the criterion of the obedience of faith (Rom 1:5 and 16:25) that will enable us to understand many of the Pauline last judgment texts to which we now turn.[54]

4.2.1a The Distortion of Justification in Recent Hermeneutics

The most frequent way in which justification is distorted is the failure to understand its life transforming character and the resulting ethical implications of living the "rightwised" life.[55] Characteristic of the current theology of acceptance is that the terms "justification" and "gospel" lose their profound transformative quality and tend to become slogans that are simply bandied about. Philip Turner has correctly described the starting point for such a theology of accommodation with regard to contemporary culture: "the incarnation is to be understood as merely a manifestation of divine love. From this starting point, several conclusions are drawn. The first is that God is love, pure and simple. Thus, one is to see in Christ's death no judgment upon the human condition. Rather, one is to see an affirmation of creation and the persons we are. The life and death of Jesus reveal the fact that God accepts and affirms us."[56]

Craig Nessan maintains that the "doctrine of justification preserves the gospel-character of the gospel of Jesus Christ."[57] By leaving these terms vague and ill-defined and by excising the ethical rigor from both the teaching of Jesus and Paul, he contends that although "justification is the central conviction of the church" that does not mean the church is "required to have unanimity about every ethical question" and, further, that "the freedom of the gospel generally allows for a range of viewpoints on challenging ethical issues."[58] Having so reduced the content of these major concepts, he is able to tolerate a wide range of contradictory opinions concerning an assortment of controversial ethical issues. Thus, when discussing the issue of homosexuality Nessan can conclude that the "gospel is that message by which people on every side of the discussion are each justified by grace and forgiven for Christ's sake. . . . In classical Lutheran terms, to identify any ethical position on a particular issue with the gospel itself is to fail to properly distinguish between law and gospel."[59] As a result of anachronistically imposing the concept of "law and gospel" on the New Testament he can then proceed to dispense with the ethical mandates in the teaching of Jesus. By disregarding the commandments of Jesus as well as the exhortations of Paul to his congregations, Nessan leads his readers into the docetic realm of generalities that vitiate any sense of obedience to the teachings of the gospel. In this classic example of theological reductionism, grace simply becomes another word for accommodation to cultural norms rather than an orientation toward the transforming reality of New Testament ethics.

Once one has reduced the heart and soul of Jesus' teaching, one is then free on the basis of "new hermeneutical methods"[60] to emphasize whatever text or theme one wishes to the exclusion of others. For Nessan, the authority of the Bible does not mean "a biblical literalism that reads every verse of the Bible as having equal importance. Lutherans understand that those sections of the Bible that point to grace, love, and forgiveness of God in Jesus Christ have more significance than any other part. In fact, Lutherans teach that all the rest of the Bible needs to be interpreted on the basis of this gospel message about Jesus Christ."[61] Alien ideologies are often concealed behind such indistinct and benign sounding language. Surely the opposite of literalism is not some form of antinomianism that urges that "the well-being of relationships" must be put "ahead of the need to be right."[62] To dismiss right teaching by referring to it as literalism is hardly a compelling argument. Once Paul's emphasis on both the *obedience* of faith and love is discarded for the sake of good human relations, then it is easy to manipulate Pauline theology by arguing that this "approach, following that of Paul in 1 Corinthians, values the health of the community by clearly communicating our care for one another in Christ, regardless of whether we do or do not agree on any issue."[63] Such a conclusion represents a fundamental misreading of 1 Corinthians! When such fundamental themes as holiness, obedience, and the last judgment are trumped by appeal to diluted and insipid references to love and grace, then the fundamental structure of the life in Christ as articulated by Paul is eradicated. A proper understanding of the Pauline teaching of justification is required precisely to avoid such misreadings of his letters. What is essential for Paul cannot be redefined as "nonessential"[64] for the sake of cultural accommodation.

4.2.2 *The Moral Life and Accountability*

The late German theologian and resister against the Nazis, Dietrich Bonhoeffer, spoke, as we have already noted, about two kinds of grace, cheap grace and costly grace. "Cheap grace is the preaching of forgiveness without requiring repentance, baptism without church discipline, communion without confession, absolution without personal confession. Cheap grace is grace without discipleship, grace without the cross, grace without Jesus Christ, living and incarnate."[65] He warns his reader, with appropriate derision, about the world's continuing temptation in this direction.

> Cheap grace means the justification of sin without the justification of the sinner. Grace alone does everything, they say, and so everything

can remain as it was before. . . . Well, then, let the Christian live like
the rest of the world, let him model himself on the world's standards
in every sphere of life, and not presumptuously aspire to live a different life under grace from his old life under sin. . . . Let him not attempt
to erect a new religion of the letter by endeavoring to live a life of obedience to the commandments of Jesus Christ! The world has been justified by grace. The Christian knows that, and takes it seriously. He
knows that he must not strive against this indispensable grace. Therefore—let him live like the rest of the world![66]

In a commanding manner Bonhoeffer illustrates the distortion of the concept of justification and grace within the German Christianity of the 1930s.
One might well ask, however, is the situation much different today? To what
degree does the ethical gravity of contemporary Christians model itself on
the teachings of Jesus and Paul? What, for example, shapes the contemporary Christian attitude toward sexuality—Scripture or the ethic of a secu-
larized society?

The opposite of "cheap grace" is "costly grace."

Costly grace is the treasure hidden in the field; for the sake of it a man
will gladly go and sell all that he has. It is the pearl of great price to
buy which the merchant will sell all his goods. It is the kingly rule of
Christ, for whose sake a man will pluck out the eye which causes him
to stumble, it is the call of Jesus Christ at which the disciple leaves his
nets and follows him. . . . Costly grace is the sanctuary of God; it has
to be protected from the world, and not thrown to the dogs. . . . Grace
is costly because it compels a man to submit to the yoke of Christ and
follow him; it is grace because Jesus says: "My yoke is easy and my
burden is light."[67]

It is this biblical sense of costly grace that compelled Bonhoeffer to resist the
secularization and nazification of his church, even to the point of death.

The coherence of Bonhoeffer's perspective with that of Paul is remarkable. Costly grace is another way to express the "holy habits," that is, holi-
ness/sanctification, that the apostle expects of all who follow Jesus Christ as
can be seen in his exhortation to both the Galatian and Corinthian
churches. To the first group he writes: "Now the works of the flesh are obvious: fornication, impurity, licentiousness, idolatry, sorcery, enmities, strife,
jealousy, anger, quarrels, dissensions, factions, envy, drunkenness, carousing, and things like these. I am warning you, as I warned you before: those

who do such things will not inherit the kingdom of God" (Gal 5:19-21). The words of exhortation to the Corinthian Christians are remarkably similar: "Do you not know that wrongdoers will not inherit the kingdom of God? Do not be deceived! Fornicators, idolaters, adulterers, male prostitutes, sodomites, thieves, the greedy, drunkards, revilers, robbers—none of these will inherit the kingdom of God. And this is what some of you used to be. But you were washed, you were sanctified, you were justified in the name of the Lord Jesus Christ and in the Spirit of our God" (1 Cor 6:9-11). By way of reminder one will observe that this Pauline double use of the phrase "inherit the kingdom" is analogous to the words of Jesus in Matthew 25:24 and remarkably similar to the words in Matthew 5:20: "For I tell you, unless your righteousness exceeds that of the scribes and Pharisees, you will never enter the kingdom of heaven" and to the many other references in the teaching of Jesus about entering the kingdom.

Paul indicates on more than one occasion that the goal of the gospel is to move the believer toward holiness and the gift of consummated salvation.[68] Quite typical is the language expressed in 1 Thessalonians 5:9, "For God has destined us not for wrath but for obtaining salvation through our Lord Jesus Christ. . . ." While salvation begins already now in the present (2 Cor 6:2), its final fulfillment is to be found only in the future (Rom 13:11; 1 Thess 5:8-9). As has previously been observed, justification can never be equated with this final gift of salvation, which includes resurrection from the dead; justification is the beginning and foundation of the Christian life, while salvation is its consummation and fulfillment. Salvation is the natural and expected end effect for the justified person living in holiness/sanctification, that is, leading a life in which faith is lived out in the context of costly grace that produces holy habits. The relationship of eschatology and ethics is as closely correlated in the theology of Paul as in the teaching of Jesus. And so the apostle can write to the Corinthians: "Since we have these promises, beloved, let us cleanse ourselves from every defilement of body and of spirit, making holiness perfect in the fear of God" (2 Cor 7:1). Only through "holiness" will one be pure and blameless on the day of Christ. To be pure and blameless on the day of Christ is an overriding concern of Paul for all his congregations (Phil 1:10-11; 1 Cor 1:8).

A concise summary of Paul's theology can be found in the deutero-Pauline letter to the Colossians. In describing who will be found irreproachable on the last day, it presents a significant Pauline stricture: "provided that you continue securely established and steadfast in the faith, without shifting from the hope promised by the gospel that you heard . . ." (Col 1:23). It is only the one in Christ who remains steadfast and firm,[69] in short, obedient to the hope of the gospel, who will receive the promised, final gift of salvation. The apostle's entire moral and ethical exhortation is anchored in the eschatological perspective that fulfilled salvation is a future event. Because the believer must stand firm in sanctification, in costly grace, dependence on the grace and the strengthening power of Jesus Christ becomes indispensable: "He will also strengthen you to the end, so that you may be blameless on the day of our Lord Jesus Christ" (1 Cor 1:8). And so Paul repeatedly urges his churches to be "blameless" (1 Thess 3:13; 5:23; Phil 2:15), "pure" (Phil 1:10), and "holy" (Rom 12:1). In short, Paul urges the one in Christ to "work out your own salvation with fear and trembling; for it is God who is at work in you, enabling you both to will and to work for his good pleasure" (Phil 2:12-13).

Even though Paul stresses that justification is purely an act of God's mercy and that sanctification is entirely the gift of God's spirit, he is quick to warn his audience that these gifts involve their active openness toward, participation in, and obedience to God's continued goodness. Otherwise they will be like the men of Israel with whom God was not pleased: "and they were struck down in the wilderness. Now these things occurred as examples for us, so that we might not desire evil as they did" (1 Cor 10:5-6). And so, because Paul wants to present his bride pure and blameless on the last day (2 Cor 11:2), he reminds his congregation of this last day in no uncertain terms. No man should transgress "because the Lord is an avenger in all these things . . ." (1 Thess 4:6). We must be careful not to despise our brother because we must all appear "before the judgment seat of God" (Rom 14:10) where "each may receive recompense for what has been done in the body, whether good or evil" (2 Cor 5:10). To simply dismiss these texts as relics from Paul's Jewish past is to fundamentally misunderstand the scope and richness of Pauline theology as well as to misread Paul's insistence on both "the kindness and severity of God" (Rom 11:22).

This theme of final accountability before the God of Jesus Christ is also confirmed by another set of texts, a series of passages that postulate a negative outcome for disobedient Christians on the last day. Texts such as these stand in direct opposition to scholars who maintain that once the believer has been justified, salvation will result in an irrevocable manner. Several passages not only warn Christians about a possible rejection by God if they abandon the hope of the gospel, but also unequivocally state that God can and will reject disobedient Christians. Such warning is explicitly found in 1 Corinthians 10 and 11:27-32, and is implied in Galatians 6:7, the text dealing with sowing and reaping. Reference has already been made to 1 Corinthians 6:9, where the rhetorical question is raised, "Do you not know that wrongdoers will not inherit the kingdom of God?"and to Galatians 5:21b, "I am warning you, as I warned you before: those who do such things will not inherit the kingdom of God." Since the last two texts[70] are found in contexts of exhortation addressed to Christians, they serve as a warning to those "in Christ" not to fall back into their prior, non-Christian patterns of behavior.

These preliminary references bring us to the single most important passage in this category of judgment texts: 1 Corinthians 5:1-8. It is one of the most troublesome Pauline judgment texts and the one most frequently used as a support for the argument that the baptized Christian is guaranteed salvation, particularly v. 5: "you are to hand this man over to Satan for the destruction of the flesh, so that his spirit may be saved in the day of the Lord." One scholar concludes his discussion of this passage with two unanswered questions: ". . . the saving of the πνεῦμα [Spirit]. This is an enigmatic statement. Does the baptized man possess a *character indelebilis*? Or is the intention precisely that the Spirit should be taken from him?"[71]

Those who interpret this verse as an indication of assured salvation in the present are all dependent on what has become the widely accepted translation of the Greek text, typified by the Revised Standard Version: ". . . you are to deliver this man to Satan for the destruction of the flesh, that his spirit may be saved in the day of the Lord Jesus." But where in the Greek text does one find any "his" [*autou*] that would allow for the translation "his spirit" rather than "the spirit"? It simply does not exist! Is there any other contextual warrant for translating "spirit" as the condemned person's spirit, other than the exegetical bias of "the introspective conscience of the West"?[72] Much to be preferred is the more literal translation of the King James Version: "To deliver such a one into Satan for the destruction of the flesh, that the spirit may be saved in the day of the Lord Jesus."[73]

This more literal translation does assist us in understanding Paul's intention, for by taking seriously the fact that Paul refers to "the spirit" rather than "his spirit," one is forced to rethink the entire meaning of these verses. Paul, in fact, is not at all referring to the offender's spirit, but to *God's* Spirit present in the Corinthian congregation.[74] He is telling the Corinthians to cast out the work of the flesh and to return it to its proper source, Satan, so that God's Spirit may continue to be present and thus preserve the congregation for the last day (see 1 Cor 1:7-8). This understanding stands parallel to the succeeding verses, which speak of the old and the new lump, and it coheres very well with 1 Corinthians 3:16-17: "Do you not know that you are God's temple and that God's Spirit dwells in you? If anyone destroys God's temple, God will destroy that person. For God's temple is holy, and you are that temple." In fact, this understanding concurs with much of the exhortation present in 1 Corinthians, namely, that the presence of God's spirit in the Corinthian church by no means leads to guaranteed assurances about their status before God (e.g., see 1 Cor 10:5-6, 12). Thus, the focus of Paul's concern in 1 Corinthians 5 is not primarily on one person's sin, but the arrogance of a congregation which would tolerate this and fail to realize that the presence of such "fleshly" actions jeopardizes the entire church's standing before God. His mandate is clear: rid yourselves of all corruption so that God's spirit may be saved, that is, may continue to dwell in your midst (1 Cor 3:16). Commenting on the function of the Spirit in this verse, one leading commentary on 1 Corinthians asserts that "for Paul the Spirit is not a habitual possession, but a gift, and moreover a gift to the community."[75]

This interpretation found in 1 Corinthians 5:5 of the Spirit's function within the life of the Corinthian congregation is similar to other statements made by Paul. In 1 Corinthians itself, in addition to 3:16-17, one should note the relevant discussion about the Spirit and the flesh in 2:10–3:4, which serves as the substructure of the practical implications and actions taken in chapter 5. Also, Paul's comment in Galatians 5:5 is helpful for an understanding of 1 Corinthians 5:5: "For through the Spirit, by faith, we eagerly wait for the hope of righteousness." Since it is only through the Spirit that one hopes for the final gift on the last day, it is critical for the congregation, by faith, to permit God's Spirit to dwell in its midst. It is for this reason that Paul must outline so carefully the radical difference between the desire of the flesh and of the Spirit in Galatians 5:16-26, and must categorically state in 5:21b: "I am warning you, as I warned you before: those who do such things will not inherit the kingdom of God." Paul is quite explicit that the gift of the Spirit at baptism (1 Cor 12:12-13) does not grant an indelible mark that inevitably leads to salvation. Rather, the one who has been baptized must continue to receive and share in the gift of God's Spirit (Phil 2:1) and, as a result, be obedient to his will. Even the deutero-Pauline letter to the Ephesians (4:30) recognizes that it is possible to "grieve the Holy Spirit." Apparently, both the Corinthians and the Galatians were in danger of confusing the gift of the Spirit with the full payment, rather than recognizing it to be only the first installment (2 Cor 1:22) of that which is yet to come if the one in Christ continues to participate in the gifts of the Spirit.

Although Paul's primary concern in 1 Corinthians 5 is with the Christian community, his comments concerning the sinner do have important implications for the overall theme concerning the relationship between justification and last judgment. The apostle's conclusion with regard to this offender appears to be clear and consistent: anyone who is baptized, justified, and a member of the church but who is not obedient to the gift and possibility of the new existence resulting from Christ's death and resurrection becomes like a cancerous growth within the Body of Christ, which is also the point of his language in 1 Corinthians 5: "Do you not know that a little yeast leavens the whole batch of dough? Clean out the old yeast so that you may be a new batch, as you really are unleavened. For our paschal lamb, Christ, has been sacrificed. Therefore, let us celebrate the festival, not with the old yeast, the yeast of malice and evil, but with the unleavened bread of sincerity and truth" (1 Cor 5:6-8). He who is disobedient lives in the realm of Satan, in the realm of the flesh, and thus corrupts the Body of Christ. Both in his formula of exclusion in 1 Corinthians 5:5 and in his citation of Deuteronomy 17:7 in 1 Corinthians 5:13, "Drive out the wicked person from among you," Paul is very consistent: the church member who is flagrantly disobedient no longer belongs to the realm of those who are being saved, but to the realm of those who are perishing (1 Cor 1:18). The apostle urges his congregation to acknowledge the obvious for the sake of the Spirit.

Not unimportant to this entire discussion concerning the moral life and accountability as well as to the more immediate dialogue concerning the Holy Spirit in selected Pauline texts is the ethical reminder that Paul gives to the believers in Thessalonica:

> Finally, brothers and sisters, we ask and urge you in the Lord Jesus that, as you learned from us how you ought to live and to please God (as, in fact, you are doing), you should do so more and more. For you know what instructions we gave you through the Lord Jesus. For this is the will of God, your sanctification: that you abstain from fornication; that each one of you know how to control your own body in holiness and honor, not with lustful passion, like the Gentiles who do not know God; that no one wrong or exploit a brother or sister in this matter, because the Lord is an avenger in all these things, just as we have already told you beforehand and solemnly warned you. For God did not call us to impurity but in holiness. Therefore whoever rejects this rejects not human authority but God, who also gives his Holy Spirit to you. (1 Thess 4:1-8)

The importance of this new lifestyle in Christ, so radically different from the paganism of Roman Thessalonica, is reinforced by references to God, the Lord Jesus, and the Holy Spirit; and the fact that the Holy Spirit is linked to the moral life in general and its sexual expression in particular is striking. The similarity to 1 Corinthians 5 is unmistakable.

By way of summary, Käsemann's remarks with regard to 1 Corinthians 11:26-34 are appropriate to this discussion: "The self-manifestation of Christ calls men to obedience and this means that, at the same time it calls them to account before the final Judge who is already today acting within his community as he will act towards the world on the Last Day—he bestows salvation by setting men within his lordship and, if they spurn this lordship, they then experience this act of rejection as a self-incurred sentence of death."[76]

4.2.3 Discipleship and the Corinthian Church[77]

The earliest extant literature of the New Testament is the Pauline corpus of letters (ca. 43-55 CE). While the gospels refer to events prior to Paul, that is, to Jesus and his ministry, they are actually written in their present form at a considerably later time (ca. 68-95 CE). In what follows I hope to show how Paul applies with consistency the principle of dynamic actualization. In virtually every one of his letters he is attempting to clarify and actualize the dynamic word as he had proclaimed it previously in oral form to his congregations. It is evident from these letters that Paul never preaches inarticulate messages to generalized audiences; rather he attempts at all times to communicate the gospel of God (Rom 1:1; 1 Thess 2:2) to the appropriate and specific needs of the congregation addressed. By taking each of his audiences and their requirements with utmost seriousness, Pauline theology is given its power and, at times, its stinging specificity.

As is evident in the gospel of Matthew, the life of the disciple needs guidance to avoid the various perils and temptations, both moral and intellectual, that continually confront the faithful. Although in a radically different setting at the center of the Graeco-Roman world, the apostle Paul needs to give similar direction to the church that he had helped to establish in Corinth. Throughout this communication Paul is concerned not merely with repeating the gospel and the tradition of the church but with explaining their meaning and relevance for day-to-day Christian existence. One specific example of this process can be caught sight of in 1 Corinthians 15, the most extensive treatment of the resurrection of the body in the New Testament.

Some familiarity with the Greek city of Corinth and its setting in Hellenistic culture will be helpful to understand 1 Corinthians 15. Situated on the Isthmus of Corinth and serving as the capital of the Roman province of Achaia, Corinth was an important seaport and commercial center linking east with west. The Romans destroyed the city in 146 BCE, but after some one hundred years Julius Caesar refounded the city as a Roman colony. The old Corinth was often referred to in literature as a center of immorality and vice, and from Paul's correspondence with the Corinthian church one has every reason to believe that the new Corinth carried on this reputation. The well-known proverb "not for every man is the voyage to Corinth"[78] became synonymous with practices such as fornication. These features, together with the biannual celebration of the Isthmian games, indicate the cosmopolitan nature of Corinth.

Corinth was influenced in many ways by Roman Hellenism, a civilization that spread throughout the Mediterranean world as a result of Alexander the Great's military adventures and conquests in the period 334–325 BCE. One of the characteristics of this period was religious individualism; the state no longer controlled worship; hence citizens chose their own gods. Foreign deities became commonplace, and the identification of Greek gods with foreign deities was not unusual. Foreign gods such as Isis and Serapis as well as the Greek deities Apollo and Aphrodite were well known in Corinth. The ruins of the temple of the goddess Aphrodite can still be seen on the acropolis (highest point) of Corinth, and the remnants of the majestic temple to the god Apollo are still present in the area adjacent to the *agora* (marketplace) of ancient Corinth. In addition, an inscription discloses that there was a Jewish synagogue in the city. Briefly, then, the Corinth Paul knew was a place of religious pluralism and syncretism. It is precisely such an environment that led to so many of the ethical dilemmas that confronted the Corinthian believers in Christ.

4.2.3a *Resurrection and the Theology of the Body*

In 1 Corinthians 15 Paul must address some in the Corinthian church who either deny or fundamentally misunderstand the significance of bodily resurrection for the Christian believer. It is interesting to observe how he deals with this problem. Does he simply tell them they are wrong and that they ought to believe what they were first taught? No; he indeed reminds them in only seven verses of the gospel he taught them, but he then proceeds with fifty-one verses of explanation! A closer look at the opening of the chapter will be instructive.

This chapter is a classic example of how Paul tries to actualize the contents of the gospel in a particular situation, in this case in reference to a misunderstanding about resurrection. Paul begins: "Now I would remind you, brothers and sisters, of the good news that I proclaimed to you, which you in turn received, in which also you stand, through which also you are being saved, if you hold firmly to the message that I proclaimed to you—unless you have come to believe in vain" (vv. 1-2). For Paul, the way to tackle the problem is not in the first place to listen to everyone's opinion on the matter or to give his own opinion; the starting point is the gospel he proclaimed to them and that they have received. Their existence as believers in Christ is rooted in this very gospel, and only as they hold fast to it will the salvation already initiated and experienced be culminated on the last day. Characteristic of Paul's understanding of Christian existence is the realization that one can believe in vain, a state of affairs that develops when one no longer clings to the content of the gospel in a steadfast manner. In short, although there can be great confidence, there is no *guaranteed* conclusion to the process of salvation begun in baptism.

Paul, having indicated to the Corinthians that the starting point for a discussion of the current situation must be the gospel, proceeds to give a summary of it. That Paul himself did not write this summary is suggested by his use of the technical terms "to receive" and "to hand on," terms used in Judaism to indicate the transmission of tradition. Paul continues: "For I handed on to you as of first importance what I in turn had received: that Christ died for our sins in accordance with the scriptures, and that he was buried, and that he was raised on the third day in accordance with the scriptures, and that he appeared to Cephas, then to the twelve" (vv. 3-5). According to this account, the foundation of the Christian proclamation is Jesus' death, burial, resurrection, and postresurrection appearances, with death and resurrection standing at the center. As we shall see, virtually every element of this traditional confession is explained in the course of chapter 15. But before Paul proceeds to a further elaboration, he adds in verse 11: "Whether then it was I or they, so we proclaim and so you have come to believe." Not only Paul, but also the other Christian leaders with whom the Corinthians were acquainted (Apollos and Peter), proclaim this identical gospel.

Which early Christian groups would have urged that "there is no resurrection of the dead" (v. 12)? There are two possibilities: (1) Some Christians in Corinth might have been influenced by the general Hellenistic anti-body attitude that would look at a concept such as physical resurrection as absurd. Virtually every church father in the early centuries of Christianity had to write a tract in defense of the resurrection because of this widespread dualistic attitude, which argued that the body was an evil prison from which the soul would be liberated at death. (2) Some Corinthians might have been attracted to a perspective, or elements thereof, that developed more fully in its Christian form during the second century, a heresy commonly referred to as gnosticism. Given the syncretism of the age one should not draw too rigid a distinction between these alternatives.

Although gnosticism originated as a pre-Christian movement, it rapidly merged with aspects of early Christian thought and became a major deviant movement. The development of a canon, ecclesiastical authority, creeds, and doctrines, just to cite a few examples, were in direct response to the threat of gnosticism by the catholic and orthodox church. Since the term *gnosticism* is a catch-all term that covers widely divergent movements that are syncretistic in nature, it is difficult to give it a precise definition. Features characteristic of some gnostic movements include a sharp dualism between the heavenly worlds and this evil world, and the belief that this world came into being accidentally or by an inferior god; that some humans contain a divine spark in the midst of their evil, corrupt bodies; that a heavenly redeemer, often Jesus, descends from above to rescue through knowledge (*gnōsis*, thus "gnosticism") those who have this spark; that since this world and the body are evil, ethics are of no consequence. In view of such beliefs most gnostic Christians would be reluctant to assert that the present physical body would be transformed at some future point. This perspective may have influenced some in the Corinthian church.

This second possibility, that the believers in Corinth were influenced by some aspects of a Christian proto-gnosticism, as opposed to the more fully mature developments of the second century, is more likely since it is against a less established perspective that Paul appears to be arguing in the remainder of chapter 15. After initiating his argument in verses 12-19 with reference to the fact of Christ's resurrection as previously summarized in the confession and then developing its implications, Paul proceeds to dwell on primarily two facts, the first of which is that the resurrection of the Christian has not yet taken place but will take place in the future. This argument is contained in verses 20-34, and we receive good insight into his perspective in verse 23: "But each in his own order: Christ the first fruits, then at his coming those who belong to Christ." Not in the present, not immediately after death, but at the consummation of history is the moment of resurrection for those who have died in Christ. In other words, the apostle is stressing the futurity of the resurrection. Paul, in verses 35-37, argues against the idea of the immortality of the soul; he attempts rather, to demonstrate to these Corinthian Christians that the future resurrection will be a *bodily* resurrection. Representative of Paul's thinking is verse 46: "But it is not the spiritual that is first, but the physical, and then the spiritual."

The thrust of the argument makes more sense when one takes note of a passage in 2 Timothy 2:16-18 where the writer refers to "Hymenaeus and Philetus, who have swerved from the truth by claiming that the resurrection has already taken place." When one reads this together with a noncanonical document known as the *Letter to Rheginus*,[79] one realizes that there were Christians in the first and second centuries who believed that they had already experienced a *spiritual* resurrection; for many this experience of a spiritual resurrection was conflated with the moment of baptism. To such a distortion Paul responds: by no means! Resurrection is future, and it is to be bodily. Both of these dimensions need to be examined with some care.

First, Paul's stress on the future consummation of salvation is consistent throughout his correspondence. Particularly relevant to the theme of future resurrection is Philippians 3:8 and following, especially verses 10-11: "I want to know Christ and the power of his resurrection and the sharing of his sufferings by becoming like him in his death, if somehow I may attain the resurrection from the dead." Paul stresses that the gift of resurrection is future, and it is not something immediately guaranteed, a point underscored by his use of the subjunctive (indicating something indefinite or possible, rather than a fact) in this verse and by his further elaboration in verses 12-14: "Not that I have already obtained this or have already reached the goal; but I press on to make it my own, because Christ Jesus has made me his own. Beloved, I do not consider that I have made it my own; but this one thing I do: forgetting what lies behind and straining forward to what lies ahead, I press on toward the goal for the prize of the heavenly call of God in Christ Jesus." As we have already had opportunity to observe, the beginning of the Christian life is marked by justification; but that is only the *beginning* of a trajectory of growth. The first fruits of salvation that are experienced in the process of justification/baptism continue to be worked out in the course of living the new life in Christ ("work out your own salvation with fear and trembling," Phil 2:12c) but are only consummated and brought to fulfillment on the last day.

Second, as a corollary to this stress on the futurity of resurrection there is the emphasis that it will be bodily. At this point an unmistakable tension exists between the Pauline conception and the Platonic conception because the ultimate objective of the apostle's teaching is not separation of the body and the spirit but transformation of the body. Two verses in 1 Corinthians 15 in particular deserve some further comment: verse 35, "But someone will

ask, 'How are the dead raised? With what kind of body do they come?'"
and verse 44, "It is sown a physical body, it is raised a spiritual body. If there
is a physical body, there is also a spiritual body." Paul is stressing both a
continuity between our present and future existence by his use of the term
"body" (Greek: *sōma)* as well as a discontinuity between the two, a fact
suggested by the distinction made between physical and spiritual.

If one follows the argument in verses 35-37 carefully, Paul appears to be
saying that there is a continuity of our individual existence (body), although
the form of that existence will be transformed from a physical to a spiritual
body on the last day: "For the trumpet will sound, and the dead will be
raised imperishable, and we will be changed. For this perishable body must
put on imperishability, and this mortal body must put on immortality"
(vv. 52-53). Upon further reflection this thought process is not really so
unimaginable as some might think. Just think of yourself for a moment at
ages five, twenty, forty-five, and seventy. Quite obviously your physical
appearance will be substantially different from decade to decade, yet those
who have known you well as a child would readily recognize your unique
personality at age seventy. Despite the fact that virtually all the cells in your
body have been replaced with new cells, there is still something distinctively
recognizable about you. It is likely that this is what Paul means by the term
"body." To use more contemporary language, each of us has a unique
genetic program from the moment of conception that remains the same
despite fairly radical physical changes during growth. This program determines a specific development that makes each of us unique, and who has
not wondered at the overwhelming and momentous transition from *in utero*
to *ex utero* that makes manifest the miracle of human life? Paul appears to
be suggesting that, although there is continuity of individual existence that
can be likened today to a genetic program, after death at the resurrection
there will be a further transformation, and at that time the believer will
receive a new spiritual body. Comparable perhaps to the change between *in
utero* and *ex utero* will be the transformation from this physical, in-the-
world existence to a spiritual one with the Lord. At that point of consummation the words of the prophets Isaiah and Hosea will be fulfilled:

"Death has been swallowed up in victory."
"Where, O death, is your victory?
    Where, O death, is your sting?"
The sting of death is sin, and the power of sin is the law. But thanks
be to God, who gives us the victory through our Lord Jesus Christ.
(1 Cor 15:54-57)

Thus far, then, it has been possible to show how Paul creatively and dynamically actualizes the gospel message so as to meet the specific needs of the Corinthian church in connection with his interpretation of the resurrection. Chapter 15 is not, by any means, an isolated example of this process. All of 1 Corinthians, from beginning to end, is an illustration of the process of dynamic actualization.

4.2.3b Life in Christ as Cruciform Existence

Another dimension of the gospel that Paul preached to the Corinthians was "that Christ died for our sins in accordance with the scriptures" (1 Cor 15:3). The fact that their Lord suffered and died should have important ethical implications for his followers, central among them the characteristic of humility and openness toward the needs of the neighbor. Owing to a high degree of immaturity and arrogance in the Corinthian church, however, a sizeable proportion in this congregation misunderstood the gospel as a message that allowed them to think of themselves as superior religious beings; they understood the gospel as giving them insight and knowledge that elevated them above ordinary folk, a misinterpretation quite intelligible in light of their Hellenistic philosophical background. For this reason Paul states: "Your boasting is not a good thing" (1 Cor 5:6a). Elsewhere he warns them: "But some of you, thinking that I am not coming to you, have become arrogant. But I will come to you soon, if the Lord wills, and I will find out not the talk of these arrogant people but their power. For the kingdom of God depends not on talk but on power" (1 Cor 4:18-20).

This arrogance leads to the view that the new life in Christ is already perfected, a view Paul does not share and one he refutes sharply and quite sarcastically. "Already you have all you want! Already you have become rich! Quite apart from us you have become kings! Indeed, I wish that you had become kings, so that we might be kings with you!" (1 Cor 4:8). What a pity it is, Paul laments, that you really are not perfected, because I would like to share in that kind of existence myself! Instead, the reality of the situation is that we "are fools for the sake of Christ, but you are wise in Christ. We are weak, but you are strong. You are held in honor, but we in disrepute" (1 Cor 4:10). These divergent understandings of the practical implications of the Christian gospel become the subject of many discussions in 1 Corinthians.

This position of boasting and arrogance is not limited to the realm of abstract pronouncements and theologizing; it has definite implications for the day-to-day behavior of these Corinthian Christians. Their arrogance leads to dissensions bordering on disunity, criticisms of Paul himself for his lack of oratorical eloquence, as well as immorality, selfishness, disregard of the lesser brother or sister, misunderstanding of the gifts and grace of God, failure to understand the church as a community, and a distorted view of the resurrection. It is into this concrete situation that Paul must actualize the gospel message. The Corinthian church has real needs and problems, and Paul must now address them precisely, relevantly, and cogently. Before one can observe Paul's process of actualization, one needs to examine the negative consequence of the Corinthians' arrogance as well as Paul's response to it.

Pride, which lies at the root of arrogance, is hardly a characteristic that leads to community building. By its very definition it elevates an individual or a small group above others, and this has a splintering and divisive effect. As Reinhold Niebuhr put it so well, pride is nothing other than placing yourself into a position where you can spit down on your neighbor.[80] And so it is not surprising to find arrogance generating a predisposition toward disunity at the midpoint of the first century. In his opening remarks in 1 Corinthians 1, Paul appeals to the Corinthians "that there be no divisions among you" (vv. 10-11). "What I mean is that each of you says, 'I belong to Paul,' or 'I belong to Apollos,' or 'I belong to Cephas,' or 'I belong to Christ'" (v. 12). Then Paul comes to the heart of the matter with the question "Has Christ been divided?" to which the unmistakable response must be negative (v. 13).

The view that early Christianity is a perfect model for all successive followers of Jesus Christ to imitate literally is clearly undermined in 1 Corinthians, as well as elsewhere in the New Testament. The early church had the same frailties and difficulties as every other subsequent Christian generation. Since this is the case, the way in which such difficulties are resolved should be particularly illuminating for the contemporary church, where many similar issues are replicated, not least the tendencies toward disunity and fragmentation present in the early Jesus movement.

Already in the mid-first century these Corinthian Christians are rallying around different heroes: Paul, Apollos, Cephas, Christ. For this reason Paul writes with a sense of despair that "when you come together it is not for the better but for the worse. For, to begin with, when you come together as a church, I hear that there are divisions among you" (1 Cor 11:17b-18). What is the logic for these divided loyalties? Some wished to elevate Paul as their leader/hero for the obvious reason that he was both an apostle and the founder of the community. Apollos, Paul's successor, apparently possessed oratorical skills that pleased many in this Hellenistic environment, skills that Paul by his own testimony did not possess (1 Cor 2:1-5) and for the absence of which he was roundly criticized (see 2 Cor 10:10). Acts 18:24 describes Apollos as "an eloquent man, well versed in the scriptures." The references to Cephas and Christ are more difficult. Cephas was clearly the most important figure in the Jesus movement at this time and perhaps had even visited Corinth; either way he was well known. If one is going to select a hero, some are undoubtedly asking, "Why not go directly to the head man in Jerusalem?" This group may also have been attracted to Peter's more conservative Jewish-Christian background. Whether the reference to Christ represents the leader of a fourth party of arrogant elitists or represents those disgusted with the party strife is difficult to determine. Given the tone of the remainder of 1 Corinthians, there is much to be said for the position of some recent commentators that the "Christ party" is a fourth group of arrogant, elitist Christians to whom much of the remainder of the letter may be addressed. "Has Christ been divided? Was Paul crucified for you?" (1:13). In demonstrating the absurdity of giving a positive answer to these questions, Paul must defend himself and the message he proclaims, as well as deflate the boasting of the Corinthians and clarify the relationship of apostles and servants to Jesus Christ. The task for Paul is not an easy one since he has to contend with religious presuppositions and philosophical categories of thought alien to his understanding of the gospel, a situation not dissimilar to what the Church Catholic confronts in the contemporary situation.

Paul forcefully asserts that their arrogance is at odds with the gospel as it was originally proclaimed to them. Its content, the power of the cross of Christ, is not a path to overconfident religious perfection. The religious hero of Christianity is not some divine being who is elevated above ordinary men and women, but one who was crucified. At this point the Jesus movement breaks sharply with its culture. "For Jews demand signs and Greeks desire wisdom, but we proclaim Christ crucified, a stumbling block to Jews and foolishness to Gentiles, but to those who are the called, both Jews and Greeks, Christ the power of God and the wisdom of God" (1 Cor 1:22-24). The ethical consequence that the religious hero for the early followers of Jesus is a crucified messiah will be given attention throughout 1 Corinthians, and it will issue in a repeated call to humility, concern for the weaker brother, and the upbuilding of the church.

Already here in chapter 1, Paul draws some conclusions from the fact that the messiah whom the Corinthians proclaim is a crucified messiah. When one says "yes" to the call of Christ, it implies neither immediate perfection nor an automatic guarantee of salvation. Rather, the life of the disciple is a process in sanctification, and here in 1:18 it is appropriately expressed in participial form: "For the message about the cross is foolishness to those who are perishing, but to us who are being saved it is the power of God." Note well the phrase "to us who are *being* saved." This understanding of the life of discipleship as both a process of growth and obedience to the will of God is a quality many of the Corinthians overlooked; for this reason the apostle must frequently and in varied ways call attention to these distinctive characteristics throughout this first letter to the Corinthians.

Paul must also challenge the Corinthian perception of what it means to be an apostle. Here, too, he must demonstrate that the call to be an apostle of Jesus Christ is not at all similar to the expectations of Hellenistic culture. The criteria for evaluation are not philosophical erudition or rhetorical skill but faithfulness to the gospel of the crucified Lord. "When I came to you, brothers and sisters, I did not come proclaiming the mystery of God to you in lofty words or wisdom. For I decided to know nothing among you except Jesus Christ, and him crucified" (1 Cor 2:1-2).

The Corinthian view of apostleship, significantly influenced by Hellenistic culture, leads them to misunderstand the relation of Christian workers to one another. The relationship is not marked by competition to outperform the others as is the case among some of the wandering preachers and missionaries in their environment. Rather, all teachers and preachers are subject to the Lord: "What then is Apollos? What is Paul? Servants through whom you came to believe, as the Lord assigned to each. I planted, Apollos watered, but God gave the growth. So neither the one who plants nor the one who waters is anything, but only God who gives the growth" (1 Cor 3:5-7). Thus Paul must call attention to the fact that the foundation of the church is Jesus Christ and that this decisive factor reduces to absurdity the rivalry that is developing in Corinth. Appropriately Paul concludes the chapter with this exhortation: "So let no one boast about human leaders" (1 Cor 3:21).

It should now be increasingly apparent that when Paul first proclaimed the gospel to these Corinthians they perceived it through the religious, philosophical, and cultural perspective of their situation. This led to misunderstandings and distortions. Paul's task, having been alerted to these problems by Chloe's people and a letter from some in the Corinthian congregation (1 Cor 7:1), is to clarify, redefine, and make concrete the gospel of the cross for these Corinthians in the midst of their cultural enticements. Similarly, contemporary biblical scholarship employing a Trinitarian hermeneutic has a responsibility to guide Western Christianity living in the midst of relativistic secular/pagan societies that produce similar temptations. Let us now examine more closely how Paul applied the gospel to the cultural contradictions present in ancient Corinth.

4.2.3c *The Community of Love*

The arrogance of the Corinthian Christians led to a distorted view of discipleship. Specific issues included the relationship of the individual to the community as well as the question of individual freedom and rights within the ethical structure of the church as the Body of Christ existing in the midst of a pagan environment.

As was explored more fully in the discussion of Paul's use of the term "justification," the apostle essentially views the person as belonging to one of two specific social arenas: the world or the Body of Christ, the church. The world is dominated by the power of sin, and this life in Adam results in behavior characterized by "fornication, impurity, licentiousness, idolatry, sorcery, enmities, strife, jealousy, anger, quarrels, dissensions, factions, envy, drunkenness, carousing, and things like these" (Gal 5:19-21). The church, in contrast, is characterized by the power of the Holy Spirit, and this life in Christ results in a lifestyle characterized by "love, joy, peace, patience, kindness, generosity, faithfulness, gentleness, and self-control" (Gal 5:22-23).

According to the Pauline letters there is no such thing as "individual" freedom because every human being is bound within one of these two groups; this immediately puts a severe limitation on "freedom" and specifically diminishes the view that an individual is *free* to act at will. In fact, Paul argues that human beings do not inherently have the ability to move from life under the power of sin to life in the power of the spirit. The agonizing cry of Rom 7:15 ("I do not understand my own actions. For I do not do what I want, but I do the very thing I hate") refers precisely to this human dilemma. The ability to move from Adam to Christ, from the world to the church, is a gift and a capability given by Jesus Christ and can only be received but not generated by the believer. Freedom for Paul has clearly defined limits; it involves a movement generated by Christ from one well-defined social realm to the other. Freedom is the transition from one to another, and this is a *gift*: it is not and cannot be claimed as a human achievement.

Paul uses the term "slavery" to define the human situation. One is a slave either to the power of sin or to the power of the Spirit; freedom is the transition from one form of servanthood to the other, from one that leads to death to one that leads to life. This perspective of Paul should not really startle us if we have some acquaintance with Paul Tillich's phrase "ultimate concern."[81] Every human being, argues Tillich, has an ultimate concern, for example, power, ambition, wealth, God; and it is this ultimate concern that shapes decisions and activities. We are free to act only within the parameters of our ultimate concern; we are, Tillich argues, slaves to that ultimate concern, a point that Paul articulates in Rom 6:16: "Do you not know that if you present yourselves to anyone as obedient slaves, you are slaves of the one whom you obey, either of sin, which leads to death, or of obedience, which leads to righteousness?"

Given their cultural context, the Corinthians misunderstood Paul's initial preaching and held a quite opposite view of freedom. They imagined that their new religion released them from all human limitations and empowered them toward an unrestricted spiritual elitism. This view not only elevated the individual above the community so that superiority was encouraged but it also made the existence of shared responsibility and concern within the community of disciples difficult, if not impossible.

Some of the problems that result from a distorted view of freedom as well as Paul's reaction to them on the basis of the gospel dominate much of the discussion in 1 Corinthians 5 to 14. Chapter 5 reviews the situation of a man for whom moral restraints have vanished to the point that he is having sexual relations with his father's wife! The apostle is incensed at this flagrant violation of the ethical behavior that is to characterize the community in Christ. The only appropriate response that the gospel allows is one of reprimand and discipline.

Those who have been influenced by a permissive culture might well ask whether this is not a rigid and narrow understanding of the gospel? What about mercy and grace? Is not Paul's attitude incongruent with the teaching of Jesus? Paul would surely challenge such an assertion and would, undoubtedly, be supportive of Dietrich Bonhoeffer's efforts to halt the ever-present danger of gospel reductionism, and his words are worth repeating. "Cheap grace means the justification of sin without the justification of the sinner. Grace alone does everything, they say, and so everything can remain as it is. . . . Well, then, let the Christian live like the rest of the world, let him model himself on the world's standards in every sphere of life, and not presumptuously aspire to live a different life under grace from his old life under sin. . . ."[82] Is not the challenge to such a distortion of grace and ethics as urgent today as it was to German Christianity in the 1930s? With Bonhoeffer one might well ask to what degree the ethical perspective as well as the public conversation of contemporary Christianity is decisively rooted in the teachings of Scripture?

Costly grace demands obedience to the will of God and understands that growth in discipleship requires discipline. As Paul affirms in Galatians 5, the believer in Christ is enabled by the Spirit here in the present to do the will of God and to separate from the behavior of the world. And so he can remind the Corinthian church: "But now I am writing to you not to associate with anyone who bears the name of brother or sister who is sexually immoral or greedy, or is an idolater, reviler, drunkard, or robber. Do not even eat with such a one" (1 Cor 5:11). Those in Christ have broken with a way of life dominated by the power of sin, which previously led to alienation from God; thus a return to such behavior cannot be tolerated. Here again this dual understanding of existence as either dominated by Adam or Christ, world or church, is a basic presupposition of Pauline theology. He emphasizes this in 1 Corinthians 6:9-11: "Do you not know that wrongdoers will not inherit the kingdom of God? Do not be deceived! Fornicators, idolaters, adulterers, male prostitutes, sodomites, thieves, the greedy, drunkards, revilers, robbers—none of these will inherit the kingdom of God. And this is what some of you used to be. But you were washed, you were sanctified, you were justified in the name of the Lord Jesus Christ and in the Spirit of our God." Precisely because those in Christ have been "washed," "sanctified," and "justified," the kind of immoral behavior referred to in 1 Corinthians 5 is unacceptable. And if persons persist in such behavior, as is apparently the case in Corinth, they must be removed from the community, not only because a contradiction exists between their confession and their behavior but also because their actions do genuine damage to the community.

Essential for the realization of Paul's perspective with regard to ecclesial discipline is his understanding of the church as the Body of Christ. For the apostle the new community in Christ is so tightly knit, such a cohesive social unit, that he can explicitly compare it to the human body in 1 Corinthians 12. The body is made up of many parts: fingers, eyes, ears, feet, and so forth. As one infected organ weakens the human body and must be attended to, so individual misbehavior must be healed lest it further infect and diminish the church's capacity to proclaim and live the gospel. The one member is so bonded to the others that "if one member suffers, all suffer together with it; if one member is honored, all rejoice together with it" (1 Cor 12:26). Given this standpoint, Paul is concerned not only about the one person who has disobeyed the will of God but also with the effect of that person's actions upon the whole. Precisely because the church is God's new batch of dough the apostle can urge: "Clean out the old yeast so that you may be a new batch, as you really are unleavened. For our paschal lamb, Christ, has been sacrificed. Therefore, let us celebrate the festival, not with the old yeast, the yeast of malice and evil, but with the unleavened bread of sincerity and truth" (1 Cor 5:7-8). What still belongs to the realm of flesh and not to the Spirit must be removed from the church as the Body of Christ.

The apostle and the community must provide correction and admonition so that each follower of Christ, and the congregation as a whole, will be sustained in obeying the will of God. Baptism does not bestow perfection, and when discipline and mutual support are absent it is possible to fall back into the old way of life and therefore to have believed in vain. Paul summarizes this matter well in 1 Corinthians 11:32: "But when we are judged by the Lord, we are disciplined so that we may not be condemned along with the world." As a result, the gospel must be specified and made relevant to every dimension of the new life in Christ.

The problem of individual freedom in relation to one's participation in the community of Christ can be seen from another dimension as well. In 1 Corinthians 6:1-8 the apostle raises another urgent issue of ecclesial life:

> When any of you has a grievance against another, do you dare to take it to court before the unrighteous, instead of taking it before the saints? Do you not know that the saints will judge the world? And if the world is to be judged by you, are you incompetent to try trivial cases? Do you not know that we are to judge angels—to say nothing of ordinary matters? If you have ordinary cases, then, do you appoint as judges those who have no standing in the church? I say this to your shame. Can it be that there is no one among you wise enough to decide between one believer and another, but a believer goes to court against a believer—and before unbelievers at that? In fact, to have lawsuits at all with one another is already a defeat for you. Why not rather be wronged? Why not rather be defrauded? But you yourselves wrong and defraud—and believers at that.

For those of us who live in a litigious society where many relationships of trust have broken down, these words may sound as strange as they did to the Corinthians living in the midst of a pagan society. Paul objects to those in Christ having lawsuits against one another because it is an exercise in pride that is bound to create animosity rather than reconciliation. When Paul argues in verse 7 that to "to have lawsuits at all with one another is already a defeat for you" he may well have in mind the words of Jesus about turning the other cheek. Further, to have lawsuits against one another is a very direct violation of *agapē,* love, the fundamental criterion for all decisions made in Christ. Since lawsuits must be decided in secular law courts, a distinctive responsibility of the church is undermined. It is the "saints [who] will judge the world" (6:2), the apostle argues, and not the other way around. In such situations the new ethic and lifestyle of the Body of Christ granted by the Holy Spirit has capitulated to the ethic of the world that was to have been discarded at baptism; for Paul such compromise cannot be tolerated. For Christians to believe that they are free to step outside the structures permitted by life in the new community in the service of self-interest must be repudiated. It is not accidental that the next verse reads: "Do you not know that wrongdoers will not inherit the kingdom of God? Do not be deceived!" (v. 9a).

Toward the middle of 1 Corinthians 6 we receive very specific insight into the Corinthian misunderstanding of the gospel. Their slogan is, "All things are lawful for me" (v. 12); yet Paul cautions, "not all things are beneficial" (10:23). 1 Corinthians 10:23 and 24 get to the heart of the misunderstanding between individual freedom and community responsibility: "'All things are lawful,' but not all things build up. Do not seek your own advantage, but that of the other." For the apostle, the sign of being a believer is not talk, but action—deeds that are concerned with the common good of the community as well as of its specific members.

The Corinthians attempted to justify a variety of activities with the slogan that in Christ "all things are lawful," including such things as temple prostitution and eating food offered to idols.[83] The Corinthians defended their freedom to eat food offered to idols on the basis of their "knowledge," and Paul is undoubtedly repeating their slogan in 8:1: "All of us possess knowledge." As is known from 1 Corinthians 12:8, Paul recognizes the importance of knowledge as a gift of the Spirit, but it, like all gifts of the Spirit, is subservient to the most important gift of all, love *(agapē).* Knowledge "puffs up"; whereas love "builds up" (8:1). Knowledge has the tendency to make individuals arrogant insofar as they believe that they have greater knowledge than others and are therefore superior. Love, however, is concerned with the other, especially the weak neighbor for whom Christ died, and it is such compassion that leads to the building up of the community. The incompleteness of knowledge is also referred to in verse 2: "Anyone who claims to know something does not yet have the necessary knowledge." A little knowledge has the tendency to make one heady, causing one to imagine that one knows more than one really does. To know as one ought to know is to be truly wise, and the more one knows, the more one is aware of how little one really does know! True knowledge leads to humility. For as Paul observes correctly in 1 Corinthians 13:9, our present knowledge is imperfect. These, then, are some of the reasons why Paul does not place knowledge in a central position in his efforts to advise the Corinthians on food offered to idols.

But what is the content of this knowledge to which the Corinthians refer? Paul apparently repeats their language in 8:4: "We know that 'no idol in the world really exists,' and that 'there is no God but one.'" On this basis some of the members of the congregation argued that it was perfectly acceptable to eat food that had been offered to pagan idols because a believer knows that such idols really do not exist, because "there is one God, the Father, from whom are all things and for whom we exist, and one Lord, Jesus Christ, through whom are all things and through whom we exist" (v. 6). Theoretically, Paul has no problem with this theological position; it is a correct assertion about the lordship of Christ. But to use this theological insight to support eating food offered to idols overlooks one important human dimension: "It is not everyone, however, who has this knowledge" (8:7). Indeed, some members of the church in Corinth are weak. Because their consciences are not yet fully mature in Christ they might believe that eating food that had been offered to an idol would in fact be an act of worship to such idols. And the result for such weak persons would be that "their conscience, being weak, is defiled" (v. 7).

The heart of the matter is expressed by the apostle in 8:9: "Only take care lest this liberty of yours somehow become a stumbling block to the weak." Freedom and knowledge do have a specific boundary beyond which they become demonic; that boundary is the point at which they cause the weak brother or sister to stumble. Thus, while sitting at table in an idol's temple is theoretically a possibility for the believer, it is to be avoided because "if others see you, who possess knowledge, eating in the temple of an idol, might they not, since their conscience is weak, be encouraged to the point of eating food sacrificed to idols?" (v. 10). The result of such action is that "by your knowledge this weak man is destroyed, the brother for whom Christ died" (v. 11).

The weak brother or sister is not to be viewed as some abstract and anonymous entity, but, rather, as the one for whom Christ died and therefore of infinite value; such a person dare not be disregarded, overlooked, or trampled upon. In verse 12 Paul intensifies the worth of this weak member. He urges the Corinthians to remember that when their personal freedom becomes more important than their concern for the weak among them, they are involved in sinning against members of their community and they "wound their conscience when it is weak" and, as a result, "you sin against Christ" (v. 12). This identification of the brother with Christ in 1 Corinthians is quite similar to the point being made in Matthew 25:40, "Truly I tell you, just as you did it to one of the least of these who are members of my family, you did it to me."

Paul's final conclusion to the argument in chapter 8 is this: "Therefore, if food is a cause of their falling, I will never eat meat, so that I may not cause one of them to fall" (8:13). A modern analogy might be this: if I am at a cocktail party with a friend who has a problem with alcohol, although I may be at liberty to drink a martini I will forgo this liberty for the sake of my friend and request instead a ginger ale. My freedom and my knowledge must never violate the law of love; to do so would allow my brother or sister to fall.

Just as the apostle had clarified such misunderstood topics as resurrection and idol meat, he also examines the tradition of the Lord's Supper in light of the Corinthian abuse of that communal meal. Paul's irritation with the Corinthian practice of the Lord's Supper is evident in 11:17: "Now in the following instructions I do not commend you, because when you come together it is not for the better but for the worse." When they gather together there are divisions and factions (11:18), and Paul is bold enough to tell the Corinthians that when they meet together "it is not really to eat the Lord's supper" (v. 20).

In order to understand the nature of Paul's concern one must realize that early Christians originally celebrated the "Lord's Supper" in the context of a common meal. It was, in fact, a supper; but because it was done in the name of their Lord it was quite naturally called "the *Lord's* Supper." The abuse set in when some members of the congregation set aside the communal nature of the meal and simply ate and drank their fill quite unmindful that by so doing there would not be enough for all. It appears as if members of the leisure class may have arrived early and began filling themselves without any regard for those of lesser status who might be delayed because of work-related responsibilities. Thus Paul chides them in verse 22: "What! Do you not have homes to eat and drink in? Or do you show contempt for the church of God and humiliate those who have nothing? What should I say to you? Should I commend you? In this matter I do not commend you!"

1 Corinthians 11:23-26 contains the earliest account of the words of institution. Paul adds in verse 26: "For as often as you eat this bread and drink the cup, you proclaim the Lord's death until he comes." Participation in the Lord's Supper is not intended as an opportunity for overindulgence or as some magical guarantee of salvation (so the tendency in 1 Corinthians

10) or merely another religious rite, but, rather, it must be understood as a participation in and remembrance of the death of their Lord. Participation in his death means participation in his community, and that should result in a lifestyle of humility that results in service to others and not some private ego trip resulting in boasting. The death of Jesus Christ must be proclaimed and lived "until he comes" (11:26). As the apostle already made clear in chapter 1, the follower of Jesus lives as a result of his death as well as in anticipation of God's final judgment and the fulfillment of his promises.

Since the confession of Christ's name alone is not an automatic assurance of God's favor on the last day, Paul adds some firm warnings in verse 27, proceeding in a manner similar to his earlier warnings in chapter 10. Having briefly reviewed the history of Israel, he concludes with these words in 10:5-6: "Nevertheless, God was not pleased with most of them, and they were struck down in the wilderness. Now these things occurred as examples for us, so that we might not desire evil as they did." And then in verse 12 we read, "So if you think you are standing, watch out that you do not fall." In like manner Paul exhorts this congregation in 11:28-29: "Examine yourselves, and only then eat of the bread and drink of the cup. For all who eat and drink without discerning the body, eat and drink judgment against themselves." Participation in the Lord's Supper is not a matter of inconsequence: it can result in either blessing or curse, salvation or condemnation. Given such critical consequences, those in Christ must examine themselves to be certain that they do not partake in "an unworthy manner" (v. 27) since the consequence of such participation would lead to their "condemnation" (v. 34, RSV).

In 1 Corinthians 12 Paul discusses the nature of the church in relationship to spiritual gifts. As is evident from Paul's letter, these believers in Christ prided themselves in having received such gifts. Paul must remind them that gifts of the Spirit are not to be used for personal glorification but for "the common good." God is the giver and provides a diversity of gifts for the upbuilding of the church but not as a source of individual boasting over the other. "To each is given the manifestation of the Spirit for the common good" (v. 7). To further illustrate "the common good," Paul develops the analogy of the church as the Body of Christ. "Indeed, the body does not consist of one member but of many" (v. 14). While such an assertion may strike us as obvious, it is essential to call the Corinthians' attention to this matter because of their hyperindividualism and their failure to grasp that their existence in Christ involves participation in a new social relationship. Some are singing their own praises, including the fact that they can speak in tongues (1 Cor 13:1; 14). Precisely because of such tendencies Paul writes:

"If the foot would say, 'Because I am not a hand, I do not belong to the body,' that would not make it any less a part of the body. And if the ear would say, 'Because I am not an eye, I do not belong to the body,' that would not make it any less a part of the body. If the whole body were an eye, where would the hearing be? If the whole body were hearing, where would the sense of smell be? But as it is, God arranged the members in the body, each one of them, as he chose" (1 Cor 12:15-18). The point is this: God chose what gift he was to give each member of the Body of Christ, gifts that are to be used in a cooperative and complementary way for the effective functioning of the church. The cohesive interaction must be such that "there may be no dissension within the body, but the members may have the same care for one another. If one member suffers, all suffer together with it; if one member is honored, all rejoice together with it" (1 Cor 12:25-26). Just as when one human organ is infected it has an effect on the whole body, in like manner the church as the Body of Christ is deeply affected by the actions of the individual believers.

One could well argue that Paul's discussion of love (*agapē*) in 1 Corinthians 13 is the high point of his letter to the Corinthians as well as the basic criterion he uses in applying the gospel to the challenges presented by this congregation. Not only in this chapter but in 1 Corinthians 14 as well, he expects that the gift of love is to be the criterion used in all decisions affecting the life of the church. For Paul *agapē* has its source in God's self-giving and self-sacrifice, demonstrated in the suffering and death of his son. Love is the supreme gift of the Spirit without which the other gifts have no inherent value. Since this cruciform love is anchored in the suffering and generous love of God in Christ, its constant concern is for the other, the neighbor, the weak person, so that it will lead to the "upbuilding and encouragement and consolation" (1 Cor 14:3) of the Body of Christ. *Agapē* uses the individual as an instrument for the edification of the common good.

Paul begins chapter 13 by citing a number of spiritual gifts the Corinthian Christians held in high regard: speaking in tongues, having prophetic power, understanding mysteries and knowledge, having faith, being charitable, and even being willing to die as a martyr. If these gifts are not performed in the context of love, that is, for the edification of the church rather than for self-enhancement, such gifts are empty and void. It is particularly noteworthy that Paul makes faith, even a faith that can "remove mountains" (1 Cor 13:2), subservient to love. Faith, as the apostle says in Gal 5:6, must always be active in love. Faith that does not manifest its relationship with God in acts of concrete love is without value. This point is underlined in the conclusion to chapter 13: "And now faith, hope, and love abide, these three; and the greatest of these is love" (v. 13).

In verses 4-7 the characteristics of love are described, and in verses 8 and following the apostle gives support for the superiority of love to the other spiritual gifts. "Love never ends" because it has an enduring value whereas all other gifts have only a temporally limited efficacy for the community (v. 8). Prophecies, that is, the critical application of God's word to specific situations, whether they be of Amos, Jeremiah, or Martin Luther King, Jr., are partial and time constrained by the very focus of their intention. The condition of inspiration that allows one to speak in tongues does not continue without end. Knowledge, it is said, is only partial and "will come to an end" (vv. 8-10). All one has to do is to reflect on the status of any scientific discipline, for example, physics, at the beginning and the end of the twentieth century to realize how quickly knowledge advances and revises previously held hypotheses. Paul concludes his great exposition on love with the reminder that existence in Christ is still being lived in a situation of eschatological reservation, in an "already/not yet" situation. Already now we share in the good gifts of God's act of salvation in Christ Jesus, but not yet in its final, fulfilled, and consummated state, a hope that is still before us. For this reason, knowledge and prophecy, articulated in this "not yet" form, are still partial and incomplete (v. 10). "For now we see in a mirror, dimly, but then we will see face to face. Now I know only in part; then I will know fully, even as I have been fully known" (v. 12).

To make absolutely sure that his point about the necessity and primacy of love has not been misunderstood, Paul singles out one gift of the Spirit, speaking in tongues, for special attention in 1 Corinthians 14. It is a splendid chapter in which Paul impressively attempts to actualize the gospel, specifically concerning the relationship of love to speaking in tongues; in addition, it contains a whole host of practical suggestions for the life of the church.

Already the first verse is filled with rich insight: "Pursue love and strive for the spiritual gifts, and especially that you may prophesy" (14:1). Here, as in Gal 5:22, love is preeminent over every other gift of the Spirit; in fact one might say that all other gifts of the Spirit flow from this greatest gift of all, love, and that the others are applications of it. Of the various concrete manifestations of love, Paul gives prophesy a very high status, particularly when compared to speaking in tongues. The basic problem with speaking in tongues is this: "For those who speak in a tongue do not speak to other people but to God; for nobody understands them, since they are speaking mysteries in the Spirit" (v. 2). It is evident that the believer's relation to God must always involve the other. There can be no private, individualistic Christianity that involves only the believer and God; Paul has serious reservations about speaking in tongues, a phenomenon with parallels in the Hellenistic religions of the day, since it includes only this singular relationship with God but overlooks the edification of the neighbor. One must accentuate the word *reservations*, for he does not reject it. The key to its acceptability is interpretation for the sake of the entire Corinthian church. If there are those who can interpret that which is normally unintelligible to the worshiping congregation, then and only then can speaking in tongues become a useful contribution for the church. "If anyone speaks in a tongue, let there be only two or at most three, and each in turn; and let one interpret. But if there is no one to interpret, let them be silent in church and speak to themselves and to God" (vv. 27-28).

The reason the apostle speaks so approvingly about prophecy is that "those who prophesy speak to other people for their upbuilding and encouragement and consolation" (v. 3). As he further stresses in verse 26, "all things" must be done for the edification of the community. All the activities of those in Christ have this singular goal: to support the church in obedience to the call of God in Jesus Christ. Here, as in several of the previous chapters, the obvious tension between Paul's understanding of the church and the individualistic tendencies of the Corinthians is evident. As the freedom of those with knowledge must be restrained by the concern for the weak in 1 Corinthians 8, so in 1 Corinthians 14 the phenomenon of speaking in tongues must be interpreted so that the "other person" who cannot understand tongues is edified. This is described with forcefulness in 1 Corinthians 14:13-19:

> Therefore, one who speaks in a tongue should pray for the power to interpret. For if I pray in a tongue, my spirit prays but my mind is unproductive. What should I do then? I will pray with the spirit, but I will pray with the mind also; I will sing praise with the spirit, but I will sing praise with the mind also. Otherwise, if you say a blessing with the spirit, how can anyone in the position of an outsider say the "Amen" to your thanksgiving, since the outsider does not know what you are saying? For you may give thanks well enough, but the other person is not built up. I thank God that I speak in tongues more than all of you; nevertheless, in church I would rather speak five words with my mind, in order to instruct others also, than ten thousand words in a tongue.

It is important to observe that when the faithful in Christ sing or pray they do so with "the spirit" and "with the mind." For Paul, the life in Christ is a combination of the spirit and the mind. The apostle uses the classical Greek word *nous* for the critical, reflective principle, namely, the mind. Life in the spirit alone would lead toward emotionalism, whereas life in the spirit infused by the critical thinking of the mind allows the Christian to "test everything" (1 Thess 5:21) and to critically discern whether one's actions and those of the community truly effect the building up of all. Guided only by the mind, one would be led to that kind of arrogance and insensitivity toward the other that Paul rejects in 1 Corinthians 8. The mind, however, operating in the context of the spirit, allows the Christian to be critically sensitive to the neighbor and to the common good. The gifts of the spirit and the mind, together, have their origin in God. Working in concert they excel in building up the church; but working without each other they lead either to an emotionalism that is immature or to an abstract theological activity that has no relevance to life. In verse 19 Paul argues that those outside the community of faith cannot be instructed with unintelligible, inarticulate babble; there must be solid content. Yet even such substance cannot be communicated effectively and with sensitivity if it is not presented in the context of love.

With insight and simplicity Paul has applied the gospel and made it concrete to specific situations in Corinth. In the same way that the apostle urges individual members to look beyond themselves toward the common good, he twice exhorts the Corinthian church to transcend local limitations and to acknowledge partnership with the universal church. First, in 1 Corinthians 1:2 he reminds them that they are "called to be saints, together with all those who in every place call on the name of our Lord Jesus Christ, both their Lord and ours." This, together with the reference to "the church of God that is at Corinth" (1:2), is a clear indication that the Corinthian church is only a part, an important one to be sure, of God's much larger strategy. Second, in 1 Corinthians 16:1 and beyond Paul speaks about a "collection for the saints." There are several other such references in the Pauline corpus. Especially helpful is Rom 15:25-27:

> At present, however, I am going to Jerusalem in a ministry to the saints; for Macedonia and Achaia have been pleased to share their resources with the poor among the saints at Jerusalem. They were pleased to do this, and indeed they owe it to them; for if the Gentiles have come to share in their spiritual blessings, they ought also to be of service to them in material things.

From these remarks in 1 Corinthians and Romans, it becomes apparent that in this particular reference the "saints" are members of the Jesus movement in the Jerusalem church who are in financial difficulty. Paul calls not only upon Corinthian compassion for the poor as motivation for the contribution, but also upon a sense of mutual interdependence with the Jerusalem church. For "if the Gentiles have come to share in their spiritual blessings, they ought also to be of service to them in material things" (Rom 15:27). The Corinthians are indebted to the Jerusalem church for their spiritual blessings since it was from and through them that the gospel was proclaimed to the Gentiles. In this sense, Jerusalem had a gift that it shared with the Graeco-Roman world, and the Corinthian Christians, along with others, were its recipients. Now, in a new moment in the historical trajectory, the Gentile Christians have the financial means needed by the Jerusalem Christians. Thus Paul encourages them, based on the theological principle of mutuality and interdependence, to give generously to "the poor among the saints at Jerusalem," and in so doing to look beyond themselves and toward the global church. Already in the earliest days of the church there is a social consciousness in the context of a universal perspective but always one that is rooted in the Christ event.

By way of summary, then, it can be said that, for Paul, justification and the moral life, grace and good works, faith and love, baptism and participation in the believing community are inseparable and indissoluble. The gospel of Jesus Christ calls all to new life in holiness and sanctification in the presence of the redeeming God who showers his grace on those who will receive this gift and bear new fruit through the guidance of the Holy Spirit in anticipation of the final accountability that will have to be given to the Lord on the last day. Paul's first letter, 1 Thessalonians, underscores the gravity of doing the will of God in the conduct of one's moral life: "For God did not call us to impurity but in holiness. Therefore whoever rejects this rejects not human authority but God, who also gives his Holy Spirit to you" (4:7). A relativism that evokes the theme of public justice while overlooking this foundational mandate of the gospel has become captive to an alien hermeneutic and no longer speaks in the name of the Triune God of Scripture.

Notes

1. The "sense of the faithful," that is, what teachings the faithful people of the church believe, accept, and reject as being in harmony with the authentic faith of the church.

2. Philip Turner, "An Unworkable Theology," *First Things* 154 (June/July 2005) 10-12, here 12.

3. Joseph Ratzinger, *Principles of Catholic Theology: Building Stones for a Fundamental*

Theology (San Francisco: Ignatius, 1987) 281. The task of Christian theology for Ratzinger is "to build and to be, not near him [Jesus Christ], but only in him and thus, by making him the all-inclusive center, to let his necessary exclusivity—which, by its inclusivity, does not destroy but liberates all things—become reality."

4. Elisabeth Sifton, *The Serenity Prayer: Faith and Politics in Times of Peace and War* (New York: Norton, 2003) 338.

5. Sifton, *Serenity Prayer*, 334-35

6. Raymond E. Brown, *An Introduction to the New Testament* (Anchor Bible Reference Library; New York: Doubleday, 1997) 171-224 provides an excellent introduction to the Gospel of Matthew as well as relevant literature. A guide to commentaries can be found in D. A. Carson, *New Testament Commentary Survey* (Grand Rapids: Baker, 2001) 42-49.

7. See Krister Stendahl, *The School of St. Matthew and Its Use of the Old Testament* (Philadelphia: Fortress, 1969) 8; W. D. Davies, *The Setting of the Sermon on the Mount* (Cambridge: Cambridge University Press, 1964).

9. See Günther Bornkamm, *Tradition and Interpretation in Matthew* (Philadelphia: Westminster, 1963).

10. This position contrasts with that of Hans Dieter Betz in his commentary on the Sermon on the Mount as well as in his essays on the Sermon on the Mount: *The Sermon on the Mount: a commentary on the Sermon on the mount, including the Sermon on the Plain (Matthew 5:3-7:27 and Luke 6:20-49)* (Minneapolis: Fortress, 1995) and *Essays on the Sermon on the Mount* (Philadelphia: Fortress, 1985).

11. W. F. Albright and C. S. Mann, *Matthew* (Garden City, N.Y.: Doubleday, 1971) 45ff.

12. Q is the abbreviation for the German word *Quelle,* which means "source." Q represents those places where Matthew and Luke agree but where there is no parallel in Mark.

13. Dietrich Bonhoeffer, *The Cost of Discipleship* (New York: Collier, 1963) 45-47.

14. See the important book by Joachim Jeremias, *New Testament Theology: The Proclamation of Jesus* (New York: Scribner, 1971) 193-203.

15. Jeremias, *Proclamation of Jesus*, 199-200.

16. Ibid., 201-3.

17. See Turner, "An Unworkable Theology."

18. Karl Paul Donfried, "The Allegory of the Ten Virgins (Matt 25:1-13) as a Summary of Matthean Theology," *Journal of Biblical Literature* 93 (1974) 415-28.

19. John Dominic Crossan, *In Parables* (New York: Harper & Row, 1973) 14.

20. Dan O. Via, Jr., *The Parables* (Philadelphia: Fortress Press, 1967) 5.

21. See Donfried, "Allegory of the Ten Virgins," 427-28.

22. Ernst Käsemann, "Righteousness of God," in *New Testament Questions of Today* (Philadelphia: Fortress, 1969) 168-82, here 170 (italics mine).

23. See also the reference to "light" in Matt 5:13-16.

24. See the previous discussion on page 7 in this volume.

25. See *Peter in the New Testament*, ed. Raymond E. Brown, Karl P. Donfried, and John Reumann (Minneapolis: Augsburg, 1973) 83-101.

26. *Peter in the New Testament*, 92.

27. Raymond E. Brown, *An Introduction to the New Testament*, 407-680, will provide a solid introduction to Paul and the Pauline letters as well as relevant secondary literature. For an excellent guide to Pauline theology, see Joseph A. Fitzmyer, *Paul and His Theology: A Brief Sketch* (Englewood Cliffs, N.J.: Prentice Hall, 1989). A guide to commentaries can be found in D. A. Carson, *New Testament Commentary Survey* (Grand Rapids: Baker, 2001) 72-110.

28. *Joint Declaration on the Doctrine of Justification/The Lutheran World Federation and the Roman Catholic Church* (Grand Rapids: Eerdmans, 2000), paragraph 15.

29. Italics mine.

30. Rom 3:9-20.

31. 1QS 9-11 (Community Rule); 1QH (Thanksgiving Hymns).

32. Martin Luther, "A Treatise on Christian Liberty," in *Three Treatises* (Philadelphia: Muhlenberg Press, 1943) 271.

33. See here, Henri J. M. Nouwen, *The Wounded Healer: Ministry in Contemporary Society* (Garden City, N.Y.: Image, 1979).

34. See note 28.

35. See note 22.

36. The term also occurs in 2 Corinthians 5:21.

37. Rudolf Bultmann, "ΔΙΚΑΙΟΣΎΝΗ ΘΕΟΎ," *Journal of Biblical Literature* 83 (1964) 12-16.

38. Ernst Käsemann, "Righteousness of God," in *New Testament Questions of Today* (Philadelphia: Fortress, 1969) 168-82, here 180.

39. Ibid., 176.

40. Ibid., 170 (italics mine).

41. Some relevant texts include 2 Corinthians 5:10 and Romans 14:10.

42. See further J. A. Ziesler, *The Meaning of Righteousness in Paul: A Linguistic and Theological Inquiry* (Cambridge: Cambridge University Press, 1972) 160. What is disappointing here is that Ziesler's rich insights are not carried through more consistently, especially with regard to the relationship between justification and last judgment.

43. For details of the discussion see Donfried, "Justification and Last Judgment in Paul," in *Paul, Thessalonica and Early Christianity* (Grand Rapids: Eerdmans, 2002) 253-92.

44. See Romans 6:16.

45. A term used by Gordon Scruton, the Episcopal bishop of the diocese of Western Massachusetts.

46. See further the discussion in George T. Montague, *Growth in Christ* (Fribourg: Regina Mundi, 1961).

47. A similar point is made in 1 Thessalonians 5:23-24.

48. C. F. D. Moule aptly comments that ". . . the baptized Christian is no safer in playing fast and loose with his privileges than were the Israelites who had been 'baptized' in the land and the sea" ("The Judgment Theme in the Sacraments," in *The Background of the New Testament and Its Eschatology*, ed. W. D. Davies and D. Daube [Cambridge: Cambridge University Press, 1956] 472).

49. Krister Stendahl, "Justification and the Last Judgment," *Lutheran World* 8, no. 7 (1961) 7, comments: "Consequently, to be a member of the church is by definition to be justified, and he who remains in the church will be saved. If someone backslides, he will not be saved."

50. See the further discussion in Karl P. Donfried, *The Setting of Second Clement in Early Christianity* (Leiden: E. J. Brill, 1974) 142-44.

51. Although taken from an earlier ecclesial tradition, Paul fully endorses this theology, and it is for this reason that he incorporates it in his letter.

52. But not for the Pauline school, for example, Ephesians 2:5-8.

53. Stendahl, "Justification and the Last Judgment," 5, puts the matter well: "The danger is not to get a little worse, and the hope is not to get a little better (ethically, or in terms of faith). It is sharpened in the simplified black and white of all eschatological situations: the dangers of apostasy."

54. See Paul S. Minear, *The Obedience of Faith* (Studies in Biblical Theology 19; London: SCM Press, 1971).

55. "To rightwise" is a literal translation of the Greek verb normally translated "to justify."

56. Turner, "An Unworkable Theology," 10-11.

57. Craig L. Nessan, *Many Members Yet One Body: Committed Same-Gender Relationships and the Mission of the Church* (Minneapolis: Augsburg Fortress, 2004) 12.

58. Nessan, *Many Members Yet One Body*, 18.

59. Ibid., 20.

60. Ibid., 46.

61. Ibid., 84.

62. Ibid., 62.

63. Ibid.

64. Ibid., 83.

65. Bonhoeffer, *The Cost of Discipleship*, 47.

66. Ibid., 46.

67. Ibid., 47-48.

68. See Romans 1:16; 10:1; 10:10; 2 Corinthians 7:10; Philippians 1:19.

69. Philippians 1:27-30; 4:1; Romans 14:4; 1 Corinthians 7:37; 15:50-58; 16:13; Galatians 5:1; 1 Thessalonians 3:8; 2 Thessalonians 2:5.

70. Calvin J. Roetzel, *Judgment in the Community: A Study of the Relationship between Eschatology and Ecclesiology in Paul* (Leiden: E. J. Brill, 1972) 129, holds with Käsemann that Paul is seeking to restore the important dimension of "eschatological reservation" in 1 Corinthians 6:9-11. Paul is stressing two factors: "(1) He challenges the eschatological certainty of the Corinthians. You do wrong, Paul says, and 'you know, don't you, that wrongdoers will not inherit the Kingdom of God.' . . . Paul thus underscores the point that apart from continued vigilance in Christ there is no guarantee of salvation. (2) He speaks of the Kingdom of God as a future inheritance not a present possession."

71. Hans Conzelmann, *1 Corinthians: A Commentary of the First Epistle to the Corinthians* (Hermeneia; Philadelphia: Fortress, 1975) 98.

72. See Krister Stendahl, "The Apostle Paul and the Introspective Conscience of the West," in *Paul among the Jews and Gentiles and Other Essays* (Philadelphia: Fortress, 1976) 78-96.

73. This verse is correctly translated by both Roetzel, *Judgement in the Community*, 123, and Robert Jewett, *Paul's Anthropological Terms* (Leiden: E. J. Brill, 1971) 124.

74. Roetzel's study *Judgement in the Community* is helpful by its very title in moving emphasis away from the purely individual aspects of judgment in Pauline thought to that of the entire congregation. ". . . Paul's emphasis falls on the corporate aspects of judgment. This finding is apparent in the prominent role the church plays in Paul's judgment allusions. In both the present and the future, the church stands at the center of Paul's thought about the Day of the Lord. . . . If the church attempts to take the fruits of salvation without assuming the responsibilities that go with them the judgment portends loss and possible ruin. . . . While Paul . . . is not unmindful of the individual believer, the individual member of the church is first and foremost a social being" (178). These perceptive insights are not, unfortunately, applied with consistency to 1 Corinthians 5:5-15, where the salvation of the individual is the primary concern for Roetzel (123-24). See the further discussion in Donfried, *Paul, Thessalonica and Early Christianity*, 253-92.

75. Conzelmann, *1 Corinthians*, 78 n. 92.

76. Ernst Käsemann, *Essays on New Testament Themes* (London: SCM Press, 1964) 126.

77. Those wishing to probe 1 Corinthians more deeply may wish to consult the commentaries by Gordon D. Fee, *The First Epistle to the Corinthians* (NICNT; Grand Rapids: Eerdmans, 1987); and Raymond F. Collins, *First Corinthians* (Sacra Pagina; Collegeville, Minn.: Liturgical Press, 1999).

78. See Donfried, *The Setting of Second Clement in Early Christianity*, 7; Strabo, *Geography*, 8.378 (Loeb 4:191).

79. James M. Robinson, *The Nag Hammadi Library in English* (San Francisco: HarperSanFrancisco, 1990).

80. A comment often made in the classroom. Included among Niebuhr's important contributions to the field of theology and ethics is his now classic *The Nature and Destiny of Man: A Christian Interpretation* (New York: Scribner's, 1949).

81. Paul Tillich, *The Dynamics of Faith* (New York: Harper, 1957).

82. Bonhoeffer, *The Cost of Discipleship*, 46-47.

83. Eating idol food is the practice of eating meat from an animal sacrificed to a heathen god as part of cultic worship.

5

The Bible and the Church

Toward the Application of a Trinitarian Hermeneutic

5.1 The Body, Sexuality, and the Moral Life

In the preceding pages considerable effort has been invested in an initial attempt to evaluate the conflicting interpretations of the Bible present in contemporary Western culture;[1] additionally, the contours of a Trinitarian hermeneutic that might assist the Church Catholic to recover the proper context for interpretation of Scripture have been proposed. In addition, especially since they are intrinsic for the proper expression for such a hermeneutic, considerable attention has been given to the intimate inter-relationship between the gift of faith and the demands of discipleship as well as the decisive integration between justification and the holiness of life for both Jesus and Paul. With this foundational work in place, another additional step needs to be taken: the application of a Trinitarian hermeneutic to one of the most pressing issues for the Christian church in the twenty-first century: sexuality, and, more specifically, the challenge of homosexuality. Given the primary focus of this volume what follows must of necessity be more programmatic than comprehensive. At this point some preliminary considerations will be introduced relating to sexuality, covenant, the holiness of the body, and justice before reviewing current arguments to override the biblical understanding of homosexuality.

Contributing to the conflicting conversations on the topic of sexuality and the Bible is the ambiguity of the term "sexuality" itself. Essentially a nonbiblical term, "sexuality" may well convey both explicit as well as subtle cultural presuppositions that may not be in accord with biblical per-

118

spectives; therefore this term will be described more carefully in the next paragraph. Another source of conflict in the current debate about whether or not the Bible approves of same-sex relationships has been the incorrect first step that isolates those texts that speak about homosexual relationships from their broader canonical context and then, depending on one's hermeneutical presuppositions, either defending the applicability or non-applicability of these individual passages. This is, however, a false starting point because homosexuality must be seen as belonging to a far broader biblical perspective that includes such basic themes as (1) the covenantal[2] relationship of God with his people, together with his creation of man and woman, (2) the sacredness of sexuality, and, (3) the holiness of the body. These topics must not only precede but must also frame the far more particular discussion of homosexuality. When this more comprehensive context is absent, the hermeneutics of ambiguity, dissonance, and antinomianism reign supreme and lead to distorted results, often in the guise of "responsible biblical scholarship."[3]

Both for the Old and the New Testament, covenant creates a new relationship between the parties involved and is foundational for the community that results. For the Old Testament the Exodus event and the covenant at Sinai and for the New Testament the death of Jesus and the New Covenant in his blood are fundamental and indispensable; for each testament the understanding of covenant is essential for their inner coherence. Thus, when the second creation account in Genesis 2:4b-25 is read within the larger framework of covenant in the Old Testament, it is evident that the extraordinary devotion and faithfulness required by God from his covenant people in general are also to characterize the more specific commitment of spouses to each other since a strong marital unit is essential for the well-being of the larger community. God created man and woman, male and female, to be in covenant relationship and fidelity, that is, for the capacity of self-donation to the other, and the seal of this particular oath and possibility is their "nakedness," that is, their sexual intimacy. This is, as John Grabowski expresses it, "the embodied gesture that expresses the new relationship that their covenant creates between them. Sexuality, therefore, as a recollection and enactment of the covenant oath, takes on a liturgical function within the marriage relationship akin to other covenant-making gestures (e.g., the sprinkling with blood, table fellowship). . . ."[4] Although the intimacy of the sexual act seals the marital bond, this bond only receives its complete meaning in the context of the more foundational Old Testament covenant oath between God and his people.

As with all covenants, sin enters, and the original hopes and potentials

are compromised and carried on within a "markedly diminished existence";[5] one needs only to review the history of Israel and the prophetic cri-
tiques of Israel's "adultery" to appreciate this line of reasoning. Jeremiah's
indictment of Israel speaks for itself (5:7):

> How can I pardon you?
> Your children have forsaken me,
>   and have sworn by those who are no gods.
> When I fed them to the full,
>   they committed adultery
>   and trooped to the houses of prostitutes.

In fact, one will note that the relationship of idolatry and adultery applies
both to God's covenant with Israel as well as to the covenant of marriage
that he has established. Israel was consistently called upon to separate herself from the various idolatrous practices of her neighbors and to reject their
cosmological mythologies as well as their ritual practices. The call to holiness is for the people of God as a whole as well as for the act of sexual intimacy within the covenant of marriage. Thus, it is not surprising that one
can find the term adultery applied to the infidelity between man and woman
as well as to the idolatrous practices of Israel as, for example, in the inci-
dent of the Golden Calf (Exod 32:21-31). Similarly, the analogous relationship between the marriage covenant and that between Yahweh and his
people is found throughout Scripture, particularly deepened by the
prophets, and, in the New Testament, by the writer of Ephesians in describing the relationship between Christ and his church. There we read:

> Be subject to one another out of reverence for Christ. Wives, be sub-
> ject to your husbands as you are to the Lord. For the husband is the
> head of the wife just as Christ is the head of the church, the body of
> which he is the Savior. Just as the church is subject to Christ, so also
> wives ought to be, in everything, to their husbands. Husbands, love
> your wives, just as Christ loved the church and gave himself up for her,
> in order to make her holy by cleansing her with the washing of water
> by the word, so as to present the church to himself in splendor, with-
> out a spot or wrinkle or anything of the kind—yes, so that she may be
> holy and without blemish. In the same way, husbands should love
> their wives as they do their own bodies. He who loves his wife loves
> himself. For no one ever hates his own body, but he nourishes and ten-
> derly cares for it, just as Christ does for the church, because we are

members of his body. "For this reason a man will leave his father and mother and be joined to his wife, and the two will become one flesh." This is a great mystery, and I am applying it to Christ and the church. Each of you, however, should love his wife as himself, and a wife should respect her husband. (Eph 5:21-33)

A Trinitarian hermeneutic interpreting for the church questions related to sexuality and the body must recognize that for both Jesus and Paul chastity is a form of self-possession that permits the other to be viewed as a person worthy of love and respect. Owing to the covenant relationship established by God with his people and between male and female, persons can never be viewed or treated as mere objects for one's conquest, use, or enjoyment. Paul summarizes this concisely in the earliest extant Christian document, 1 Thessalonians, addressed to believers in Christ who lived in the midst of pagan cultic and sexual practices: "For you know what instructions we gave you through the Lord Jesus. For this is the will of God, your sanctification: that you abstain from fornication; that each one of you know how to control your own body in holiness and honor, not with lustful passion, like the Gentiles who do not know God; that no one wrong or exploit a brother or sister in this matter" (1 Thess 4:2-6). In fact so holy is the body that Paul can write to the Corinthians: "Shun fornication! Every sin that a person commits is outside the body; but the fornicator sins against the body itself. Or do you not know that your body is a temple of the Holy Spirit within you, which you have from God, and that you are not your own? For you were bought with a price; therefore glorify God in your body" (1 Cor 6:18-20). Emphases such as these remind us that the basic presuppositions with regard to sexuality and the body for both Jesus and Paul are Jewish and not Graeco-Roman; neither participate in the regularly negative Greek attitudes toward women and sexual practice. The issue at stake is considerably more profound: sexuality gone astray, like murder, was a threat not only to the survival of Israel but also for the early Christian communities; participation in forbidden sexual relationships would pollute and eventually destroy both the individual and the holy community. A perspective such as this makes intelligible Paul's insistence that the unrepentant sexual offender in 1 Corinthians 5 be removed from the community of believers.[6]

Finally, a few words about "justice," a theme that is frequently injected into the contemporary discussions about sexuality. Since it is often ill-defined, it generates great ambiguity and lack of clarity. Some activists utilize it as a synonym for radical inclusion within the people of God with minimal ethical boundaries or responsibility; as a result the demands of discipleship are obscured and, in some cases, obliterated. Here, again, it is the biblical perspective, and not the relativism of secular culture that must be primary and dominant. In the Old Testament, justice[7] is firmly anchored in the fact that the people of Israel are a people covenanted to the God who, as Creator and covenant partner, is himself the author of justice. Since justice and righteousness belong to the very nature of Israel's God it is understood that he is both its source as well as its unrelenting advocate. In the words of Psalm 99:4: "Mighty King, lover of justice, you have established equity; you have executed justice and righteousness in Jacob." Further, for the Christian, justice is a theme that must always be related to and anchored in the righteousness of God as revealed in the new covenant of Jesus the Christ, a righteousness that "rightwises," that is, "justifies," the believer and that incorporates and integrates "gift" with "responsibility."[8] Justice as inclusion, biblically understood, must always involve "exclusive inclusivity,"[9] namely, ethical and virtuous living, which Augustine describes so aptly as "a good quality of mind, by which we live righteously, of which no one can make bad use. . . ."[10] A Trinitarian hermeneutic must insist that the content and shape of justice, as well as sexuality, be defined and shaped by Scripture in its canonical wholeness and not by the political agendas of the left or the right.

5.2 Arguments for Overriding the Biblical Understanding of Homosexuality

Several Protestant churches are currently attempting to determine the appropriateness of ordaining practicing gay persons as well as blessing gay partnerships as similar or equivalent to heterosexual marriage. The universal church's understanding of Scripture, and especially the New Testament, allows only one kind of sexual activity, namely, that which takes place within a monogamous, heterosexual marriage. Those opposed to this interpretation assert that the "church has over-ridden what has been interpreted as the clear teachings of Scripture in favor of more just practices which better serve the neighbor and community. The church, for example, remarries divorced persons, ordains women and opposes slavery. . . ."[11] Before these arguments related to divorce, ordination of women, and slavery are examined more closely, a few thoughts about the coherency of the gospel and the contingency of its application(s) are called for.

The language of "coherency" and "contingency" is found in the writings of J. Christiaan Beker, and many have found these categories to be a useful way in distinguishing between the coherent, consistent message of the gospel and its specific, contingent actualization and application at a particular time and place. Because the New Testament is dynamic and always attempts to actualize and make concrete the words of the risen Jesus, it contains not one gospel volume abstractly summarizing Jesus' complete and coherent message and teaching, but rather four, Matthew, Mark, Luke, and John, each applying and interpreting selected dimensions of Jesus' activity to meet the contingent needs of the specific audiences for whom they were written.

The Pauline letters, with their repeated contingent, specific application of the one unified, generative and coherent message of the gospel, are a classic example of how this dynamic application functions. In his letter to the Corinthians Paul writes in this way:

> Now I would remind you, brothers and sisters, of the good news that I proclaimed to you, which you in turn received, in which also you stand, through which also you are being saved, if you hold firmly to the message that I proclaimed to you—unless you have come to believe in vain. For I handed on to you as of first importance what I in turn had received: that Christ died for our sins in accordance with the scriptures, and that he was buried, and that he was raised on the third day in accordance with the scriptures, and that he appeared to Cephas, then to the twelve. (1 Cor 15:1-5)

Although these verses make clear that the generating force of the gospel as a way of life and salvation is at the root of all Pauline proclamation, the precise application of these insights can be found only in his individual letters, all of which are written to contingent, specific situations that take seriously the intended congregation's culture, identity, and integrity, as our previous examination of 1 Corinthians has shown. In this sense there is no "pure" gospel that can be easily abstracted or summarized from its contingent applications. To think otherwise places one into a fundamentalist mindset that distorts Scripture primarily through a narrow, one-dimensional approach. And herein lies the hermeneutical difficulty: given the fact that biblical actualization is a dynamic and not a static process (i.e., there is no single conflated, summary gospel, but rather four), one is obligated to realize that the cohesive message of salvation assumed by the writers of the New Testament cannot initially be understood apart from the varied ways in which it is embodied in the particular situations to which it is addressed. But given the hermeneutical confusions present in the current discussions about sexuality, a critical question must be raised: does the recognition of contingent applications of the gospel, as we have seen throughout 1 Corinthians, automatically relegate such an application as time-bound, inadequate, and, thus, irrelevant?

In the contemporary situation a crucial hermeneutical issue, broadly put, is how to recognize the one, coherent message of God's work of redemption in Jesus Christ while distinguishing this proclamation from its contingent application within Scripture? The challenge is to understand the reciprocal relationship between the two. When the tension between them is eliminated it results either in a fundamentalism of the liberal left in which the contingent is trivialized or of the conservative right in which it is absolutized; by such means, however, each, in its own way, falsifies the gospel message. Given such tendencies to misapprehend the gospel, an urgent practical question arises: how can practitioners of a Trinitarian hermeneutic distinguish between *authentic* and *inauthentic* ways of interpreting and living out the gospel of Jesus Christ in a post-Christian world? Although this is a wide-ranging and complex question capable of a variety of correct answers, given our immediate context one criterion in particular may be especially relevant and applicable: *an ethical application or claim of the gospel made by the authors of the New Testament, whether contingent or not, can only be revised or modified when Scripture itself provides such a justification.* In other words, before a contingent application of the gospel can be decreed as having been overridden, that is, declared as no longer valid, there must be a generative force within Scripture itself that would make such a declaration reasonable and justifiable. In the absence of such a self-generated, internal scriptural critique, a contingent application of the gospel would have to be recognized as a genuine and authentic part of the coherent whole of the gospel.

5.2.1 Divorce

Not only has Western culture in general severed itself from the biblical norms with regard to divorce, but also, even more tragically, those who understand themselves to be disciples of Jesus Christ. Although divorce causes incalculable harm to the parties involved and to society as a whole, as well as profound psychological damage to the children caught up in these traumatic rejections, many mainline Protestant churches increasingly accept this situation as normal.[12] No longer are clergy, traditionally understood as providing a modeling function for those whom they shepherd, reprimanded for adultery and other extramarital shenanigans and asked to resign from their ministerial functions, but in some cases, alas, their new "life-long" commitments are even celebrated in seminary chapels and churches as paradigms of "love" for the entire community.

Permissiveness is not only the order of the day with regard to the uncritical acceptance of divorce as a routine occurrence, but it has also extended itself to the area of premarital counseling and the marriage liturgy itself. In many places the preparatory sessions seeking to prepare man and woman for the sacred mystery of Christian marriage are minimal, often superficial, and in certain cases nonexistent. Such shallowness is reflected in self-constructed wedding services that more often than not mirror the current expectations and whims of secular society rather than the holiness of the union of woman and man in Jesus Christ. Given the amnesia that surrounds this subject it will be well to review a passage from Matthew's gospel (19:3-9):

> Some Pharisees came to him, and to test him they asked, "Is it lawful for a man to divorce his wife for any cause?" He answered, "Have you not read that the one who made them at the beginning 'made them male and female,' and said, 'For this reason a man shall leave his father and mother and be joined to his wife, and the two shall become one flesh'? So they are no longer two, but one flesh. Therefore what God has joined together, let no one separate." They said to him, "Why then did Moses command us to give a certificate of dismissal and to divorce her?" He said to them, "It was because you were so hard-hearted that Moses allowed you to divorce your wives, but from the beginning it was not so. And I say to you, whoever divorces his wife, except for unchastity, and marries another commits adultery."

According to the gospel accounts (see also, for example, Mark 10:2-12) Jesus reaffirms Genesis 1:27, that God created humankind as "male and female," and Genesis 2:24, that man and woman "become one flesh," and then proceeds with the declaration that divorce within the ethic of the kingdom of God is not a possibility except for unchastity. Joseph Fitzmyer maintains that "unchastity" within Matthew's Jewish context does not mean licentiousness, that is, "fooling around," but rather refers to an illicit marriage between relatives. This exemption does, according to Fitzmyer, give the church the authority to annul marriages that were never authentic marriages from the outset.[13] This, however, is unmistakably the exception and not the norm, and the original context of Jesus' teaching on these matters is certainly in need of reappropriation by contemporary Christianity.

The argument is often advanced today that since many contemporary churches no longer take seriously the New Testament prohibition of divorce, similarly prohibitions against homosexual relations should be removed. One wonders whether this argument might not be fueled, at least partially, by those who feel guilt or discomfort with the circumstances that led to their own divorce and the tensions between this state of affairs and the biblical norms? Would it not be hypocritical, it is asked, to insist on the biblical normativity of the one but not the other? And thus, some would argue, one should insist on neither the wrongness of divorce nor of homosexual behavior. Nevertheless, attention must be called to the fact that Matthew not once but twice presents a great exception to Jesus' unmistakable response to the question about divorce. Once in 5:31-32 and again in Matthew 19:9, as just cited: "And I say to you, whoever divorces his wife, *except* for unchastity, and marries another commits adultery." Similarly, Paul grants some latitude on a related issue; in 1 Corinthians 7:13-15 he advises that "if any woman has a husband who is an unbeliever, and he consents to live with her, she should not divorce him. . . . But if the unbelieving partner separates, let it be so; in such a case the brother or sister is not bound." The situation does not involve illicit marriage between relatives, as in Matthew's context; rather, for Paul, separation is possible when one member in an originally non-Christian marriage has believed in Christ and the other, who has remained a nonbeliever, wishes to leave. In both cases a unique and limited set of circumstances is not elevated to the status of a universal norm that can be applied arbitrarily.

Two factors, then, need to be taken into consideration when discussing divorce. First, although the New Testament position against divorce is consistent, it does allow for unique exceptions in unusual situations. Second, the widespread carelessness in recent application of the New Testament perspective by many churches with reference to the sacredness and indissolubility of marriage can never be an argument for the exclusion of the primary perspective of Scripture regarding divorce. Not irrelevant is the old adage, *abusus non tollit usum* ["abuse does not preclude proper use"]. Although many Christians recognize the unfortunate and limited need for the annulment of some marriages, this must always be carried out in an ecclesial process marked by prayer, repentance, spiritual direction, and thoughtful reflection. Both the recognition of an aborted marriage and the decision to bless a new one must be primarily ecclesial and not secular decisions; otherwise churchly blessings become disingenuous and hypocritical.

Conclusion: To argue that the Church Catholic has overridden Scripture with regard to divorce is a blatant misstatement of the facts. That churches have often handled the serious matters of marriage preparation, marriage counseling and divorce carelessly is, unfortunately, all too evident. But the neglect of proper practice is not to be confused with "overriding" or "modifying" Scripture. Therefore by applying the hermeneutical principle that *an ethical application or claim of the gospel made by the authors of the New Testament, whether contingent or not, can only be revised or modified when Scripture itself provides such a justification,* it can be demonstrated that such a justification, in limited circumstances, is indeed present in Scripture with regard to the troubling and complicated subject of divorce.

5.2.2 Ordination of Women

The argument is put forward by some that since many churches reversed the New Testament position prohibiting the ordination of women in the twentieth century these same churches have the authority to change the biblical position both with regard to the ordination and marriage of practicing homosexuals. This is a specious argument for at least two reasons:

1. Ordination, as a formal ecclesial process for the setting aside of persons for a ministry of Word and Sacraments, is not known in the New Testament. There are two passages in the New Testament that may indicate by the use of the phrase "laying on of hands" in specific contexts the first steps toward such a trajectory; nevertheless, one needs to avoid reading them anachronistically. These texts include the following:

1 Timothy 4:11-16
These are the things you must insist on and teach. Let no one despise your youth, but set the believers an example in speech and conduct, in love, in faith, in purity. Until I arrive, give attention to the public reading of scripture, to exhorting, to teaching. Do not neglect the gift that is in you, which was given to you through prophecy with the *laying on of hands* by the council of elders. Put these things into practice, devote yourself to them, so that all may see your progress. Pay close attention to yourself and to your teaching; continue in these things, for in doing this you will save both yourself and your hearers.

2 Timothy 1:6-7
For this reason I remind you to rekindle the gift of God that is within you through the *laying on of my hands*; for God did not give us a spirit of cowardice, but rather a spirit of power and of love and of self-discipline.

If these texts are linked, for which a plausible argument can be made, then presumably Paul and the elders together participated in this event that conferred the proper authority on Timothy for a specific task, one that I. Howard Marshall describes as "a kind of 'superintendent' in the Pauline mission field with the approval of the congregations themselves."[14] The intention of these texts is both to encourage Timothy and to remind the elders regarding the responsibility that they had given him; nothing beyond that is implied.

2. There are manifold texts in the Bible that demonstrate the extraordinary leadership of women. In the New Testament none can be more fundamentally affirmative about the equality of women in the life of the church than Paul's remarks to the believers in the Galatian churches: "There is no longer Jew or Greek, there is no longer slave or free, there is no longer male and female; for all of you are one in Christ Jesus"(3:28). This is a compelling message that intentionally removes within the new community of believers the cultural barriers imposed by both Jewish and Graeco-Roman society and, even more explicitly, is determined to liberate women in the churches from these limitations. At the practical level Paul repeatedly commends female leaders in the church and works closely with them. This is evident both in Romans 16:1-2, "I commend to you our sister Phoebe, a deacon of the church at Cenchreae,[15] so that you may welcome her in the Lord as is fitting for the saints, and help her in whatever she may require from you, for she has been a benefactor of many and of myself as well," and Philippians 4:2-3, "I urge Euodia and I urge Syntyche to be of the same mind in the Lord. Yes, and I ask you also, my loyal companion, help these women, for they have struggled beside me in the work of the gospel, together with Clement and the rest of my co-workers, whose names are in the book of life."

The citation from Romans 16, as well as the remainder of the chapter, requires further comment. The relevant portion of the chapter includes the first sixteen verses:

> I commend to you our sister Phoebe, a deacon of the church at Cenchreae, ²so that you may welcome her in the Lord as is fitting for the saints, and help her in whatever she may require from you, for she has been a benefactor of many and of myself as well.
> ³Greet Prisca and Aquila, who work with me in Christ Jesus, ⁴and who risked their necks for my life, to whom not only I give thanks, but also all the churches of the Gentiles. ⁵Greet also the church in their

house. Greet my beloved Epaenetus, who was the first convert in Asia for Christ. [6]Greet Mary, who has worked very hard among you. [7]Greet Andronicus and Junia, my relatives who were in prison with me; they are prominent among the apostles, and they were in Christ before I was. [8]Greet Ampliatus, my beloved in the Lord. [9]Greet Urbanus, our co-worker in Christ, and my beloved Stachys. [10]Greet Apelles, who is approved in Christ. Greet those who belong to the family of Aristobulus. [11]Greet my relative Herodion. Greet those in the Lord who belong to the family of Narcissus. [12]Greet those workers in the Lord, Tryphaena and Tryphosa. Greet the beloved Persis, who has worked hard in the Lord. [13]Greet Rufus, chosen in the Lord; and greet his mother—a mother to me also. [14]Greet Asyncritus, Phlegon, Hermes, Patrobas, Hermas, and the brothers and sisters who are with them. [15]Greet Philologus, Julia, Nereus and his sister, and Olympas, and all the saints who are with them. [16]Greet one another with a holy kiss. All the churches of Christ greet you.

It should be observed that: (1) Phoebe is not only a deacon (or, alternatively, minister) in Cenchreae, a port city of Corinth, but also a *prostatēs*, that is, a benefactor, patron, or protector. She is a woman of means encouraging the work of the church in a variety of substantial ways. (2) Twenty-seven individuals are cited in this list of names; ten are those of women. (3) As John D. Crossan and Jonathan L. Reed have noted, Paul uses the verb *kopiaō* to refer to "hard work"; he uses it not only with regard to himself (Gal 4:11; 1 Cor 15:10) but also four times in Romans and exclusively of women: Mary, Tryphaena, Tryphosa, and Persis.[16] (4) In Romans 16:7 one meets Andronicus and Junia, ". . . my relatives who were in prison with me; they are prominent among the apostles, and they were in Christ before I was." Here Paul unmistakably refers to a female as an apostle.

This association and collaboration with women, in such marked contrast to societal expectations, is an impulse that originates in the ministry of Jesus. Luke 8:1-3 is sufficient testimony to this fact:

Soon afterwards he went on through cities and villages, proclaiming and bringing the good news of the kingdom of God. The twelve were with him, as well as some women who had been cured of evil spirits and infirmities: Mary, called Magdalene, from whom seven demons had gone out, and Joanna, the wife of Herod's steward Chuza, and Susanna, and many others, who provided for them out of their resources.

This text foreshadows the role of women both at the cross and resurrection as well as in the formation of the early communities of the Jesus movement.

Some will correctly assert that this is not the entire story concerning the role of women in the New Testament, especially within the Pauline and deutero-Pauline correspondence. There are three texts (1 Cor 14:33b-36; 1 Cor 11:2-16; 1 Tim 2:11-15) in particular that have been invoked against the ordination of women. However, a brief examination of these texts will reveal that the question of ordination is not under discussion. The first of these texts is found in 1 Cor 14:33b-36:

> (As in all the churches of the saints, women should be silent in the churches. For they are not permitted to speak, but should be subordinate, as the law also says. If there is anything they desire to know, let them ask their husbands at home. For it is shameful for a woman to speak in church. Or did the word of God originate with you? Or are you the only ones it has reached?)

We have retained the parentheses of the NRSV translation since they suggest what many scholars believe, namely, that this text does not derive from Paul but is, rather, a subsequent insertion into the text of 1 Corinthians reflecting a later situation more similar to that found in the Pastoral Epistles. The basis for such a decision is the obvious inconsistency in the assertions about women made here in 1 Corinthians 14 with those of the other Pauline texts that have just been examined. Other scholars who would argue for a noninterpolation from a later period advise that Paul is responding to a specific and contingent situation in the Corinthian congregation influenced by the nearby Eleusian mysteries or the cultic practices at Delphi; at both sites there is evidence of the intimate relationship of women and ecstatic speech, a concern that might be reflected in 1 Corinthians 14. If so, this would help explain the omission of the phrase "there is no longer male and female" in 1 Cor 12:13, an expression that is included in Gal 3:28: "There is no longer Jew or Greek, there is no longer slave or free, there is no longer male and female; for all of you are one in Christ Jesus."

But perhaps this omission of the words "no longer male and female" might be more appropriately explained by the second troublesome text related to the question of the equality of women in the New Testament, one also found in 1 Corinthians. In 11:2-16 of that Pauline letter he writes these words to the Corinthian Christians:

> I commend you because you remember me in everything and maintain the traditions just as I handed them on to you. [3]But I want you to

understand that Christ is the head of every man, and the husband is the head of his wife, and God is the head of Christ. [4]Any man who prays or prophesies with something on his head disgraces his head, [5]but any woman who prays or prophesies with her head unveiled disgraces her head—it is one and the same thing as having her head shaved. [6]For if a woman will not veil herself, then she should cut off her hair; but if it is disgraceful for a woman to have her hair cut off or to be shaved, she should wear a veil. [7]For a man ought not to have his head veiled, since he is the image and reflection of God; but woman is the reflection of man. [8]Indeed, man was not made from woman, but woman from man. [9]Neither was man created for the sake of woman, but woman for the sake of man. [10]For this reason a woman ought to have a symbol of authority on her head, because of the angels. [11]Nevertheless, in the Lord woman is not independent of man or man independent of woman. [12]For just as woman came from man, so man comes through woman; but all things come from God. [13]Judge for yourselves: is it proper for a woman to pray to God with her head unveiled? [14]Does not nature itself teach you that if a man wears long hair, it is degrading to him, [15]but if a woman has long hair, it is her glory? For her hair is given to her for a covering. [16]But if anyone is disposed to be contentious—we have no such custom, nor do the churches of God.

This text presents a variety of difficulties, particularly in the area of translation, since Paul's rhetoric involves the use of polyvalent puns including "head" (*kephalē*; vv. 3, 4, 5, 7, 10) and "authority" (*exousia*; v. 10). So, for example, should the Greek word *kephalē* be translated as "head" or "source"? Should *exousia* be translated as "to have authority" or "to have the right to choose"? Further, is this text really, as John Shelby Spong states, intended to demonstrate the inferiority of women?[17] Such a suggestion is categorically refuted by the unambiguous statement of mutuality and equality in v. 11, "Nevertheless, in the Lord woman is not independent of man or man independent of woman." A careful reading of these verses makes clear that the goal is not hierarchical but relational. Given the contentious situation within the Corinthian church, Paul insists on the maintenance of gender distinctions; he does not, however, advocate that one must be subordinate to the other.

Before reaching dogmatic conclusions about the meaning of this exceptionally complicated text, one must first inquire: what problem is Paul reacting to within the Corinthian church? If the issue centers on gender confusion and not the status of women, then the distinctions that the apostle is making between male and female become more comprehensible and the unmistakable omission of the phrase "there is no longer male and female" in 1 Corinthians 12:13 becomes transparent. In short, this text has nothing to do either with denigrating the role of women in the Corinthian church or with the issue of their ordination but avoiding gender, and thereby, ecclesial confusion.

The third text that discusses women in a critical manner is 1 Timothy 2:11-15; and, as we noted earlier, this text has certain elements in common with the interpolation found in 1 Corinthians 14:33b-36:

> Let a woman learn in silence with full submission. I permit no woman to teach or to have authority over a man; she is to keep silent. For Adam was formed first, then Eve; and Adam was not deceived, but the woman was deceived and became a transgressor. Yet she will be saved through childbearing, provided they continue in faith and love and holiness, with modesty.

Once again it is imperative to distinguish between the coherent message of the New Testament and its contingent application. 1 Timothy, like any other New Testament writing, is addressed to a specific congregation with an identifiable set of problems and challenges. The initial question, then, that must be addressed is the kind of situation the author of this deutero-Pauline letter, probably addressed to Christians in Ephesus, is attempting to prove false. A fuller exposition of these verses would need to take into account that some women converts to the church had a good deal to unlearn as a result of their previous participation in the Artemis cult, especially in the area of sexuality, fertility practices, and the prohibition of marriage. In addition, it is likely that the heretics who are being refuted asserted that sexual intercourse, marriage, and procreation were by nature evil and should be avoided by religious persons.[18] Contrary to such assertions, the author of 1 Timothy is communicating to Christian women living in an alien environment such as this that marriage, sexual relations, and the bearing of children will indeed not hinder their salvation in the Lord.[19] Observations like these suggest that probing the deep structure of a text, as, for example, 1 Timothy 2:11-15, makes it far less likely to transform it into a general disparagement of women by means of ideological and fundamentalist misreadings of the historical situation.[20] A Trinitarian hermeneutic must alert readers to the fundamentalists on the left and right who remove texts from their contingent and specific context and make them normative in illegitimate ways.

Conclusion: There is no evidence to suggest that those churches that ordain women have overridden Scripture. Therefore by applying the hermeneutical principle that *an ethical application or claim of the gospel made by the authors of the New Testament, whether contingent or not, can only be revised or modified when Scripture itself provides such a justification,* it can be argued that those churches that have inaugurated augmented forms of ecclesial service for women have done so in a manner consistent with the affirmative perspectives of both Jesus and Paul and, further, that they have been sensitive to the original contexts of various contingent New Testament texts resulting from the proper application of the historical-critical method.

5.2.3 Freeing the Oppressed

Another of the arguments presented for altering the normativity of Scripture with regard to sexual matters concerns the issues of slavery and oppression. Since, so it is argued, both the New Testament churches and subsequent forms of Christianity have endorsed slavery, then its rejection by contemporary Christianity represents an elimination of a major early Christian practice; if such a paradigm can be changed others can as well. "According to the contextual hermeneutic, just as historical interpretations of the Bible eventually led to a change in the institution of slavery or the role of women in the church (by allowing ordination of women), so now the blessing of committed same-gender relationships may be warranted."[21]

A number of assumptions in this proposition are problematic. Chief among them is the failure to distinguish between slavery as practiced in the antebellum South and in the Roman Empire. Although there are major differences between the two, they tend to be merged in a superficial way. The divergences are several, and with reference to slavery in Roman society, the following perspectives need to be remembered as background to a variety of comments made in the New Testament. First, Roman jurists considered slavery to be morally right and legitimate. Second, racism is not a necessary component of slavery. Third, although the Roman moralist Seneca condemns the severe punishment of slaves, he has no difficulty with the moderate discipline. Fourth, for the most part Roman slaves were not segregated from freeborn persons with regard to the type of work they carried out. Slaves could be found in all economic categories, and they served, for example, as teachers, philosophers, physicians, shopkeepers, and architects; and they were known to have been able to amass substantial wealth. Fifth, manumission of Roman slaves is not to be confused with the emancipation of slaves in modern societies. The former was a legal, not a political procedure, and often served as a reward for those slaves considered worthy.[22]

For some contemporary scholars to presume that Paul endorses slavery is a bit disingenuous. In the first place, how likely is Paul, as one persecuted by the Roman Empire, to have influence in overthrowing an institution that involved some 20 to 33 percent of the population? As a member of contemporary society I may well be furious about the excessive compensation received by many corporate CEOs as well as their insensitivity to the pay, pensions, and health care of the employees entrusted to them. By urging them to treat their employees more respectfully am I thereby necessarily endorsing the corruptions of a capitalist system? Further, I can work toward reform and even replacement of the system, but do I have instantaneous and extraordinary powers to accomplish this immediately? Is Paul's situation significantly different? Hardly. Given a social system that Paul does not have control over he is nevertheless direct and forceful in his ethical admonitions addressed to that particular context. To slavemasters he writes: "Masters, treat your slaves justly and fairly, for you know that you also have a Master in heaven" (Col 4:1); "And, masters, do the same to them. Stop threatening them, for you know that both of you have the same Master in heaven, and with him there is no partiality" (Eph 6:9). What is a Roman slave to do once he has received a new perspective on life as a result of his spiritual liberation in Jesus Christ? Paul does not hesitate to give advice: "Slaves, obey your earthly masters with fear and trembling, in singleness of heart, as you obey Christ; not only while being watched, and in order to please them, but as slaves of Christ, doing the will of God from the heart. Render service with enthusiasm, as to the Lord and not to men and women, knowing that whatever good we do, we will receive the same again from the Lord, whether we are slaves or free" (Eph 6:5-8).

Paul is aware of the possibility of manumission, unusual as it was, but he is also aware that it is not wise for the believer to become obsessed with this prospect and so he asks: "Were you a slave when called? Do not be concerned about it. Even if you can gain your freedom, make use of your present condition now more than ever" (1 Cor 7:21). Whatever their social situation, their new life in Christ will allow them to transcend their specific situation the more they experience the depth of love and grace that has been poured into their heart (Rom 5:1-5). That Paul is not adverse to manumission should be obvious from his communication with Philemon, in which he attempts to persuade him to consider having Onesimus "back forever, no longer as a slave but more than a slave, a beloved brother" (Phlm 3:15-16).

And, finally, not to be overlooked is the important text in Galatians 3:28, which we have already cited, namely, that in Christ there is "no longer Jew or Greek, there is no longer slave or free, there is no longer male and female; for all of you are one in Christ Jesus." Having addressed the Galatian churches in this way Paul does not, however, assume that the proclamation of Jesus Christ in the Roman Empire will lead to the eradication of ethnic groups and slaves, or that hierarchical differences between male and female will be eliminated.[23] Rather, he expects only that such dichotomies will no longer exist *within* the community of believers. Although, for example, master sergeants and brigadier generals in the U.S. Army do not normally associate socially, I have been present at Christian Bible study groups meeting in private homes when the external boundaries between the commissioned and noncommissioned were held in abeyance within the community of faith.

Conclusion: Therefore by applying the hermeneutical principle that *an ethical application or claim of the gospel made by the authors of the New Testament, whether contingent or not, can only be revised or modified when Scripture itself provides such a justification,* it can be determined that many churches, no longer living in societies where slavery is part of the social structure, have been able to transcend such patterns of bondage on the basis of the freedom-generating texts found in Scripture itself. But to argue that the church has contradicted the New Testament in these matters is mistaken, because there is no evidence that the early church either advocated the maintenance of slavery nor that they, or the Romans for that matter, recognized slavery to be comparable to the exclusion of civil rights as defined by contemporary societies.

5.2.4 The Inclusion of the Gentiles

It is frequently argued that the early church's struggle for the inclusion of Gentiles is directly parallel to the current situation involving the inclusion of practicing homosexuals and that the former is a warrant for the latter. Is this indeed the case? Moreover, one must ask: What is at issue in the New Testament's multiple arguments for the admission of believing Gentiles into the fellowship of the church, and does this situation, in fact, have relevance for the current discussions regarding practicing homosexuals?

To begin with, it will be important to understand what is meant by the term "Gentile." As far back as Genesis 12:3 the Lord promises to Abram that "I will bless those who bless you, and the one who curses you I will curse; and in you all the families of the earth shall be blessed"; and in Genesis 18:18 the promise is repeated "that Abraham shall become a great and mighty nation, and all the nations [*goyim*] of the earth shall be blessed in him." Throughout the Old Testament the term that describes all the nations outside of or beyond Israel is *goyim*. This comes into Greek as *ethnē* and into Latin as *gens/gentis*, the transliteration of which is *gens/gentis* and leads to the term "Gentile." Contrary to common misperceptions, Gentile is not synonymous with the term Christian; from an Israelite perspective the term simply designates all the *other* nations outside of physical Israel.

That God's intention from the beginning was to extend his blessings to the other nations, that is, to the Gentiles, is specifically stated in the New Testament with explicit reference to the promises of the Old Testament. Thus Luke, the author of Acts, understands Isaiah 49:6 in such a way, and he cites that text in Acts 13:47 to demonstrate that Paul and Barnabas, as a result of Jesus' death and resurrection, are now fulfilling God's promises to the Gentiles:

> For so the Lord has commanded us, saying,
> "I have set you to be a light for the Gentiles,
> so that you may bring salvation to the ends of the earth."

Certain actions during the ministry of Jesus anticipate such a postresurrectional outreach to the Gentiles, among them his encounter with the Syrophoenician woman, a Gentile, despised by Jews, from an area northwest of Galilee, who asks him to heal her daughter. The dialogue and healing continue in this way:

> He said to her, "Let the children be fed first, for it is not fair to take the children's food and throw it to the dogs." But she answered him, "Sir, even the dogs under the table eat the children's crumbs." Then he said to her, "For saying that, you may go—the demon has left your daughter." So she went home, found the child lying on the bed, and the demon gone. (Mark 7:27-30)

A similar account can be found in Matthew 15:21-28 with the difference that the Syrophoenician woman is a Canaanite; in both cases, however, a non-Jew. In expanding on this theme in his gospel, Matthew in 12:21 cites Isaiah 42:4, "And in his name the Gentiles will hope," and has Jesus conclude the gospel with these words: "Go therefore and make disciples of all nations, baptizing them in the name of the Father and of the Son and of the

Holy Spirit, and teaching them to obey everything that I have commanded you" (Matt 28:18-20a). To be remembered, of course, is that the word "nations" in the Greek is identical to "Gentiles."

The great struggle for the inclusion of Gentile believers in the early church can be observed in the Pauline letters, especially Galatians and Romans. Paul is convinced that one of the distinctive features of the messianic age is the incorporation of believing Gentiles into the people of God. The justification for this lies in the providence of God as witnessed by his prophets. Especially important are Hosea 1:10 and 2:23, texts that he cites in Romans 9:25-26:

> Those who were not my people
> I will call "my people,"
> and her who was not beloved I
> will call "beloved."
> And in the very place where it
> was said to them, "You are not my people,"
> there they shall be called
> children of the living God.

The early Jesus movement was Jewish, but not all Jews who believed in the Christ were convinced that the gospel should be proclaimed to Gentiles. After centuries of cultic separation from the nations it was difficult for Jewish believers in Jesus as the messiah to imagine another possibility, especially because they thought that inattention to dietary regulations and other aspects of ritual purity would result in their loss of identity. Would not eating with non-Jews put at risk the identity of the early church as the messianic community of God?

Given this background the controversy between Paul and Peter (Cephas) in Antioch becomes intelligible. Paul describes the controversy in his letter to the Galatians (2:11-14):

> But when Cephas came to Antioch, I opposed him to his face, because he stood self-condemned; for until certain people came from James, he used to eat with the Gentiles. But after they came, he drew back and kept himself separate for fear of the circumcision faction. And the other Jews joined him in this hypocrisy, so that even Barnabas was led astray by their hypocrisy. But when I saw that they were not acting consistently with the truth of the gospel, I said to Cephas before them all, "If you, though a Jew, live like a Gentile and not like a Jew, how can you compel the Gentiles to live like Jews?"

It appears that James, the brother of Jesus and the leader of the Jerusalem church, could not comprehend entirely the far-reaching consequences resulting from Jesus' death, resurrection, and postresurrectional appearances,[24] namely, that those Gentiles who believed in Jesus Christ were to be fully welcomed into the Israel of God. In fact, they were elected by God for that very purpose, a theme that Paul already emphasizes in his first letter, 1 Thessalonians, and, therefore, also the earliest extant Christian document.[25] He reminds the Gentile believers in Christ that they are beloved by God and that "he has chosen you" (1:4). As a result there is now an equality of salvation that allows those in Christ, whether Jew or Gentile, to share bread together without barriers regarding the type of food to be eaten. That such a monumental change to the Jewish way of thinking would not come without controversy can be appreciated, and the sharpness of the polemical situation evident in Paul's letter to the Galatians reflects this intense conflict. At issue also was circumcision as a sign of Jewish ethnic identity, but here the potential for reinterpretation may have been somewhat less controversial given the earlier emphasis on a "circumcision of the heart" both in the Dead Sea Scrolls[26] and by Paul himself in his letter to the Romans.[27] That the apostle Paul correctly interpreted the prophetic tradition concerning the inclusion of Gentile believers in light of both the Christ event and his understanding of election is evident from the fact that his letter to the Galatians was preserved in the canon and that his perspective became the dominant one.

The debates concerning the incorporation of believing Gentiles into the Israel of God[28] were both volatile and lengthy, and they are still very much alive as Paul writes his final letter to the church in Rome. Additional evidence for this contentious situation is its considerable discussion in the book of Acts, a volume that is written considerably later than the period of Paul's ministry, probably sometime in the 90s of the first century. Among the many intentions of this secondary account of Paul's apostolic activities is the suggestion that controversies between Paul and others were settled early and that these difficulties were concluded in a harmonious manner.[29] Thus the extended narratives in Acts 10 and 11 dealing with Peter and Cornelius, as well as Acts 3:25-26, aim to demonstrate not only that God intended from the beginning that the Gentiles share in the blessing of Abraham but that this was revealed to Peter prior to the beginning of Paul's ministry. The account in Acts must be a considerably later rereading of the actual situation because Peter gives no indication whatsoever in Galatians 2:11-14 that he fully comprehends that it is possible to go to the uncircumcised and eat with the Gentiles, particularly when those from James challenge him on this matter. The decisive revelation to Peter that what "God has made clean, you must not call profane" (Acts 10:15) is clearly not in his consciousness with any degree of clarity. The acute difficulty of this situation in the early Jesus movement is reflected by the several repetitions of the essential narrative with reference to the inclusion of Gentiles in Acts 10 and 11. In fact, according to the book of Acts the question of Gentile believers is finally resolved only in Acts 15 when James stands before the council in Jerusalem and reaches the following conclusion: "Therefore I have reached the decision that we should not trouble those Gentiles who are turning to God, but we should write to them to abstain only from things polluted by idols and from fornication and from whatever has been strangled and from blood" (15:19-21). This highly stylized historical rereading shares only a distant correlation to Paul's account of the meeting he had in Jerusalem with James, Cephas/Peter, and John as recorded in Galatians 2.

For some to appeal to the events surrounding the inclusion of Gentile believers into the messianic people of God as a parallel to the church's acceptance of homosexual activity fully misses the mark; it is an emblematic example of a non sequitur. The situations are not only radically different, but they are fundamentally contradictory. Just as the members of the Qumran community believed that the Bible, and especially the prophets, were being fulfilled in their own day within their eschatological community, so did the members of the Jesus movement. Thus, what the prophets had predicted about the inclusion of the Gentile believers into the people of Israel was now being fulfilled as a result of the death and resurrection of Jesus Christ. From Genesis to the prophets to Jesus and to Paul there is a trajectory of inclusion that is now in the process of being actualized. With regard to those who engage in homosexual acts, however, there is unanimous exclusion of such activity within the holy people of God, and there is not the slightest clue in either the teaching of Jesus or the proclamation of Paul that this situation is in any way to be altered. Quite the contrary! Jesus specifically reaffirms both Genesis 1:27 and Genesis 2:24 as part of his longer teaching narrative in Matthew 19:4-6:

> He answered, "Have you not read that the one who made them at the beginning 'made them male and female,' and said, 'For this reason a man shall leave his father and mother and be joined to his wife, and the two shall become one flesh'? So they are no longer two, but one flesh. Therefore what God has joined together, let no one separate."

Paul reaffirms the sacredness of sexuality as well as its proper exercise only within the covenant of heterosexual marriage. Moving from this normative situation he pointedly excludes homosexual activity in both Romans 1:24-27 and in 1 Corinthians 6:9-11. Also not to be overlooked is the fact that one of the primary texts in Acts (15:19-21) for the inclusion of Gentiles explicitly excludes "fornication," that is, the practice of sexual intimacy outside the covenant of heterosexual marriage. Thus to argue that what is specifically intended from Genesis through the New Testament can be likened to that which is explicitly excluded from Genesis through the New Testament defies reasonable logic.

The theme of Gentile inclusion has been particularly susceptible to application in the sexuality debate because it represents the inclusion of a group that had previously not been part of Israel. Since many modern commentators exploit the language of inclusion without regard for its full biblical or theological meaning, it will be important to pick up a previous thread in our discussion and ask whether a Trinitarian hermeneutic, based on a theology of redemption, denies the significance of being "inclusive"? Quite the contrary! The gospel of Jesus Christ is radically inclusive in its call for all persons to repent, to believe, to be forgiven, and to take up the cross of discipleship. But inclusion of this sort might more appropriately be referred to as "exclusive inclusivity,"[30] since only a Trinitarian hermeneutic can lay proper claim to the biblical meaning for the term "inclusive"; it alone insists on the inclusiveness of Christ, a comprehensive inclusivity that calls for the absolute unity of faith and the moral life so that "Christ will never be isolated, as the Risen Christ, from his body, his church. [Further] this inclusiveness of Christ involves Trinitarian dynamism. Christ is present, giving his body his Spirit and guiding his people to the Father."[31] It is in the richness of this exclusive inclusivity that believing Gentiles were incorporated into the holy people of God.

Conclusion: Therefore by applying the hermeneutical principle that *an ethical application or claim of the gospel made by the authors of the New Testament, whether contingent or not, can only be revised or modified when Scripture itself provides such a justification,* we find that the discussion of Gentile inclusion in Scripture has no relevance whatsoever for the ordination of practicing homosexuals nor the blessing of such partnerships/marriages. The alleged parallels for inclusion simply do not exist, and the naive calls for the church to be inclusive or welcoming are not in any way synonymous with the situation of the early church. For the early Christian movement, inclusion denotes that those believers outside of physical Israel may become part of God's chosen people in light of the Christ event and the continuing reality of God's election. The insider/outsider dichotomy is not transferable to any categories other than Jew/Gentile precisely because the theme of election stands at the center of the entire discussion.

5.3 Hermeneutical Probings: Sexuality and Homosexuality

A canonical approach toward the biblical study of sexuality will examine all the relevant texts in the Old and the New Testament and then interpret each within the entire theological context of Scripture guided by a Christological and Trinitarian hermeneutic. It is particularly important to begin with those passages that describe sexuality and that speak to the question of its divine intentionality. Only in light of such a broader context is one then able to evaluate those texts that discuss prohibitions of certain kinds of sexuality.

The beginning point, therefore, must be to hear the complete witness of Scripture, especially the broad setting of sexuality within the purpose of God's creation. Thus, to use Leviticus 18:22; 20:13; or Romans 1:26-28 as a starting point for a discussion of homosexuality invites distortion, because it is Scripture as a whole that norms Leviticus 18, 20, and Romans 1 and not the other way around.[32] Not only must one examine the texts dealing with sexuality within the specific and the larger theological contexts in which they are placed, but careful attention must be given to (1) the question of God's plan in the creation of man and woman; (2) what, biblically, is meant by sin; and, (c) the consequences of the life of discipleship "in Christ."

Although it is not possible in this context to develop views on human sexuality much beyond what has been said earlier,[33] it is important to re-emphasize a few basic themes. According to Mark 10:2-12 Jesus gives this testimony concerning marriage and divorce:

> Some Pharisees came, and to test him they asked, "Is it lawful for a man to divorce his wife?" He answered them, "What did Moses command you?" They said, "Moses allowed a man to write a certificate of dismissal and to divorce her." But Jesus said to them, "Because of your hardness of heart he wrote this commandment for you. But from the beginning of creation, 'God made them male and female.' 'For this reason a man shall leave his father and mother and be joined to his wife, and the two shall become one flesh.' So they are no longer two, but one flesh. Therefore what God has joined together, let no one separate." Then in the house the disciples asked him again about this

matter. He said to them, "Whoever divorces his wife and marries another commits adultery against her; and if she divorces her husband and marries another, she commits adultery."

Since these words contain a clear reference to the intention of God in creation and explicitly cite Genesis 1:27 ("So God created humankind in his image, in the image of God he created them; male and female he created them") and Genesis 2:24 ("Therefore a man leaves his father and his mother and clings to his wife, and they become one flesh"), any comprehensive study of sexuality and homosexuality will need to study these foundational texts in Genesis dealing with God's creation of man and woman as sexual beings. Other relevant texts that need to be examined include Genesis 19:1-29; Leviticus 18:22; 20:13; Matthew 19:3-12; 1 Corinthians 6:9-11; 1 Timothy 1:10; Romans 1:18-32; and Ephesians 5:21-33.

Genesis 2:23-24 represents a covenant oath, with v. 23 (below) being the presupposition for v. 24 ("Therefore a man leaves his father and his mother and clings to his wife, and they become one flesh").

> Then the man (ʾādām) said,
> "This at last is bone of my bones
>   and flesh of my flesh;
> this one shall be called Woman (ʾiššâ),
>   for out of Man (ʾîš) this one was taken."

This text does not use the generic description "mankind" but rather the gender specific terms ʾiššâ and ʾîš, man and woman. Man and woman are made of the same stuff, that is, they have the same nature. Clearly, identity cannot be equated with sameness, since researchers are aware not only of biological differences but also of an entire sequence of cognitive and psychological distinctions between the sexes. Yet at the same time the answer does not lie in the overestimation of these differences either, as if men and women possess distinct natures. For those who argue this perspective one must pursue their logic and ask whether, in fact, there are not then two different human species.

This volume has argued for a Trinitarian hermeneutic as a proper way of interpreting Scripture. Analogously John Grabowski suggests that the Trinity can help in explaining the fact that women and men share in the same nature and yet are part of a different "personhood." He proposes that just as the revelation that God is both a Trinity of Persons and yet utterly one in nature provided an unexpected solution to the problem of the one and the many that so baffled ancient thought, it can shed light on the debate on sexual difference. In the Trinity, each person is utterly equal in his possession of the divine nature and yet utterly irreducible to one another as Persons. Divine Personhood is known through the relations that are constitutive of it. Only the Father begets, only the Son is begotten, and only the Holy Spirit is breathed forth as the bond of their mutual love. Personal difference exists within the unity of nature.[34]

Thus Grabowski can conclude that women and men share a common humanity but are "irreducibly different" as persons.[35] In a quite similar way Walter Kasper suggests that while men and women share the same nature they are "two equally valuable but different expressions of the one nature of humanity. . . ."[37]

In examining the biblical texts referred to in this chapter, as well as other relevant texts, one must attempt to do so in the context of Scripture as a unified and canonical whole, while simultaneously recognizing the texts as contingent,[37] spoken in specific historical moments and situations. In order to understand their intention one must also be alert to their countercultural intent, that is, what situations/challenges are being addressed. By placing specific and particular historical investigations regarding individual texts within the canonical whole, such inquiries will be considerably enhanced. To listen to Scripture in its entirety means that all relevant texts need to be examined and listened to with care; simultaneously one must also be very cautious about prejudgments that intend to jettison certain texts because of their cultic context (Leviticus 18), because they purportedly belong to Paul's Jewish-Hellenistic past (Romans 1), or because they contain a view of subordination that is no longer fashionable today (Ephesians 5). Often the ideological imperialisms of the day short-circuit both the first step of any responsible biblical interpretation, inquiry into the author's primary intention in writing at a given historical moment, and the second, the relationship of individual texts to the canon in its entirety.

The twentieth-century German biblical scholar Rudolf Bultmann has urged that there are three steps in biblical interpretation: (1) to recognize that all who come to the biblical text come to it with presuppositions; (2) to understand the text in its context and to allow it to speak in its own terms so far as possible, and; (3) to allow the examined text to confirm, alter, or reject one's initial presuppositions.[38] Keeping this process in mind when dealing with the theme of sexuality in Scripture, one must first, since no text can be approached without presuppositions, recognize that contemporary Western culture, along with other cultures, trivializes and cheapens sex at all levels. Is it coincidental, some have asked, that "permissive abortion, widespread adultery, easy divorce, radical feminism, and the gay and lesbian movement . . . [have] appeared at the same historical moment"?[39] Second, one must allow the relevant biblical texts to expose these and similar presuppositions. And, third, as a result of this difficult work, one must permit the text(s), properly understood, either to confirm the correctness of one's presuppositions or to modify, correct, or reject these initial presuppositions.

A comprehensive treatment of sexuality and homosexuality in the Bible will need to include all the relevant texts. For our more limited purpose we make reference to some of these, followed by examples of ways in which these texts might be queried.

Mark 10:2-12 (see pages 141-42 above for the complete text)

After having been in careful conversation with the text, together with its synoptic parallels in Matthew 19:3-12 and Luke 16:18, and having noted their obvious dependence on Genesis, one must ask whether the thesis of Wolfhart Pannenberg can be affirmed: "Jesus' words in Mark 10:2-9 allow the following conclusion: that the goal of the Creator's intention for humanity is the undeviating fellowship of husband and wife. The indissoluble fellowship of marriage is the reason for the creation of humans as sexual beings."[40] As the Matthean text in particular makes clear, to participate in sexual activity presupposes an unconditional and faithful self-giving within the covenant of heterosexual marriage.

Genesis 1:27-28
So God created humankind in his image,
   in the image of God he created them;
   male and female he created them.
God blessed them, and God said to them, "Be fruitful and multiply,
and fill the earth and subdue it; and have dominion over the fish of the
sea and over the birds of the air and over every living thing that moves
upon the earth."

Can it be affirmed that according to Genesis 1 sexual differentiation is "viewed as a divine gift, a mark of blessing, and a responsibility faithfully to be lived out as God's co-creators"?[41] For the church to acknowledge that

God's gift of sexuality is a call to responsible co-creatorship implies that considerably more attention and reflection be given to God's invitation to share in his work of creation, covenant making, and community building.

Genesis 2:18-25

Then the LORD God said, "It is not good that the man should be alone; I will make him a helper as his partner." So out of the ground the LORD God formed every animal of the field and every bird of the air, and brought them to the man to see what he would call them; and whatever the man called every living creature, that was its name. The man gave names to all cattle, and to the birds of the air, and to every animal of the field; but for the man there was not found a helper as his partner. So the LORD God caused a deep sleep to fall upon the man, and he slept; then he took one of his ribs and closed up its place with flesh. And the rib that the LORD God had taken from the man he made into a woman and brought her to the man. Then the man said,

> "This at last is bone of my bones
>   and flesh of my flesh;
> this one shall be called Woman,
>   for out of Man this one was taken."

Therefore a man leaves his father and his mother and clings to his wife, and they become one flesh. And the man and his wife were both naked, and were not ashamed.

One will wish to inquire from this text whether the primary significance of the relationship between male and female resides not only in the procreative potential of this relationship but also in its sexual nature at a more essential level. Do not the two opposites embrace for the purpose of bringing each other more fully toward completion?[42] The perspective of the Old Testament is that such a complementary relationship is capable of expression only heterosexually and, for this reason, homosexual relationships are viewed as contrary to God's purpose for humanity. Rodney Hutton would go even further and urge that the "aversion to homosexual practice in the Old Testament is certainly anchored in some sense of the ordered nature of creation—that Adam was given this opposite who is yet of his very bone and flesh. She is woman because she was taken from man."[43] Further reflection and careful probing of this text in its canonical fullness might help to clarify such problematical texts as 1 Corinthians 11 and might well indicate that the core issue for Paul cannot be described as "hierarchical" but "relational."[44]

Can Genesis 1 and 2 be read apart from Genesis 3 and the reality of sin? Sexuality in both testaments is repeatedly described as a gift that is not simply "dysfunctional," as we moderns are prone to say, but one that has been distorted and perverted by the power of sin and thus often becomes a sign of the brokenness of creation. According to the witness of Scripture, sin is not simply the result of personal choice in which the autonomous self is the sole arbiter of moral authority; rather, it is defined as an evil force reflecting "the power of chaos lying caged beneath God's created world."[45] As a result of the Fall *all* sexuality is now lived in a strikingly diminished way. Only when the chaotic and transpersonal nature of sin is taken seriously can one begin to understand how the partnership between male and female, created out of opposition for the purpose of complementarity, can be disfigured as alienation and oppression. Thus, it should come as no surprise that all men and women living in a disordered world are involved, to one degree or another, with disordered inclinations. What is ethically and morally relevant is not so much that persons are tempted by such inclinations but whether, in fact, they act on such disordered inclinations.

In the context of this discussion it is relevant to make reference to Romans 1:26-28:

> For this reason God gave them up to degrading passions. Their women exchanged natural intercourse for unnatural, and in the same way also the men, giving up natural intercourse with women, were consumed with passion for one another. Men committed shameless acts with men and received in their own persons the due penalty for their error. And since they did not see fit to acknowledge God, God gave them up to a debased mind and to things that should not be done.

It is frequently asserted that Paul is not here referring to persons with a homosexual orientation but only to those homosexual acts committed by *heterosexual* persons who "exchanged" natural intercourse for unnatural. Paul, however, has no interest whatsoever in questions of sexual orientation. The apostle intends only to describe the condition of sinful Gentiles who have exchanged the truth about God for a lie (1:25). Ancients did not think that there was a *class* of people with same-sex "preferences"; this is a modern notion and one that has no basis in the Western tradition. Thus, to try to use it as an interpretative category promotes misunderstanding, and to apply it to Paul is a classic example of *eisegesis,* namely, a reading *into* the text rather than allowing the text itself to speak (i.e., exegesis). Those interpreters who impose this argument on the text attempt thereby to deploy the text for their reconstruction of what Paul *really* meant and, in turn, dismiss the interpretation that the church fathers and the vast majority of modern commentators give to it. For Paul, homosexual practice is not merely a matter of specific, private sexual acts, because these acts have moral and communal consequences. By undermining the union of male and female, which is at the heart of the Creator's intention, homosexual sexual practices alienate human beings from one another and from God. "Paul," according to E. P. Sanders, "condemns both male and female homosexuality in blanket terms and without making any distinctions."[46]

Paul reaches a similar conclusion in 1 Corinthians 6:9-11:

> Do you not know that wrongdoers will not inherit the kingdom of God? Do not be deceived! Fornicators, idolaters, adulterers, male prostitutes [*malakoi*], sodomites [*arsenokoitai*], thieves, the greedy, drunkards, revilers, robbers—none of these will inherit the kingdom of God. And this is what some of you used to be. But you were washed, you were sanctified, you were justified in the name of the Lord Jesus Christ and in the Spirit of our God.

With regard to the use of the terms *malakoi* and *arsenokoitai* Sanders's commentary is unambiguous and pierces through much current illusory rhetoric:

> Paul names both the effeminate partner, the *malakos*, "soft" one, and the active one, the *arsenokoites*. Some scholars propose that the words are uncertain as to meaning and thus that perhaps Paul did not really condemn homosexuality. The words, however, are quite clear. "Soft" was a common term for the passive partner, and nothing could be more explicit than "one who buggers males." We noted the word in the Sibylline Oracle 2:73, and both that passage and Paul's reflect the terminology of Leviticus 18:22 and 20:13: *meta arsenos koiten*, "he who has coitus with a male."[47]

Reference must be made not only to the frequent misreadings of 1 Corinthians 6:9-11 but also to authors like John Shelby Spong, who will not engage in the diligent and conscientious examination of Pauline texts but prefer rather to embrace unsubstantiated speculations about the person of Paul himself. To dismiss Paul as a "religious fanatic"[48] who "was a gay man, deeply repressed, self-loathing, rigid in denial, bound by the law that he hoped could keep this thing, that he judged to be so unacceptable, totally under control, a control so profound that even Paul did not have to face this fact about himself"[49] simply does not further the cause of responsible scholarship nor reasonable dialogue. Such impulsive assertions would suggest that Spong's hermeneutic of suspicion might more effectively be applied introspectively to ascertain his own social location and those of his associates.

Leviticus 18:6-23; 20:13; Genesis 19:1-11

Leviticus 18

None of you shall approach anyone near of kin to uncover nakedness: I am the LORD. You shall not uncover the nakedness of your father, which is the nakedness of your mother; she is your mother, you shall not uncover her nakedness. You shall not uncover the nakedness of your father's wife; it is the nakedness of your father. You shall not uncover the nakedness of your sister, your father's daughter or your mother's daughter, whether born at home or born abroad. You shall not uncover the nakedness of your son's daughter or of your daughter's daughter, for their nakedness is your own nakedness. You shall not uncover the nakedness of your father's wife's daughter, begotten by your father, since she is your sister. You shall not uncover the nakedness of your father's sister; she is your father's flesh. You shall not uncover the nakedness of your mother's sister, for she is your mother's flesh. You shall not uncover the nakedness of your father's brother, that is, you shall not approach his wife; she is your aunt. You shall not uncover the nakedness of your daughter-in-law; she is your son's wife; you shall not uncover her nakedness. You shall not uncover the nakedness of your brother's wife; it is your brother's nakedness. You shall not uncover the nakedness of a woman and her daughter, and you shall not take her son's daughter or her daughter's daughter to uncover her nakedness; they are your flesh; it is depravity. And you shall not take a woman as a rival to her sister, uncovering her nakedness while her sister is still alive. You shall not approach a woman to uncover her nakedness while she is in her menstrual uncleanness. You shall not have sexual relations with your kinsman's wife, and defile yourself with her. You shall not give any of your offspring to sacrifice them to Molech, and so profane the name of your God: I am the LORD. You shall not lie with a male as with a woman; it is an abomination. You shall not have sexual relations with any animal and defile yourself with it, nor shall any woman give herself to an animal to have sexual relations with it: it is perversion.

Leviticus 20
If a man lies with a male as with a woman, both of them have committed an abomination; they shall be put to death; their blood is upon them.

Genesis 19
The two angels came to Sodom in the evening, and Lot was sitting in the gateway of Sodom. When Lot saw them, he rose to meet them, and bowed down with his face to the ground. He said, "Please, my lords, turn aside to your servant's house and spend the night, and wash your feet; then you can rise early and go on your way." They said, "No; we will spend the night in the square." But he urged them strongly; so they turned aside to him and entered his house; and he made them a feast, and baked unleavened bread, and they ate. But before they lay down, the men of the city, the men of Sodom, both young and old, all the people to the last man, surrounded the house; and they called to Lot, "Where are the men who came to you tonight? Bring them out to us, so that we may know them." Lot went out of the door to the men, shut the door after him, and said, "I beg you, my brothers, do not act so wickedly. Look, I have two daughters who have not known a man; let me bring them out to you, and do to them as you please; only do nothing to these men, for they have come under the shelter of my roof." But they replied, "Stand back!" And they said, "This fellow came here as an alien, and he would play the judge! Now we will deal worse with you than with them." Then they pressed hard against the man Lot, and came near the door to break it down. But the men inside reached out their hands and brought Lot into the house with them, and shut the door. And they struck with blindness the men who were at the door of the house, both small and great, so that they were unable to find the door.

The urgent questions that must be raised with regard to these texts are, (1) whether Leviticus 18 and 20 can be dismissed because they are merely "cultic"; and (b) whether Genesis 19 is really dealing with inhospitality rather than sexually offensive behavior. With regard to the Leviticus texts, employing both historical biblical criticism as well as a canonical approach, it must be asked on what basis one is able to dismiss the warrants against male homosexuality but not those dealing with incest and bestiality? Also not unimportant is the positive influence of Leviticus 18 on Pauline theology (see 1 Cor 6:9-11 above), an early Christian thinker who can hardly be accused of his uncritical acceptance of the law. With regard to Genesis one must inquire whether the remainder of the canon actually understands Genesis 19:1-11 only as inhospitality. The use of the verb *yādaᶜ* in Genesis[50] with the meaning "to have sexual intercourse" and the reference to the Sodom tradition in Ezekiel 16:47-52 as the doing of "abominable things" make clear that sexual offenses, and specifically, homosexual activity, are the focus.[51] An examination of the entire canonical witness, including not only Ezekiel 16:47-52 but also Jeremiah 23:14; Isaiah 1:9; 13:19; Amos 4:11; Zephaniah 2:9; Jude 7; 2 Peter 2:4-8; and Matthew 11:23-24 make it difficult to sustain the argument that the reference to Sodom and Gemorrah is ever primarily cited as an example of "inhospitality" in any biblical text. Rather, the themes of "total destruction" and "sexual offense" are the ones in the foreground.[52]

A canonical study of sexuality, after having explored all the relevant texts in detail and in dialogue with one another, will have to ask whether, in fact, the Old Testament's negative understanding of "homoerotic behavior is consistent and is coherent with its view of the nature of God's intent for sexual expression within the context of patterns of justice and righteousness which permeate creation"?[53] Also to be explored is the Pauline theme of justification as God's sovereign reclamation and restoration of his broken creation and whether the apostle is not contrasting the revelation of God's righteousness in Jesus Christ (Rom 3:21-31) with the sinfulness described in Rom 1:18-32.

Perhaps it may be helpful to ask a negative question: at what points would the biblical texts cited above, viewed in their entire canonical context, not yield the following results: (1) That heterosexual marriage is linked with the procreative power of and responsibility to the Creator God; that marriage represents the complementariness of male and female; that such marriage is the only arena for the expression of sexual desire, a desire that is powerful, often unpredictable, and capable of grotesque deformations. Consistent with this reading of Scripture, it can be argued that marriage "is a place where, in a singular manner, our waywardness begins to be healed and our fear of commitment overcome, where we may learn to place another person's needs rather than our own desires at the center of life."[54] (2) That there is not one biblical text that contradicts Paul's negative evaluation of homosexuality; further, that homosexuality is repeatedly declared to be a path that deviates from God's intention for creation; and that, finally, today's cultural situation is not new: Paul unwaveringly speaks against a culture with a radically divergent sexual ethic. Thus for Craig Nessan to assert that "the scriptural witness is far more ambiguous with regard to homosexuality than it is, for example, about racism or hunger" constitutes an unmistakable misrepresentation of the evidence.[55]

The New Testament unequivocally maintains that sexuality is to be practiced in the context of lifelong heterosexual marriage. Those who would deny such a conclusion on the grounds that Jesus never spoke against homosexuality simply miss a fundamental point: Jesus was thoroughly a Jew and on this issue there was complete agreement among the various expressions of Judaism in the first century. The only biblical alternatives to lifelong heterosexual marriage are abstinence or celibacy. All other forms of sexual expression are repeatedly referred to as "impurity, sexual immorality or licentiousness" (2 Cor 12:21). This matter is of such magnitude that Paul not only addresses the issue of appropriate sexual behavior in his earliest letter, 1 Thessalonians, but specifically declares that what he writes is the will of the Lord Jesus: "For you know what instructions we gave you through the Lord Jesus. For this is the will of God, your sanctification: that you abstain from fornication; that each one of you know how to control your own body in holiness and honor, not with lustful passion, like the Gentiles who do not know God" (1 Thess 4:2-5).[56]

Conclusion: Therefore by having applied the hermeneutical principle that *an ethical application or claim of the gospel made by the authors of the New Testament, whether contingent or not, can only be revised or modified when Scripture itself provides such a justification* it has become unmistakably clear that there are no texts in Scripture dealing with sexuality that provide the Church Catholic justification to modify or revise its long-established teaching with regard to the issue of homosexuality. A Trinitarian hermeneutic has to acknowledge that human interpretations of Scripture can be corrected, but only a compelling generative force within Scripture itself can justify such an alteration. In the case of homosexuality, Scripture gives no warrant whatsoever for any deviation from a position maintained with consistency throughout the canon and throughout the history of the Church Catholic.

Notes

1. For a further discussion see chapter 6 in this volume.

2. With regard to the relationship of covenant to sexuality I have been instructed by John S. Grabowski, *Sex and Virtue: An Introduction to Sexual Ethics* (Washington, D.C.: Catholic University of America, 2003). Also influential has been Carlo Maria Martini, *On the Body: A Contemporary Theology of the Human Person* (New York: Crossroad, 2001).

3. See further the discussion in chapter 6 of this volume.

4. Grabowski, *Sex and Virtue*, 38.

5. Ibid., 39.

6. See the previous discussion of this text on pages 89-91 in this volume.

7. Often in the Old Testament the terms "righteousness" (*sĕdāqâ*) and "justice" (*mišpaṭ*) are used synonymously as, for example, in Genesis 18:19 and Amos 5:24.

8. See pages 78-83 in this volume for the discussion of this terminology.

9. See page 7 in this volume.

10. Grabowski, *Sex and Virtue*, 79

11. "A response to *The Church and Human Sexuality: A Lutheran Perspective* by members of the faculty at Luther Northwestern Theological Seminary, St. Paul, Minnesota, April 5, 1994," 3. The Faculty Drafting Group includes Robert H. Albers, Terence E. Fretheim, Arland J. Hultgren, Diane L. Jacobson, and Paul R. Sponheim [henceforth referred to as LNTS]. A remarkably similar approach is taken by Craig L. Nessan, *Many Members Yet One Body: Committed Same-Gender Relationships and the Mission of the Church* (Minneapolis: Augsburg Fortress, 2004).

12. See, for example, Nessan, *Many Members Yet One Body*, 72-73.

13. Joseph A. Fitzmyer, "The Matthean Divorce Texts and Some New Palestinian Evidence," in *To Advance the Gospel: New Testament Studies* (Biblical Resource Series; Grand Rapids: Eerdmans, 1998) 79-111.

14. I. Howard Marshall, *A Critical and Exegetical Commentary on the Pastoral Epistles* (ICC; Edinburgh: T & T Clark) 569.

15. Cenchreae was the port of ancient Corinth about 6.5 miles east of the city on the Saronic Gulf.

16. John D. Crossan and Jonathan L. Reed, *In Search of Paul: How Jesus' Apostle Opposed Rome's Empire with God's Kingdom* (New York: HarperSanFrancisco) 115.

17. John Shelby Spong, *The Sins of Scripture: Exposing the Bible's Texts of Hate to Reveal the God of Love* (San Francisco: HarperSanFrancisco, 2005) 22.

18. Paul rejects similar emphases in 1 Corinthians 7.

19. For a further elaboration of a similar perspective, see Sharon H. Gritz, *Paul, Women Teachers, and the Mother Goddess at Ephesus: A Study of 1 Timothy 2:9-15 in Light of the Religious and Cultural Milieu of the First Century* (Lanham, Md.: University Press of America, 1991).

20. See Spong, *The Sins of Scripture*.

21. Nessan, *Many Members Yet One Body*, 35

22. For a more detailed discussion of slavery in the Roman world, see J. A. Harrill, "Slavery," in *Dictionary of New Testament Background*, ed. Craig A. Evans and Stanley E. Porter (Downers Grove, Ill: InterVarsity, 2000) 1124-27, as well as the literature cited there.

23. See the previous discussion of 1 Corinthians 11, pages 130-32 in this volume.

24. See 1 Corinthians 15.

25. For a further discussion on election, see Karl P. Donfried and I. Howard Marshall, *The Theology of the Shorter Pauline Letters* (Cambridge: Cambridge University Press) 28-30.

26. 1QpHab 11:13 (Commentary on Habakkuk).

27. Romans 2:29. One might also observe that the theme of circumcision does not occur in the final letter of the Jerusalem Council to the Gentiles (Acts 15:22-30).

28. A term that Paul uses in Galatians 6:16.

29. Note the emphasis on *homothoumodon* in Acts.

30. See the discussion on pages 7 and 44 in this volume.

31. Richard John Neuhaus, *Biblical Interpretation in Crisis: The Ratzinger Conference on Bible and Church* (Grand Rapids: Eerdmans, 1989) 166.

32. Arland Hultgren, "Being Faithful to the Scriptures: Romans 1:26-27 as a Case in Point," *Word & World* 14 (Winter 1994) 315-25.

33. See pages 118-22 in this volume.

34. Grabowski, *Sex and Virtue*, 110.

35. Ibid.

36. Ibid.

37. By the term "contingent" is meant the specific actualization of the will of God for the purpose of salvation; it does not refer to something as irrelevant or as "discardable."

38. See the insightful article by Rudolph Bultmann, "Is Exegesis Without Presuppositions Possible?" in *Existence and Faith: Shorter Writings of Rudolf Bultmann*, ed. Schubert M. Ogden (Cleveland: World, 1965) 289-96.

39. "The Homosexual Movement: A Response by the Ramsey Colloquium," in *First Things* 41 (March, 1994) 15-21, here 17.

40. Wolfhart Pannenberg, "'Einem männlichen Wesen darfst du nicht beiwohnen' Maßstäbe zur kirchlichen Urteilsbildung über Homsexualität," *Zeitwende* 65/1 (January 1994) 1-4; here, 1 (translation mine).

41. Rodney Hutton, "Old Testament Perspectives on Human Sexuality" (unpublished typescript) 8.

42. Ibid., 13-14.

43. Ibid., 13.

44. *Kephalē* is not concerned with "head" as authority but as the source of life. Although man is the source of woman's life, she is man's glory, and without her he would not be complete—a remarkable parallel to Genesis 2:18-25. See further, Gordon D. Fee, *The First Epistle to the Corinthians* (Grand Rapids: Eerdmans, 1987) 498-512.

45. Hutton, "Old Testament Perspectives," 22.

46. E. P. Sanders, *Paul* (Oxford: Oxford University Press, 1991) 112-13.

47. Ibid. See also Robert A. J. Gagnon, *The Bible and Homosexual Practice: Texts and Hermeneutics* (Nashville: Abingdon, 2001) 303-32.

48. Spong, *The Sins of Scripture*, 137.

49. Ibid., 140.

50. Genesis 4:1, 17, 25; 24:16; 38:26.

51. Hutton, "Old Testament Perspectives," 18: *to eba* in Ezekiel 16:50a is the same term used for homosexual activity in Leviticus 18:22 and 20:13.

52. See also the discussion of the specific texts in Gagnon, *The Bible and Homosexual Practice*.

53. Hutton, "Old Testament Perspectives," 21.

54. "The Homosexual Movement: A Response by the Ramsey Colloquium" 17.

55. Nessan, *Many Members Yet One Body*, 77.

56. See further Karl P. Donfried, "The Cults of Thessalonica and the Thessalonian Correspondence," in *Paul, Thessalonica and Early Christianity* (Grand Rapids: Eerdmans, 2002), 21-48.

6

The Bible and the Church

Hermeneutics Once Again

6.1 Confronting Alien Hermeneutics

Misleading approaches to Scripture often fail to consider the entire canonical context of Christian Scripture as a narrational and theological whole centered in the Trinitarian God who has revealed himself definitively in the death and resurrection of Jesus Christ. As we have had repeated opportunity to observe, such alien hermeneutics remove biblical texts from a Trinitarian universe of meaning and introduce them into an alien ideological context. Characteristic of such dislodgment are the hermeneutics of ambiguity, dissonance, and antinomianism.

6.1.1 *The Hermeneutics of Ambiguity*

Usually the first step away from a Trinitarian hermeneutic is one that operates within much of the biblical narrative but refuses to take seriously the centrality of the Christ event. Marcus Borg, for example, summarizes three primary convictions that emerge from his study of the biblical traditions:

(1) "First, there is a deep sense of the reality of the sacred. God is not only real, but knowable. Moreover, the sacred is known not in a set of statements about God, but experientially, as a Mystery beyond all language."

(2) "Second, there is a strong conviction that our lives are made 'whole' and 'right' by living in a conscious relationship with the Mystery who is alone Lord."

(3) "Third, these voices are convinced that God is a God of justice and compassion."[1]

Such an interpretation, revealing as it does the subtle influences of current cultural philosophies, is so unfocused that it distorts the fundamental themes of Scripture, including the fact that the depth of sin and the far-reaching character of judgment are omnipresent throughout the biblical story. As a result there is little room, if any, in these hermeneutics of ambiguity for forgiveness and the renewed moral life in Christ; instead indistinct statements such as the "Bible is God's means of coming to us"[2] abound. Against such interpretations a Trinitarian hermeneutic insists that the God revealed in the Bible does not remain a "Mystery." Rather, the God of Israel and the God of Jesus come to us in the form of the Incarnate One and with a specific intention: for salvation, for the setting right of a broken cosmos, for the healing of sin, for reestablishing relationship with the Creator God, and for setting us on a path whereby we, through unmerited grace, can discern and do his will.

Ambiguity quickly gives way to imprecision in the explanation of biblical terminology and conceptualities. This is especially the case with regard to the use of the term "love" as a cliché in many current ecclesial discussions. Philip Turner illustrates with lucidity how the transition from a vague notion of God, much like that of Borg, ends up with a defective notion of love. In much contemporary preaching "the incarnation is to be understood as merely a manifestation of divine love. From this starting point, several conclusions are drawn. The first is that God is love pure and simple. Thus, one is to see in Christ's death no judgment upon the human condition. Rather, one is to see an affirmation of creation and the persons we are. The life and death of Jesus [merely] reveal the fact that God accepts and affirms us."[3] Love, deprived of its Christocentric focus, evolves into a theology of acceptance and ambiguity in which critical questions are no longer asked and moral demands are no longer necessary for the life of discipleship. Commenting on Romans 13:8-10, the following conclusion is reached by one Protestant study on the advisability of ordaining practicing gays and lesbians as well as the blessing of those partnerships: "This love which does 'no wrong to a neighbor' and fulfills all the commandments is pivotal for evaluating homosexual activity. Through Jesus Christ, the heart of the Law is revealed as love of God and love of neighbor. Gay and lesbian persons are indeed among the neighbors we are called by Christ to love. But what that love entails, and the implications for church policy, evoke different responses among us."[4] Indeed, this is the emblematic refrain of a quasi-deist theology whose proclamation is limited to a benevolent God who acts "neither to save us from our sins nor to raise us to new life after the pattern of Christ . . . [and that] produces an ethic of tolerant affirmation that carries with it no call to conversion and radical holiness."[5] Such an alien hermeneutic of ambiguity sanctions acceptance without reservation, whereas a theology based on a Trinitarian hermeneutic achieves a far more nuanced and comprehensive understanding both of love as well as its implications for the ethical life in Christ. Love is then no longer viewed as some abstract and inarticulate concept exempt from the corrupting power of sin, which entices us to place the love of neighbor apart from the love of God; instead one is able to come to terms with "God's difficult, redemptive love."[6] No doubt Dietrich Bonhoeffer would use the terms "cheap grace" and "costly grace"[7] as a way to distinguish between these two radically different interpretations of love.

6.1.2 The Hermeneutics of Dissonance

Because the historical study of the Bible independent of other considerations can teach us only what selected texts may have meant in their original settings, such methods offer little comprehensive guidance as to how they should be interpreted within and for the nurture of the contemporary church. When such critical approaches are used apart from a Trinitarian hermeneutic, biblical studies will be dominated by a variety of alien ideological perspectives; this presents an acute problem for the Church Catholic not least because this state of affairs exists as a largely unrecognized threat to classical expressions of the Christian faith. Before the rich model provided by understanding Scripture as a School of the Word[8] can become effective, the seriousness of the current dilemma needs to be recognized.

A hermeneutics of dissonance sets up discord and conflict between Scripture and the present mission of the church. "In the end," argues one leading theologian, "one no longer learns what the text says, but what it should have said. . . ."[9] Contributing to the confusion concerning the meaning of the biblical text for the contemporary church is Krister Stendahl's distinction between "what it meant," "what it means," and "what it might come to mean."[10] His appropriate concern is not to "freeze" provisional biblical expressions and formulations into absolute theological formulations. While recognizing the importance of this point, it must, however, be emphasized that there are fundamental witnesses to truth in Scripture that cannot simply be transformed and reshaped as a result of either the indeterminate argument of the provisional or as a consequence of the ideological winds that sweep across every generation. More accurate than the "what it meant"/"what it means" dichotomy is the recognition that there is a difference between "the truths of faith and the manner in which they are expressed. . . ."[11] Contingent articulation, however, does not negate the truth of faith expressed, nor does it mean that the ethical and moral teachings of Scripture are merely episodic comments.

In practical terms, aside from creating a fracture between the authority of Scripture as understood by the church fathers and the contemporary church, the "what it meant"/"what it means" dichotomy often implies that "what it meant" does not correspond to current cultural movements; as a result a hermeneutic of dissonance often becomes an advocate for "what the text should mean." In so doing a variety of dichotomies and dissonances are established, as can be observed in the work of Spong,[12] Nessan,[13] and Stendahl. Although acknowledging that procreation is an important dimension of sexuality in the Old Testament, Stendahl, for example, adds that the "theme of procreation is not part of Paul's reasoning about sexuality, nor is it anywhere in the New Testament."[14] Does Stendahl assume that Jesus and Paul began with a *tabula rasa* and that the community of Jesus was a new religion begun *de novo*? It is indeed puzzling that the one who has argued so vigorously against such a view and who has repeatedly urged that Paul was called to a new task and not converted to a new religion can so hastily drop the Jewishness of both Jesus and Paul when that no longer fits the needs of his hermeneutic of dissonance.

A hermeneutic of dissonance in which "what it meant" is often placed in conflict with "what it means" (i.e., "what it *should* mean") is fraught with grave danger and is filled with highly questionable exegetical maneuvers. About 1 Corinthians 7:10 and 12 Stendahl remarks that Paul is giving advice to a specific situation in Corinth and clearly affirms "I say, not the Lord. . . ." These statements become for Stendahl Paul's "personal opinions" and his "tentative advice"[15] and are then applied to Romans 1:26-28 and 1 Corinthians 6:9-11, texts in which Paul speaks of homosexuality. These clever but unsuccessful attempts at correlation conflate a misunderstood contingency with coherence, and such missteps erode Scripture as a normative source for theology and ethics.[16] What is to prevent one from applying such "personal opinions" and "tentative advice" to the theme of the resurrection and simply conflate the contingency of apocalyptic language with the divine mystery of resurrection and discard them both as outdated cultural expressions? Any canonical exegesis will want to present all of the relevant texts, as well as their underlying assumptions, within the total framework of the testimony of Scripture; only within this broader field of meaning can one adequately discuss the relationship of contingency and coherence. Stendahl's grave hesitancy to follow such a hermeneutic is also evident when he uses

Matthew 23:4 to issue warnings against "binding heavy burdens" with regard to sexuality; to do so he exploits a text that is entirely unrelated to marriage, divorce, or celibacy. This propensity to pick and choose texts at will and with blatant disregard for context is precisely why "alien hermeneutics" are so enticingly precarious and why one needs to be wary of the fundamentalism of the left. George Lindbeck remarks perceptively that such approaches tend more "to replace Scripture than lead to it."[17]

The "what it means"/"what it meant" dichotomy made explicit by Stendahl but also implicit in the work of many others is fraught with grave dangers that lead to skewed interpretations of the biblical text. In light of these provocations, a Trinitarian hermeneutic will bring to the fore some of the following concerns:

1. Since there are in the New Testament certain moral commandments that must *always* remain effective and since certain types of behavior that are not "worthy of the gospel of Christ" (Phil 1:27) must always be prohibited, the contrast between "what it meant"/"what it means" should be eliminated because of its strong potential for imprecision and distortion. A far more productive method for approaching Stendahl's appropriate apprehension that the provisional not be frozen into the absolute is instead to consider the complex correlation between the "coherent" and the "contingent," an approach that we have discussed earlier.

2. If the interpretative key for a Christologically based Trinitarian ecclesiological hermeneutic is always the crucified and risen Christ, then any claim toward liberation and freedom, claims that lay behind the hermeneutics of dissonance and expediency, must be tested against the freedom to which Christ calls his followers in discipleship. For the Church Catholic to defend unchanging moral norms is not an expression of oppression but an exercise in defending the true freedom of the Christian, a freedom gained only by the death of the crucified one whose service is perfect freedom; ambiguous calls to liberation based on dubious cultural claims can never stand in opposition to revealed truth. Thus, it is not some modern notion of freedom that becomes the source of ethical life, but the will of God as testified to in Scripture and interpreted by the Trinitarian church.

3. Since the church and the development of its canon are not a later addendum to the Christ event but integral parts of it, any modern theological treatment of sexuality will need to consider the church's struggle with this issue over many centuries, a conversation set forth skillfully by Peter Brown in his extraordinary volume *Body and Society*.[18] Were early Christians, one might ask, simply perverse in their struggle with sexuality or did they correctly recognize in it a power that, if not exercised with great care,

could have demonic consequences? Did they perhaps have an insight that we post-moderns might benefit from today, namely, that sexual activity must not become the dominating center of human existence? Once again the words of Raymond E. Brown contain much wisdom and directly refute a key presupposition of any hermeneutic of dissonance: "What the biblical text said to its first readers should be related to what the text says to me, because I am a Christian heir to the people of Israel and the people of the early church, and *not independent of them*."[19]

6.1.3 The Hermeneutics of Antinomianism

The greatest deception employed by the various manifestations of alien hermeneutics is the assumption, often unexpressed, that neither the gospel of Jesus Christ nor Paul's understanding of justification have specific ethical and moral consequences; it is at this point that we see the clearest clash between a theology of acceptance and a theology of redemption, between cheap grace and costly grace, between an alien and a Trinitarian hermeneutic. The former consistently maintains that there is a dichotomy between that which it considers to be essential and nonessential and, more specifically, that there is a separation of faith from the moral life. In effect this is a form of antinomianism, one that claims that those in Christ are not bound by moral laws.

A hermeneutic of antinomianism will often begin with a correct assertion that Scripture cannot be used as a legalistic textbook that describes and prescribes all ethical action, as is frequently the case with the fundamentalism of the religious right. From there it moves to a more ambiguous affirmation that "the Bible does indeed inform and guide us in regard to moral issues. . . ."[20] It is not too extreme a leap to move from censuring the misuse of Scripture as a legalistic textbook to then limiting its function to that of simply informing and guiding? This essentially denies Scripture the normative function of serving as a foundational source for moral teachings that contain specific parameters of behavior, the nonperformance of which places one outside the community.[21]

When the hermeneutics of antinomianism refers to the verbs "inform and guide" they are not meant in any authoritative sense; as a consequence it is fully possible, so it is thought, to argue misleadingly that the "church has over-ridden what has been interpreted as the clear teachings of Scripture in favor of more just practices which better serve the neighbor and community. The church, for example, remarries divorced persons, ordains women and opposes slavery. . . ."[22] Since Scripture is reduced to simply one source of information among others, the church is encouraged to incorporate the insights of the natural and social sciences into its moral deliberations and thus "to exercise our stewardship as persons endowed by reason and powers of observation."[23] Can the church, however, endorse a hermeneutic shaped by "more just practices" and endowments of "reason and powers of observation" that is divorced from the reality of sin? A Trinitarian hermeneutic will have to raise the challenge whether the will of God as revealed in the Christ event corrects and informs our reason, powers of observation, and definitions of love *or* whether human perceptions correct and inform our understanding of Scripture?

In opposition to such hermeneutics of antinomianism it must be insisted that the separation of faith from the moral life is impossible from a New Testament perspective and that the unfocused interpretations of love advocated by these scholars are inconsistent with its proper understanding. *Veritatis Splendor* puts the matter well:

> When the apostle Paul sums up the fulfillment of the law in the precept of love of neighbor as oneself (cf. Rom 13:8-10), he is not weakening the commandments but reinforcing them, since he is revealing their requirements and their gravity. Love of God and of one's neighbor cannot be separated from the observance of the commandments of the covenant renewed in the blood of Jesus Christ and in the gift of the Spirit.[24]

Such an understanding of the ethical life places love in the appropriate context of justification as both a gift and a responsibility and consequently holds faith and the moral life together as one.

An ecclesiological, Trinitarian hermeneutic, in which Scripture is recognized as a unified and canonical whole, would offer the following proposals in reaction to an assortment of deceptions inherent in the various hermeneutics of antinomianism:

1. With regard to the *authority of Scripture*, it is necessary to assert together with *Veritatis Splendor*[25] that "Christ is the teacher, the risen one who has life in himself and who is always present in his church and in the world. It is he who opens up to the faithful the book of the Scriptures and, by fully revealing the Father's will, teaches the truth about moral action." As a result, Scripture is and remains the "living and fruitful source"[26] of the church's ethical and moral teachings. There is in Scripture an intimate and unbreakable bond between justification and sanctification, faith and moral actions that are pleasing to God.[27]

2. With regard to the *separation of faith and the moral life* by some, it will be necessary to assert that the way of salvation is, according to Scripture, made real precisely in the obedience of the moral life. Is this not what Paul means by the "obedience of faith" in Romans (1:5; 6:16; 15:18) as well as in his reference to the "form of teaching to which you were entrusted" (Rom 6:17)? With *Veritatis Splendor* one has to ask whether it is "possible to obey God and thus love God and neighbor without respecting these commandments in all circumstances."[28] If these commandments are not respected must one not, in fact, speak of the possibility of love as sin? Can a blurred discussion of love, often ideologically driven, override the commandments?

There is a fundamental misconception among many that the divine openness of Christ to all sorts and conditions of persons is equivalent to an "I'm OK, your OK" mentality; such a perception is succinctly described in Philip Turner's essay.[29] Surely the grace of Christ welcomes all for the purpose of repentance and the renewal of a right relationship with the living God, but the message of divine openness emphatically includes the divine invitation to lead a life of discipleship: "Come, follow me" (Matt 19:21). The indicative contains an imperative! Or, to put it in a Pauline context, justification is both "*Gabe* und *Aufgabe*" (gift *and* responsibility).[30] It is surely not incidental that much of Scripture, including the New Testament, places great emphasis on exhortation and urges vigilance over the right conduct for those who are in Christ. Grace embraces not only the gift of forgiveness and reconciliation but also the power to lead a new life of discipleship in holiness and with accountability.

Some Christians, especially in the Protestant tradition, become nervous with such discussions, almost immediately suggesting that one is engaging in an ethic of "works righteousness." Luther, frequently cited in this regard, would demur: "Good works do not make a good man, but a good man does good works."[31] The life of discipleship cannot be exercised as a result of our own strength but only because a gift has been received. As Paul makes clear in Rom 8:1-4, only in the life of the Spirit is the law, that is, the will of God, fulfilled and the possibility of carrying out God's commandments given. Neither here nor in 1 Corinthians 7, however, do God's commandments become *adiaphora*, that is, optional: "For neither circumcision counts for anything nor uncircumcision, but keeping the commandments of God" (1 Cor 7:19). The maturation, progress, and transformation of the life in Christ are essential characteristics of "good works" as well as of the Pauline understanding of baptism and justification.[32]

3. Practitioners of the hermeneutics of antinomianism often advocate for "more just practices"[33] and for "the public exercise of human reasoning . . ."[34] in their desire to make the Bible relevant to modern culture. With regard to assigning the autonomous self and human reason a hermeneutical primacy of place, a Trinitarian hermeneutic will have to insist, together with the classical Christian tradition, that human beings are unable, without forgiveness and the guidance of the Spirit normed by Scripture, to really know what best serves the neighbor, what best enhances life in community, and what is just. Would not this tradition be highly skeptical of placing too high a value on "reason and the powers of observation" insulated from the corrupting power of sin? Would not Augustine and Luther agree with Paul's pronouncements in Romans 3 and insist with him that "reason and the powers of observation" are very much in bondage to sin? In many discussions of "justice" and "just practices" one also observes the disturbing tendency to separate sanctification from justification and the moral life in Christ from faith by the use of distinctly secular ethical reasoning. Such antinomian tendencies place themselves in opposition to the teaching of the Trinitarian church which has always insisted that the moral life is not established by human beings through the power of reason or through the agency of the social sciences but rather by God himself, the Holy Trinity. "Some people," *Veritatis Splendor* correctly observes, by "disregarding the dependence of human reason on divine wisdom and the need, given the present state of fallen nature, for divine revelation as an effective means for knowing moral truths, even those of the natural order, have actually posited a complete sovereignty of reason in the domain of moral norms regarding the right ordering of life in this world."[35] God and not humans *author* what is "just," and it is as a consequence of this divine *author*ship that God's justice and righteousness become *author*itative for us.

A similar perspective needs also to be applied to the frequent dependence on the behavioral sciences as an authority in the moral arena. Must not those who stand in a biblical tradition shaped by a Trinitarian center be at least suspicious that what is declared as "normal" in these human endeavors might, in fact, be warped by the power of sin? Can one concur that the hermeneutics of an autonomous self, motivated by the need to satisfy personal desire, which lies at the root of much current thinking in the behavioral sciences, is incompatible with a life of discipleship? Is experiencing the joy of the gospel dependent on every human need being acted upon? Again the contemporary Roman Catholic tradition has spoken forthrightly: "The affirmation of moral principles is not within the competence of formal empirical methods. . . . Hence the behavioral sciences, despite the great value of the information which they provide, cannot be considered decisive indications of moral norms. It is the gospel which reveals the full truth about man and his moral journey, and thus enlightens and admonishes sinners. . . ."[36]

False hermeneutical starting points together with the failure to view Scripture as a unified whole and as a fruitful source of the church's moral teaching contribute toward the widespread tendency to play "First-Century Bible Land,"[37] that is, to pick and choose those texts that cohere with the dominant ideologies; texts that stand in contradiction are discarded with the pretext that they belong to a time-conditioned and obsolete Jewish or Hellenistic worldview that should best be abandoned. Once again it is important to affirm that it is not historical biblical criticism per se that is primarily the villain, but, rather, diverse manifestations of alien hermeneutics that misappropriate and misinterpret its proposals.[38]

6.2 Some Concluding Thoughts

George Lindbeck recognizes with distressing accuracy that it is "now the scholarly rather than the hierarchical clerical elite which holds the Bible captive and makes it inaccessible to ordinary folk."[39] Some in this new scholarly elite have indeed so manipulated Scripture that no word of God could possibly emerge from biblical texts for the contemporary church. Faced with similar concerns by those who had usurped the authority to interpret the Bible in his day, Tertullian boldly asks to whom the Bible belongs, who its rightful owners are, and who is entitled to interpret its texts for the Church Catholic. His audacious reply is as remarkably accurate today as it was in the third century: "This property belongs to me; I have always possessed it, I have possessed it prior to you and have reliable title-deeds from the original owners of the estate. I am the heir of the apostles."[40] Tertullian, good lawyer that he was, adamantly insists that for accurate biblical interpretation to take place there must be a direct continuity between the normative apostolic witness to the Christ event and that of its subsequent interpreters. Anyone who rejects the indispensable components of the Christian narrative would be engaged in an *alien hermeneutic*, namely, an interpretation of the Christ event that was in effect opposed to its essential meaning and dependent on extrabiblical conceptualities.

At the beginning of his 1988 lecture in New York City on biblical hermeneutics, Joseph Ratzinger narrated a fascinating yet disturbing image in Wladmir Solowjew's *History of the Antichrist,* in which "the eschatological enemy of the Redeemer recommended himself to believers, among other things, by the fact that he had earned his doctorate in theology at Tübingen and had written an exegetical work which was recognized as pioneering in the field. The Antichrist, a famous exegete! With this paradox Solowjew sought to shed light on the ambivalence inherent in biblical exegetical methodology. . . ."[41] The objective here is not the rejection of critical biblical methods, tools, and resources, for that would only move us from a fundamentalism of the left to a fundamentalism of the right, but rather to say that the historical approach alone does not comprehensively exhaust the content of Scripture nor necessarily provide a faithful direction for its interpretation by the Christian church. When, however, these valuable aids are employed and transformed by a Trinitarian hermeneutic that acknowledges Scripture in its canonical fullness, and when these tools are used in harmony with the church that both preceded the New Testament and shaped the canon through the guidance of the Holy Spirit, then Scripture can indeed become Holy Scripture and then the Word of God will be manifested to the contemporary church with power and, through her, to the entire world.[42] The final sentences in Joseph Ratzinger's essay appropriately recognize that a Christian biblical hermeneutic "must recognize that the faith of the church is that form of *'sympathia'* without which the Bible remains a *closed* book. It must come to acknowledge this faith as a hermeneutic, the space for understanding which does not do dogmatic violence to the Bible, but precisely allows the solitary possibility for the Bible to be itself."[43]

Notes

1. Marcus Borg, *Reading the Bible Again for the First Time* (San Francisco: HarperSanFrancisco, 2001) 299-300.

2. "A response to *The Church and Human Sexuality: A Lutheran Perspective* by members of the faculty at Luther Northwestern Theological Seminary, St. Paul, Minnesota, April 5, 1994," 3. The Faculty Drafting Group includes Robert H. Albers, Terence E. Fretheim, Arland J. Hultgren, Diane L. Jacobson, and Paul R. Sponheim [henceforth referred to as LNTS].

3. Philip Turner, "An Unworkable Theology," *First Things* 154 (June/July 2005) 10-12, here 10-11.

4. "The Church and Human Sexuality: A Lutheran Perspective," First Draft of a Social Statement, Division for Church in Society, Department for Studies of the Evangelical Lutheran Church in America [henceforth, ELCA], Chicago, October 1993, 15. In the evaluation of this ELCA text that follows it is important to note that the comments are directed to the question of what is normative for Scripture and do not stand in judgment of particular individuals.

5. Turner, "An Unworkable Theology," 11.

6. Ibid.

7. See pages 85-86 in this volume.

8. See pages 32-39 in this volume.

9. Joseph Ratzinger, "Biblical Interpretation in Crisis: On the Question of the Foundations and Approaches of Exegesis Today," in Richard John Neuhaus, *Biblical Interpretation in Crisis: The Ratzinger Conference on Bible and Church* (Grand Rapids: Eerdmans, 1989) 1-23, here 2.

10. Krister Stendahl, "Biblical Theology, Contemporary" in *Interpreter's Dictionary of the Bible* (4 volumes; New York: Abingdon, 1962) 1:418-32; now reprinted with new introductory remarks in *Meanings: The Bible as Document and as Guide* (Philadelphia: Fortress, 1984) 11-44; see also 1-7.

11. *Veritatis Splendor*, in *Origins* 23/18 (October 14, 1993) 297-336; here 307 is cited. *Veritatis Splendor* is a papal encyclical issued by Pope John Paul II in 1993.

12. John Shelby Spong, *The Sins of Scripture: Exposing the Bible's Texts of Hate to Reveal the God of Love* (San Francisco: HarperSanFrancisco, 2005).

13. Craig L. Nessan, *Many Members Yet One Body: Committed Same-Gender Relationships and the Mission of the Church* (Minneapolis: Augsburg Fortress, 2004).

14. Krister Stendahl, "Memorandum on Our Bible and Our Sexuality" 4 (unpublished draft also subsequently circulated as "Letter to the Evangelical Lutheran Church in America, February 28, 1994).

15. Stendahl, "Memorandum," 2.

16. For a previous discussion of "contingency" and "coherence," see pages 122-24 in this volume.

17. George Lindbeck, "Scripture, Consensus, and Community," in Neuhaus, *Biblical Interpretation in Crisis*, 74-101, here 87.

18. Peter Brown, *The Body and Society: Men, Women, and Sexual Renunciation in Early Christianity* (New York: Columbia University Press, 1988).

19. Raymond E. Brown, "The Contribution of Historical Biblical Criticism to Ecumenical Church Discussion," in Neuhaus, *Biblical Interpretation in Crisis*, 24-49, here 46 (italics mine).

20. LNTS 2.

21. See, for example, 1 Corinthians 5:1-12.

22. LNTS 3; Nessan, "Many Members Yet One Body," 72-73; see also the previous discussion on pages 122-24 in this volume.

23. LNTS 2.

24. *Veritatis Splendor*, 320.

25. Ibid., 301.

26. Ibid., 307.

27. This theme is especially stressed in 1 Thessalonians 4:1-8.

28. *Veritatis Splendor*, 300.

29. Turner, "An Unworkable Theology."

30. Ernst Käsemann, "Righteousness of God," in *New Testament Questions of Today* (Philadelphia: Fortress, 1969) 168-82, here 170.

31. Martin Luther, "A Treatise on Christian Liberty," in *Three Treatises* (Philadelphia: Muhlenberg Press, 1943) 271.

32. See the previous discussion on pages 75-85 in this volume.

33. LNTS 2.

34. Ibid.

35. *Veritatis Splendor*, 309.

36. Ibid., 329-30.

37. Krister Stendahl, *The Bible and the Role of Women: A Case Study in Hermeneutics* (Philadelphia: Fortress, 1966) 40.

38. As Joseph Ratzinger has pointed out, not even the tools developed and employed by historical critics are without presuppositions. See his analysis, "Biblical Interpretation in Crisis," 1-23.

39. Lindbeck, "Scripture, Consensus, and Community," 90.

40. Tertullian, *Prescription against Heretics*, 37.3ff.; modified translation from S. L. Greenslade, *Early Latin Theology* (Library of Christian Classics 5; Philadelphia: Westminster, 1956) 58.

41. Ratzinger, "Biblical Interpretation in Crisis," 1.

42. Classic examples of such a Trinitarian hermeneutic include *Peter in the New Testament*, ed. Raymond E. Brown, Karl P. Donfried, and John Reumann (Minneapolis: Augsburg, 1973), and *Mary in the New Testament*, ed. Raymond E. Brown et al. (Philadelphia: Fortress, 1978).

43. Ratzinger, "Biblical Interpretation in Crisis," 16.

Biblical Index

All translations of the biblical texts follow
the New Revised Standard Version unless otherwise noted.

Modern Author Index

Topical Index